Counter-Co

Counter-Colonial Criminology

A Critique of Imperialist Reason

Biko Agozino

With a Foreword by Stephen Pfohl

Pluto Press

LONDON • STERLING, VIRGINIA

First published 2003 by Pluto Press
345 Archway Road, London N6 5AA
and 22883 Quicksilver Drive, Sterling, VA 20166-2012, USA

www.plutobooks.com

British Library Cataloguing in Publication Data
A catalogue record for this book is available from
the British Library

ISBN 0 7453 1886 X hardback
ISBN 0 7453 1885 1 paperback

Library of Congress Cataloging in Publication Data
Agozino, Biko.
    Counter-colonial criminology : a critique of imperialist reason /
  Biko Agozino ; with a foreword by Stephen Pfohl.
        p. cm.
Includes bibliographical references.
    ISBN 0–7453–1886–X (hardback) — ISBN 0–7453–1885–1 (pbk.)
  1. Criminology. 2. Imperialism. I. Title.
    HV6018 .A37 2003
    364'.09—dc21
                                                                              2003004580

10   9   8   7   6   5   4   3   2   1

Designed and produced for Pluto Press by
Chase Publishing Services, Fortescue, Sidmouth, EX10 9QG, England
Typeset from disk by Stanford DTP Services, Towcester, England
Printed and bound in the European Union by
Antony Rowe, Chippenham and Eastbourne, England

Contents

Acknowledgements

All the errors in this book are mine alone. However, as with all scholarly works, many people share the credit with me. I will first acknowledge the support of my colleagues and friends who read drafts of the manuscript and gave me the encouragement to get it published. They include Herman Schwendinger and Rosemary Galli, who wrote detailed comments that greatly helped to improve the final version; Horace Campbell, who inspired me with his belief that this work should be urgently published; Stephen Pfohl, who was very generous with praise and even offered a wonderful Foreword; and Ngugi wa Thiong'o, who offered encouraging words after reading the manuscript. Similar encouragement came from Ifi Amadiume, Olu Oguibe, Esiaba Irobi, Abubakar Momoh, Ihekweaba Onwudiwe, Nkiru Nzegwu and Oka Obono. Of course, my greatest thanks go to the editorial team of Pluto Press for their patience and support. Stuart Hall taught me a lot in London. Love to you all!

I would also like to give a shout to my students at Bendel State University (now known as Ambrose Ali University), Ekpoma; the University of Calabar; the Open University; Edinburgh University; the Liverpool John Moores University; and the Indiana University of Pennsylvania on whom I tested these ideas from when I started teaching at university level in the mid-1980s. Their questions and comments have challenged me to clarify my thinking over the years. In this respect, I would like to acknowledge the colleagues who encouraged my interest in theoretical work. These include in Ekpoma, Jerry Dibua, Bona Chizea, B.I.C. Ijeoma, the late Frank Mowah and many others. In Calabar, I learnt a lot from my teachers and colleagues, Eskor Toyo, Edwin and Bene Madunagu, Herbert Erwe-Erwe, David Johnson, Akpan Ekpo, Princewill Alozie, Yakubu Ochefu, Okonette Ekanem, Ike Anyanike, Bassey Ekpo Bassey, Tunde Ahonsi, Stella Ogbuagu, Daniel Offiong, Victor Uchendu, Joseph Ottong, Edet Abasiekong, Len Bloom and Joseph Ugal. Colin Sumner, Anthony Bottoms and Alison Morris provided inspiration at Cambridge University. At Edinburgh University, I benefited from the theoretical clarity of David Garland, Peter Young, Beverley Brown, Neil McCormick and Zenon Bankowski. Notable colleagues who assisted my scholarly growth at Liverpool John Moores University include Roger Evans, Joe Sim, Pete Gill, Steve Tombs, Alarna Barton, Dave McEvoy, Marion Price, Gill Hall, Brian Scott, Jon Binnie, George Mair, Joseph Akomode and many others. At Indiana University of Pennsylvania, I would like to acknowledge the encourgagement of my colleagues Yolanda Scott, Tim Austin, Nanci Wilson, Jake Gibbs, Rosemary Gido, Chris Zimmerman, Imogen Moyer, Kwasi Yirenkyi, Amadu Ayebo, Tony Joseph, Veronica Watson, Jim Dougherty, Brenda Mitchel, Carol Young, Yaw Asamoah, Bill Oblitey, Harvey Holtz, Carol Princes and John Orife, and my graduate assistants John Hardee and Patrick Harvey for their help with chasing up the references.

My special thanks go to the Senate Research Grants Committee at Indiana University of Pennsylvania for supporting the completion of this book with a Summer Fellowship in 2001, which enabled me to visit the East African colonial archives at Syracuse University for one week. Thanks to the family of Horace Campbell for generously hosting my family during our trip to Syracuse and for lending me the use of their rich collection on African history. Assata Zerai and Che Fanon were also very supportive of my research in Syracuse. The same Senate Research Grants Committee awarded me an international conference grant, which enabled me to present the introduction to this book at the XV World Congress of Sociology, in Brisbane, Australia, 2002. Thanks also to my Dean, Brenda Carter, for supplementing the conference grant and thereby making it possible for me to benefit from the comments of my peers before sending the manuscript to the publishers. The W.E.B. Du Bois Institute at Harvard University gave my research a boost by awarding me an unfunded fellowship for the summer of 2002. Although I was not able to take up the fellowship due to lack of funding, the fact that they selected my project for such a recognition encouraged me to work harder to complete it on schedule.

Last but not least, I would like to acknowledge the sacrifices of my immediate family who suffered my long hours in the office and constant reading at home and still provided the warmth and encouraged the laughter that sustained me during the period of writing. Also, at the back of my mind during the writing was the story told repeatedly by my father about how he liberated himself from a colonial jail by pissing against the door when they refused to let him out to ease himself following his arrest for selling gunpowder without a licence.

Finally, I wish to acknowledge that slightly different versions of some of the chapters in this book were previously published in refereed journals. These include: chapter 7, 'Social Fiction *Sui Generis*: The Fairy Tale Structure of Criminological Theory', in *The Critical Criminologist*, June 1999; chapter 9, 'Radical Criminology in African Literature', in *International Sociology*, Vol. 10, No. 3, Winter 1995; chapter 10, 'Committed Objectivity in Race–Class–Gender Research', in *Quantity & Quality: International Journal of Methodology*, Vol. 33, No. 4, November 1999; chapter 11, 'How Scientific is Criminal Justice? A Methodological Critique of Research on *McCleskey* v. *Kemp* and other Capital Cases', in *The National Black Law Journal*, December 2002; and chapter 12, What is Institutionalised? The Race-Class-Gender Articulation of Stephen Lawrence', in *British Criminology Conference: Selected Proceedings*, Vol. 3, 2000.

Foreword

> Victimisation is not always interpersonal or intergroup, it is
> sometimes also structural and institutionalised. The decolonisa-
> tion of victimisation from the expanding penal colony must come
> to terms with the fact of internal colonisation at the institutional
> level of punishment and also at the level of political space. The
> struggle involves and always has involved people who are black
> and people who are not. The important thing is to relate the
> struggle for decolonisation and against recolonisation to the
> cultural politics of the people.
>
> Biko Agozino

Since first articulated in the classical eighteenth-century writings of
Cesare Beccaria and Jeremy Bentham, the discipline of criminology
has long been part of the cultural politics of the modern/colonial
world system. Criminology's blindness to and institutional
complicity with the victimization wrought by that global system of
power are also real aspects of its contradictory history. Consider the
date 1791. In most conventional histories of criminology 1791 is
noteworthy because in that year France enacted its Revolutionary
Penal Code. The Penal Code put into practice Beccaria's and
Bentham's Enlightenment-inspired ideas about the supposed rational
choices that lead to crime as well as the legal mandate of 'equal
punishment' for all found guilty of the same criminal acts.

The date 1791 is also significant for another reason. It was in that
year that Africans in Haiti, whose legal enslavement was permitted
by French law, revolted against their European masters. As a profit-
driven system of abject terror and capitalist economic exploitation,
the institution of slavery systematically punished the innocent. But
unlike the large number of individual criminal offenses targeted for
punitive deterrence by France's Revolutionary Penal Code, slavery's
punishment of the innocent was not declared a crime.

The silence of the 1791 French Penal Code concerning slavery
represents far more than a simple omission to include slavery as yet
another form of punishable crime, alongside a long legislative list of
offenses against individual citizens, private property, and the state.
The failure to identify slavery as a crime also casts a troubling shadow

on the Enlightenment imagination of modern criminology as such. Indeed, there is something hauntingly unreal about a scholarly discipline dedicated to the study of crime, the criminal and the criminal law that focuses almost exclusively upon the actions of law-breaking individuals, while turning a blind eye to the mass terrorism imposed upon innocent people by slavery, colonialism, and their continuing legacies. A key aspect of Biko Agozino's *Counter-Colonial Criminology* involves a challenge to contemporary criminology to 'get real' about this disturbing matter.

To 'get real' about the relationship between the modern criminological imagination and what Agozino calls the logic of 'imperialist reason' is to recognize that, for those most impacted by the violence of colonization in its past and present historical forms, the widespread punishment of the innocent is typically a matter of greater urgency than is the legalized punishment of offenders alone. For many conventional western criminologists this will prove a discomforting and difficult lesson. This is because the 'imperial reason' shaping dominant disciplinary approaches to the study of crime offers a wide range of professional rewards and personal pleasures for continuing to think about crime as if criminology itself is not partially complicit with the punishment of innocent persons and groups, whose only crime is to be subordinated by power. But for those committed to both scholarly objectivity and an impassioned struggle for peace, safety, and justice, Agozino's important book will read like a long-awaited breath of fresh air.

Counter-Colonial Criminology is a transdisciplinary work of cutting-edge social theory, rigorous historical scholarship, and moving poetics. It provides a discerning genealogy of how the 'cancer of imperialist logic' has impacted the conceptual agenda, methods, and practical political implications of criminology as a modality of knowledge and power. In so doing, Agozino brings the voices of a wide variety of critical African and African Diaspora theorists, researchers, poets, novelists, playwrights, and musicians to bear upon the meaning of crime, as well as upon possible counter-colonial solutions for the crime problem. In this, the anti-imperialist scholarship of Walter Rodney, W.E.B. DuBois, Kwame Nkrumah, Ifi Amadiume, Angela Davis, Ama Ata Aidou, Frantz Fanon, bell hooks, Stuart Hall, Gani Fawehimi, Aimé Cæsaire and Patricia Hill Collins is mixed with the artistry of Ngugi wa Thiongo, Fatunde, Iyayi, Linton Kwesi Johnson, and Peter Tosh.

Although speaking directly to many questions about both the meaning of crime and social responses to crime, to date, these voices have impacted little – if at all – upon key theoretical, methodological, and ethical-political debates within the discipline of criminology. In Agozino's text these historically marginalized voices enter into engaged dialogue with a variety of more familiar figurations of progressive and radical approaches to criminology. These include advocates of labeling theory, feminist social thought, Marxism, poststructuralism, postmodern theory, cultural studies, and left realism. Sometimes the dialogue is mutually enriching. Often, it points to blind spots by otherwise sympathetic First World intellectuals. Such scholars fail or refuse to notice the complex ways in which their own truths and approaches to truth are historically mediated by what the Peruvian sociologist Anibal Quijano refers to as a continuing 'coloniality of power.' What results from this engaging dialogical mix is a model for decolonizing our understandings of crime that goes beyond existing critical thought within criminology and other western intellectual traditions. This provocative mix, in combination with Agozino's reflexive embrace of 'committed objectivity,' enables the Nigerian-born criminologist to critically address such pressing matters as collective victimization, executive lawlessness, the death penalty, racist police brutality, sexual violence in an international context, the methods of criminological research, the global prison industry, and the right to resist or rebel against unjust authority.

Throughout *Counter-Colonial Criminology* Agozino makes a compelling case for the often unconscious institutional complicity between modern criminology and the epistemological rituals of western imperial power. As a scholarly field of inquiry, criminology remains relatively undeveloped, or even nonexistent, within those African countries where the terrorism of imperialist underdevelopment has been most virulent. At the same time, criminology itself remains conceptually underdeveloped by its lack of awareness of its own 'reasoned' historical connections to the crimes of imperialism. Drawing upon the lessons of feminist standpoint epistemology, as articulated by Sandra Harding, Patricia Hill Collins, and others, and guided by an ethic of collective responsibility for socially structured harms, Agozino's challenging text seeks to redress the problematic character of both forms of underdevelopment.

Confronted with crime problems that today jeopardize the realization of democracy within a context of global political, corporate-economic, and militarized power, the people of Africa hunger for approaches to crime that go beyond the formalities of law and the lawlessness of individual offenders. The same is true for criminology. That is, it is true for a criminology that seeks to participate in, rather than impede energetic struggles for, global justice. This, perhaps, is the central challenge of *Counter-Colonial Criminology* to invite a comparative transdisciplinary study of crime and crime control that is simultaneously committed to anti-imperialist scholarship, situated objectivity, activist legal reform, and radical reconstruction of everyday social institutions for the purpose of better securing democracy, peace, and social justice.

Stephen Pfohl
Professor and Chair
Department of Sociology
Boston College, Massachusetts

Introduction

The enormous dimensions of criminological knowledge are concentrated in a few hands and create an extremely extensive network of close ties and relationships which involve not only the young and middle-aged criminologists, but also even the very young students. This, on the one hand, and on the other the bitter struggle against other disciplinary groups of scholars for the partition of the world of knowledge and the right to rule over Others – these two factors taken together cause the complete conversion of conventional criminologists to the side of imperialism. The signs of the times are a 'general' enthusiasm regarding the prospects of imperialist reason, a passionate defence of imperialism, and every possible camouflage of the real nature of imperialism and the complicity of criminology in its genealogy.[*]

Criminology is scarcely a rocket science or neuro-surgery, yet even Third World countries that have entered the nuclear arms race shy away from the institutionalisation of criminology as an autonomous discipline, despite their huge crime problems. My hypothesis is that criminology is concentrated in former colonising countries, and virtually absent in the former colonised countries, because criminology is a social science that served colonialism more directly than many other social sciences. If this hypothesis is corroborated, why is the postcolonial critique that anthropology, sociology and political science have been subjected to yet to be extended to criminology? (See Ake (1979); also Mafeje (1998) and responses to Mafeje in ibid.) *Counter-Colonial Criminology: A Critique of Imperialist Reason* is a transdisciplinary theoretico-methodological intervention aimed at decolonising theories and methods of imperialist reason in criminology.

The emphasis on the decolonisation of theory and methodology here is an important reminder that crimes have been committed in the name of colonialist science, as in the recent ethical nightmare in sociobiological anthropology concerning the scandalous investigation of the Yanomamo of Venezuela by Napoleon Chagnon (1992).

---

[*] My paraphrase of the epigraph to Kwame Nkrumah (1968) quoted from V.I. Lenin (1916, 1996). For criminology, read finance capital and for groups of scholars, read nation states in the original.

1

A human rights activist, Patrick Tierney (2000), revealed that Chagnon's research among the Yanomamo had exposed this indigeneous people to 'ethnocide' due to Chagnon's experimentation with the measles vaccine Edmonston B, which, it is alleged, triggered an unprecedented measles epidemic which almost wiped out the tribe, just as some say the HIV/AIDS epidemic in Africa is linked to eugenics experimentation under colonialism. While this is denied by Chagnon's supporters and defenders of colonial medicine, on the grounds that the Edmonston B vaccine has never triggered an epidemic anywhere in the world (which raises the doubt whether it was actually the Edmonston B vaccine or something else that was administered to the tribe), other critics emphasise that Chagnon committed an ethical blunder by claiming that the Yanomamo are a belligerent people who fight over the reproductive rights in women. Soon after the publication of his initial fieldwork in the 1960s, goldminers rushed into the gold-rich territory of the tribe and devastated their environment, polluted their fishing rivers and killed them or left them to starve.

Researchers have since discovered that the Yanomamo are actually very loving and caring people, who were misrepresented to justify imperialist eugenics. Chagnon may not be responsible for all the woes that imperialism have brought to the Yanomamo, but there is nothing in his research methodology or theory to help prevent such criminal consequences. Coincidentally, Chagnon was claiming to have discovered that aggression over reproductive rights was natural in men at the same time that American imperialism was waging a war of aggression against the Vietnamese people over economic reproductive rights! Similarly, criminologists who suggest that poor Third World people are violent terrorists (almost by nature) promote fascistic imperialist 'responses', which have the ultimate consequence of genocide.

This book goes beyond the theoretical footprints in the sand left by Stan Cohen in a paper originally presented at a conference on 'Crime and Crime Control in Developing Countries' (organised by the Research Committee on Deviance and Social Control, International Sociological Association (ISA), at the University of Ibadan, in 1980). In his paper, 'Western Crime Control Models in the Third World: Benign or Malignant' Cohen stated that 'Criminologists have either ignored the Third World completely or treated it in a most theoretically primitive fashion, and the general literature on development and colonialism is remarkably silent about crime' (Cohen, 1988: 172). He concluded that it is ironic that while critics in the West are identifying forms of social control that are traditional in the Third World as better alternatives to the neoclassical and positivistic repressive traditions of the West, others suggest that what they have found to be malignant in the West should be exported to the Third World as benign. Echoes of these neglected thoughts were heard in Brisbane, when I presented a summary of this book to the same research committee of the ISA 22 years later, in July 2002. This book goes beyond an examination of western crime control models to look at criminology itself as an imperialist science for the control of others.

It is known that, unlike any location in metropolitan Europe, colonial locations were regarded collectively by Orientalist scholarship (Said, 1978) as places characterised by lawlessness and chaos, 'inhabited by various despotic governments and roving bands of thugs and bandits ... troubled by a history of bribery and corruption, which served as poor imitations of civil jurisprudence' (Harlow and Carter, 1999: 67). This ideological justification of British rule in terms of its moral superiority was the forerunner of academic criminology, which passed in those days under the interdisciplinary field of Orientalism. Even Karl Marx, in an article published in the *New York Daily Tribune* (25 June 1853), justified the 'vilest interests' that motivated the crimes of the East India Company and the 'stupid means' by which those vile crimes were committed by the British, on the basis that Britain was an unwitting catalyst for essential social revolution in India. Marx argued that, partly due to earlier conquests, there were feudal classes in India that oppressed the masses before British colonialism emerged. He reasoned that the struggle against colonialism in India would be part of the struggle against Oriental despotism in Hindustan (Marx and Engels, 1974: 36–7).

Rodney (1972) debunked the self-serving myth that colonialism was essential for African development when all available evidence pointed to the underdevelopment of Africa through Africans' increasing loss of control over the conditions of their life. Africans' opposition to European rule and how they were suppressed by superior force, not superior enlightenment, are documented by Rodney and Fanon (among others) with an emphasis on the minority class of African collaborators who wanted to maintain the unequal relationship between Europe and Africa for their own selfish ends. In conclusion, Rodney observed that under colonialism, law and order involved the maintenance of conditions suitable for the effective expatriation of the surpluses produced by the colonised.

Rodney (1972) reasoned that it was curious that Europeans justified colonialism on the ground that they were morally opposed to the slave trade that they themselves had enthusiastically created (although they were more critical of the Arab slave trade than its European equivalent). Even undeveloped European countries like Portugal felt morally superior to Africa and justified its colonial rule in terms of the need to cast *iluminismo* over the dark continent, while genocidists like King Leopold of Belgium presided over the massacre of millions of Africans to improve forced labour as a civilising process. The dishonesty of the Europeans became transparent when they started deposing African rulers such as King Jaja, who were no longer trading in slaves but who insisted that they should be in control of the legitimate trade in raw materials. None of the criminals that worked for imperialism was ever punished, even in rare cases such as the shooting in 1905 of striking Guyaneses workers, who were demanding a minimum wage of 16 cents a day, when two senior police officers were prosecuted to appease popular anger but later acquitted (Rodney, 1981: 190–222). Not surprisingly, the imperialist agents who assassinated Rodney in 1980 for his alliance with the working people of Guyana were never arrested and put on trial. Yet, in 1844, when a poor working woman, Sophia Ross, tried to draw water from Plantation Bath to quench her thirst rather than walk miles to the nearest public source, she was prosecuted and fined four dollars for trespass (Rodney, 1981: 10).

In *Black Reconstruction in America*, Du Bois (1992: 631–4), noted how American leaders supported colonisation in Africa as a way of removing free African Americans to make it easier to justify the enslavement of the rest in the US. He went on to demonstrate that colonisation was the preferred solution to the colour problem because its advocates knew that the colonised would remain enslaved through the combined forces of finance capital, privileged workers, scientists and engineers. Although Du Bois (one of the founding fathers of conflict criminology; see Moyer, 2001; Gabbidon et al., 2002) did not specify the scientists who rallied to the service of colonialism after the abolition of slavery, he left little doubt that criminologists were among the 'wisest men of science' who defended the new oligarchy. They used the Social Darwinist ideology of the 'survival of the fittest' (the so-called criminal anthropology that won Cesare Lombroso, the father of positivist criminology, the French Legion Medal of Honour; see Moyer, 2001) to prove that African Americans and white women, like Africans and Asians, were unfit for self-determination through universal suffrage. This was justified by the fact that European countries were bearing what Rudyard Kipling called the white man's burden of enlightening white women, Native Americans, Aboriginals, Africans and Asians. In his inimitable lyrical style, Du Bois concluded that the tragic outcome of the collusion of science with colonialism was that:

> God wept; but that mattered little to an unbelieving age; what mattered most was that the world wept and still is weeping and blind with tears and blood. For there began to rise in America in 1876 a new capitalism and a new enslavement of labor. Home labor in cultured lands, appeased and misled by a ballot whose power the dictatorship of vast capital strictly curtailed, was bribed by high wage and political office to unite in an exploitation of white, yellow, brown and black labor, in lesser lands and 'breeds without the law.' ... The immense profit from this new exploitation and world-wide commerce enabled a guild of millionaires to engage the greatest engineers, the wisest men of science, as well as pay high wage to the more intelligent labor and at the same time to have left enough surplus to make more thorough the dictatorship of capital over the state and over the popular vote, not only in Europe and America but in Asia and Africa. (Du Bois, 1992: 634)

Soon enough, the same criminological justifications used to rationalise imperialism were exported to the metropole to justify the repressive control of the working classes, especially the equally colonised Irish. Even in those days, voices were heard challenging the authenticity of Orientalist criminology in terms of moral superiority. As George Bernard Shaw (1938) told his English audience, every available evidence pointed to the moral and intellectual superiority of the Irish who were ruled by the British on the basis of superior force rather than superior enlightenment.

Cæsaire (1972: 13–14) highlights how violence, rape, torture and repression of the colonised in the name of civilisation spreads back to Europe like a gangrene of savagery. As he puts it:

> People are surprised, they become indignant. They say: 'How strange! But never mind – it's Nazism, it will pass!' And they wait, and they hope; and they hide the truth from themselves, that it is barbarism, but the supreme barbarism, the crowning barbarism that sums up all the daily barbarisms; that it is Nazism, yes, but

that before they were its victims, they were its accomplices, that they tolerated that Nazism before it was inflicted on them, that they absolved it, shut their eyes to it, legitimized it, because, until then, it had been applied only to non-European peoples; that they have cultivated that Nazism, that they are responsible for it, and that before engulfing the whole of Western, Christian civilization in its reddened waters, it oozes, seeps, and trickles from every crack. (Cæsaire, 1972: 14)

This book surveys recent developments in criminology and demonstrates how imperialism used criminological knowledge and how it can be seen as a criminological project – imprisonment with or without walls, a widening of the net of incarceration, and how the close kinship between the two fields of knowledge and power, criminology and imperialism, served both. The book examines the reasons why conventional criminologists are overwhelmingly silent about the more than coincidental origin of their discipline at the height of European colonialism. The book also explores the possibility that the mechanical solidarity between colonialism and criminology is part of the reason why few postcolonial territories today have developed criminology as an institutionalised discipline.

This book develops a theory of social control from the point of view of counter-colonial scholars who are familiar with the history of resistance to colonialist (including the colonial, postcolonial, neocolonial, internal colonial and re-colonial) law and order reasoning. The book surveys the major epochal moments in criminology, especially since the 1960s, and indirectly illuminates the colonialist conditions that created changes in criminological theory from the eighteenth century to the twenty-first. Criminology emerged as a discipline for disciplining and controlling the Other at a time when colonial administrations were imprisoning most regions of the world. The book will revise existing criminological knowledge by exposing what was hidden by the carceral imperialist logic that produced earlier texts and by charting the potential consequences for criminology when its violent colonial heritage is exposed.

Given the crucial importance of (cultural) imperialism in the history of knowledge in all parts of the world, the book will attempt to explain why criminology is dominated by scholars in former colonial centres of authority and how such colonialist domination leads to theoretical underdevelopment through the concealment of the bloody legacy of colonialist criminology. The book will compare criminological theories and methods according to whether they are pro- or anti-imperialist in orientation in order to show what criminology has been missing by ignoring the marginalised voices of the Other in its institutional development or what criminology could learn from anti-colonial struggles. A few historians of law and criminologists have looked at the repressive militaristic policing of the colonised (Van Onselen, 1976; Hall et al., 1978; Fitzpatrick, 1980; Shivji, 1982; Sumner, 1990), but hardly any has demonstrated the legacy of imperialist reasoning within criminological theories of different shades or explored (with the exception of writers who are not trained in criminology or law such as Fanon, 1963; Nkrumah, 1968; Rodney, 1972; Hochschild, 1998) the possibility of punishing the crimes of slavery and colonialism through reparation or restorative justice. Outside the social sciences, the critique of imperialism is even better established in literary criticism where Achebe (1975, 1988, 2000), and many others have contributed to the canon of postcolonial literature. Wole Soyinka's Nobel lecture was a counter-colonial criminological discourse of the finest quality that is sadly rare among scholars trained in criminology (Soyinka, 1988).

Many African-American criminologists (Tatum, 1996, for example) have examined the colonial model that seeks to apply the insights of Frantz Fanon to an explanation of the over-representation of minorities in the criminal justice system. Onwudiwe (2000) did the same in his original application of world-system theories to what he called the globalisation of terrorism. Young and Turner (1985) took a similar historical approach to understanding the crimes of the state and corruption in neocolonial Zaïre under Mobutu Sese Seko. Pepinsky (1991) has argued that the geometry of violence cannot be explained without bringing into consideration the violence of imperialist powers in foreign countries. Scraton (1990) has called for the history of colonialism to be made an essential module of criminology courses. A few papers are being published by Australian and New Zealand criminologists on the incredible injustice done to the native populations as part of colonialism (see, Midford, 1992, for example). However, to my knowledge, no one has examined the extent to which criminology is inherently a colonial enterprise or why this repressive technology is monopolised by imperialist countries while the former colonised countries seem indifferent to it.

Critical scholars are usually different in orientation compared to the modernisation and liberal legalism schools of what Cohen (1988) calls 'made-for-export criminology'. The irony is that the modernisation theorists such as Clinard and Abbott (1973) and Clifford (1974), who come from countries with high crime rates, assume that they can teach countries with lower crime rates how to solve their crime problem. Their solution usually takes the form of adopting western crime control models without any evidence that these models have helped to reduce crime in their own countries. Clinard and Abbott (1973: 275–8) even recommend enthusiastically that Third World countries should adopt the apartheid pass law system as a way to reduce urban crime by controlling the population more rigorously, while suggesting that nothing can be done about white-collar crimes because these are normal paths to development. Apart from the fact that the pass laws have since been recognised as one of the crimes against humanity called apartheid, there is abundant evidence that they did not reduce 'crime' in South Africa as hundreds of black women were arrested and jailed in their irrepressible mass defiance of these laws. Cohen (1988) cautions left-wing critics of modernisation criminology, however, because they could easily fall into a trap by suggesting that current crime rates in the Third World are the inevitable consequence of capitalist development. Rather, Cohen suggests that by following Fanon's third way, instead of trying to create another Europe, Third World criminologists might discover better solutions to the crime problem. The western crime control models are the types of criminology that Cohen opposes, especially when exported uncritically to the Third World. It could be the case that one of the reasons why Third World countries have neglected the development of criminology is due to the lack of relevance of much of conventional criminology to the realities of the Third World.

Evidence for the underdeveloped state of criminology in Africa, for example, can be found in Johnson (1983). This has chapters on Egypt, Ghana, Nigeria, South Africa and Uganda. Although this descriptive and atheoretical publication is almost 20 years old, there is no evidence that criminology has been developed in African universities since the 1980s, but there is abundant evidence of the increasing criminological problems facing Africa. The chapters simply describe the teaching of criminology as parts of courses on state security (South Africa), prison administration (Ghana and Uganda) and police training (Egypt and Nigeria), without any reflection on the development of theoretical orientations suitable for explaining postcolonial crime and justice in Africa. This book will be a first attempt to challenge existing criminological theory with evidence from colonial and postcolonial history and thereby develop a new criminological theory of postcolonial authority and social control.

Whereas almost every university in America offers a degree in criminology or criminal justice from a largely administrative and uncritical orientation, there is no single such department in the numerous universities in Africa (except in South Africa), the Caribbean, Asia and, to a lesser extent, South America. Is this because corrupt postcolonial policy-makers are scared that criminologists will conduct research to expose their misdeeds and encourage a punitive attitude to fraud instead of treating it simply as civil wrong to be settled through the refund of embezzled funds, if at all? If the reason for apathy towards the institutionalisation of criminology in postcolonial locations is fear of exposure, then it is irrational because there is no evidence that administrative academic criminology has been responsible in any country for exposing imperialist corruption – that is usually left to often marginalised critical journalists and organic intellectuals.

All known administrative, empiricist and descriptive accounts of the invisibility of criminology in postcolonial locations serve to justify a more rigorous attempt to theorise the genealogy of criminology from the family tree of colonialism. This book will help to develop critical scholarship in criminology to avoid the stultifying influence of the imperialist logic that sees criminology only in terms of police training, security agency and prison administrations, especially in postcolonial universities.

OUTLINE

Chapter 1 summarises European theories of the judicial process and indicates how widespread they are today. The chapter highlights the strengths that made the spread of European ideas feasible and highlights the weaknesses in other parts of the world that made their domination by Europeans possible. The chapter concludes by highlighting how European theories of social control used the colonised for laboratory experimentation before being reflected back to internal colonies in Europe.

Chapter 2 focuses on the post-war challenge to colonialist ideas in criminology by examining questions of power and moving away from a definition of crime as otherness, which coincided with the peak of the anti-colonial struggles in Africa and South East Asia. The chapter links new theoretical insights into anti-colonial struggles around the world and the civil rights movement in America. The chapter concludes by highlighting the pluralist weaknesses in the societal reaction perspective that made it unable to shift the colonialist domination of criminological theory.

Chapter 3 deals with the fragmentation of the radical perspective in criminology into competing sub-paradigms. The chapter chronicles the origins of the radical perspectives from critical social theory and evaluates the contributions of the competing sub-paradigms to criminological theory. Finally, the chapter compares the radical paradigms to the dominant paradigms in criminology and explains the dominance of the conventional by linking them to colonialist and anti-colonialist thought.

Chapter 4 is an introduction to feminist thought in criminology. The chapter underscores what feminist writers are struggling against in the discipline and the various approaches that feminists engage in with the domineering colonialist ideas of criminology. The chapter concludes by stressing what all criminologists (feminist and otherwise) could gain from serious attention to feminist contributions.

Chapter 5 indirectly considers the loss to feminist criminology due to its complicity in the silence on the colonial genealogy of the discipline. By means of a critical evaluation of the use of the rape metaphor in international relations, the chapter suggests how the gender critique of criminology could be enriched by being sensitive to anti-colonial struggles.

Chapter 6 focuses on poststructuralist theories of relevance to criminology and how this perspective is coloured by its relation to colonialism. Borrowing from postcolonialist theory in literature, this chapter presents a critique of poststructuralism in criminology by questioning its silences while highlighting its useful contributions.

Chapter 7 illustrates the contributions of poststructuralism to criminology by presenting a comparative philosophy of science with a focus on two competing perspectives on the sociology of knowledge both published in 1996. One view is that of the German social theorist, Jürgen Habermas, who argues that modernism is still a relevant philosophy for the sociology of law; the other is the view of the French theorist, Jean Baudrillard, who argues that modernism has been overtaken by postmodernism as the guiding explanation of how criminologists work.

Chapter 8 looks at state crimes and the struggle for democracy around the world. The chapter critiques the underdevelopment of theories of crimes of the state and offers insights on structural penology for such state crimes as human rights violations.

Chapter 9 takes this look at African contributions to criminological theory further by examining the importance of radical criminology in African literature. This chapter illustrates how creative counter-colonial criminology could be in theory and methods by examining the theory of radical criminology in African literature.

Chapter 10 outlines a methodological option suitable for counter-colonial criminology: the option of being both committed and objective, instead of seeing objectivity and commitment as incompatible polarities. This chapter highlights the importance of committed objectivity in race–class–gender research.

Chapter 11 demonstrates the usefulness of committed objectivity by offering a scientific argument against the death penalty with evidence from the United States, Africa and the rest of the world. The chapter uses the scientific methodological assumptions of social science research to critique criminologists who seek scientific means to make the death penalty error-proof.

Chapter 12 reaffirms the postcolonial approach to criminology by focusing on the conditions of people of African descent in the internal colonies of metropolitan imperialist locations. The case of the racist killing of Stephen Lawrence and the insensitive police response to the murder serve to illustrate that a counter-colonial criminology is relevant not only to former colonial locations but also to the former colonial countries.

Chapter 13 concludes the chapters on the conditions of the African Diaspora under the domination of imperialist reason. This time, the case study is the African Caribbean theatre of the repressive policing of subversive popular culture. The execution of Peter Tosh for his 'criminal records' serves as a lesson and a warning to counter-colonial criminologists.

The Conclusion assesses the relevance, or otherwise, of criminology to the continuing struggle to decolonise the world. Critics might point out that following the lacunae in criminology that this book has exposed, why not follow Stan Cohen, Carol Smart and many other sociologists and declare a principled opposition to criminology as presently constituted? My answer will be in the form of a proverb rendered in the genre of folk tales which I learnt from my radically democratic Igbo culture of Nigeria. The proverb goes by way of a short story that Chinua Achebe (2000: 14–16) recounts with his legendary mastery of the narrative arts. The story goes like this:

Once upon a time, the animal kingdom called a general meeting to discuss urgent matters (the way the Igbo still do). On their way to the public meeting, the animals were surprised to see the chicken heading in the opposite direction. When asked if he had not heard of the general meeting, the chicken replied that he had some urgent matter of his own to attend to, but that he was in full support of whatever decision that would be reached at the public meeting. It turned out that the only item on the agenda was the way human beings were terrorising the animals by using them as sacrificial offerings to their gods. The animals concluded that a diplomatic solution was better than all-out war. They suggested that one animal should be offered to human beings as their preferred sacrificial offering to save the rest of the animal kingdom. Guess who was offered to the humans? The chicken, of course, since he had already pledged his allegiance to any decision reached at the meeting in his absence.

The moral of the story is that Third World countries should not chicken out of the general meeting of criminologists or they might remain the preferred sacrificial offering to the gods of imperialism. As Stephen Pfohl (1994) argues, Third World scholars should be interested in western criminology while developing their own perspectives because it was part of the technology with which they were colonised for centuries.

Of course, the arguments made in this book could be extended to other fields of study, especially in the social sciences. Sociology, anthropology, economics, political science, geography and others are old-established disciplines in postcolonial locations without a serious attempt to develop new theories and research methods from the point of view of the colonised. What Fanon (1963) and Toyo (2001) have said with reference to those that Fanon called the phantom bourgeoisie who are characterised by lack of creativity and productivity is equally applicable to psuedo-intellectuals in the Third World who have developed no theory or methods for the study of their own realities.

1. The Enlightenment and Euro-American Theories of the Judicial Process

The influence of the Roman Empire on the evolution of European penology is all too obvious. Many legal historians would emphasise the role of the Roman emperors, as well as Napoleon and German legal scholars in laying the foundation of the Romano-Germanic family of law which dominates continental Europe today. However, when it comes to modern European imperialism and the imposition (of often perverted western ideas about 'crime and punishment' on the rest of the world, and the heroic resistance to this) of a largely puzzling *criminal* justice, conventional criminology is curiously silent. This conspiracy of silence may be due to criminology's complicity in the imperialist project. The silence could also be partly due to the questionable nature of *criminal* justice in the face of resolute resistance to colonial injustice in contrast to the *relative* legal consensus among the ruling capitalist classes of Europe.

From your reading of history, you must be familiar with the socio-cultural contexts within which the Enlightenment movement developed and from which the movement broke away to found modernity. The pre-Enlightenment period was the era of supernatural explanations for power and misconduct – kings ruled because they had divine right to rule and people became deviant as a result of demonic possession from which they had to be exorcised and purified if possible, or destroyed in order to be saved in the hereafter. The demonic judicial process was characterised by public executions for serious 'offenders' or sinners, pillory and shame for cheats, the centralisation of judicial authority in the hands of religious officials, public administration of punishment in the community and, above all, a phallocentric bias against pagan women, who were executed as witches (Pfohl, 1994). In this sense, the Enlightenment, or *Iluminismo* in Portuguese, was a progressive movement in social thought, aimed at the liberation of individuals from despotic rule by the forces of nature, religious orthodoxy and political traditionalism in Europe.

Piers Beirne analysed how a Frenchman was wrongly executed in 1761 for the murder of his son who had in fact committed suicide. Three years later, Beccaria published anonymously his best-seller, *Treatise on Crime and Punishment*, condemning the arbitrary power exercised by judges and calling for the rational application of the law based on the principle of equality. He also called for the abolition of the death penalty because, according to him, the right to take life was not one of the rights that individuals possessed in a state of nature and so was not a right that people ceded to the state to be exercised on their behalf under the social contract. However, his insistence that punishment should be made to fit the crime provided his supporters with an excuse to retain capital punishment as the only penalty that fitted certain crimes. At the same time, his opponents were powerful members of the justice system and the Church who ridiculed his idea of equality before the law and convinced the Pope of the need to ban his treatise for almost 200 years (Beirne, 1993). The execution of a single innocent Frenchman counts for more in the conventional history of criminology than the genocidal trans-Atlantic slavery in which millions of Africans were destroyed or the genocide of Native Americans and Aboriginal Australians by European *conquistados*.

The European slave trade was the testing ground for the Enlightenment's credentials as a liberatory thought, but as Gilroy (1993), Fanon (1963) and Rodney (1972) – all descendants of enslaved Africans – have shown, *Iluminismo* was pathetically blinded by what Retamar (1979) calls the 'black legend'. According to the myth of the black legend, Spain was blamed by Britain and France for giving a bad name to imperialism due to its more brutal form of the civilising process. However, Retamar argues: 'If anything distinguishes the Spanish conquest from the depredations of Holland, France, England, Germany, Belgium or the United States ... it is not the proportion of crimes – in this they are all worthy rivals – but rather the proportion of scruples.'

The conquest of the New World and the development of European slavery systematised the persecution of people simply because they appeared different, long before this experiment was extended to the 'witches' of Europe. The European enslavement of Africans and the massacre of Native Americans began in the fifteenth century, but it was in the seventeenth century that the rarely enforced medieval criminal category of 'witchcraft' became a massive force of moral panic that saw millions of mostly women murdered. European enslavement of Africans and the genocidal conquest of Native Americans started before the witch craze, but all three forms of persecution continued together for many years. In fact, the Salem witch hunt was blamed on Tituba, a kitchen slave from Barbados, who was the first to be tried and murdered for allegedly bewitching young girls, who were crawling on all fours, and barking like dogs, at a time when the Royal Charter of the Puritans had just been revoked, giving rise to widespread economic stress and uncertainty (Pfohl 1994: 26; Wilson 1993).

It was at the height of the slave trade that classicism emerged to challenge the arbitrary nature of punishment in medieval Europe, but this insight was not extended to enslaved Africans who were arbitrarily victimised, even when they did no wrong. However, it was not until the height of colonialism in Africa and Asia that Europe discovered the new 'science' of criminology as a tool to aid the control of the Other – a supposed advancement on classicist philosophies of justice. This was also the time that the Marquis de Sade was writing about the pleasure of inflicting pain on innocent people, a metaphor for imperialism, except that the sadist did not live on the surpluses of sadism. However, talk of retribution and utilitarianism could well become a metaphor for the campaign by people of African descent demanding reparations for the crimes of slavery and colonialism, except that Marx rightly critiqued the gangster philosophy of Jeremy Bentham, who suggested that everyone was a calculating philistine, maximising profits and minimising losses, like the bourgeoisie, without regard to morality (Marx, 1954: 609–10). In other words, the demand for reparations is not a search for profit from slavery by people of African descent, but a search for justice which would be incomprehensible to the utilitarian Bentham, who saw the common people as objects to be manipulated with carrots and sticks instead of recognising them as active subjects who are making their own principled history. As Cæsaire put it, with his compelling poetic prose that says a lot about criminology without any need to name the discipline:

Security? Culture? The rule of law? In the meantime, I look around and wherever there are colonizers and colonized face to face, I see force, brutality, cruelty, sadism, conflict, and, in a parody of education, the hasty manufacture of a few thousand subordinate functionaries, 'boys', artisans, office clerks, and interpreters necessary for the smooth operation of business ... Between the colonizer and colonized there is room only for forced labor, intimidation, pressure, the police, taxation, theft, rape, compulsory crops, contempt, mistrust, arrogance, self-complacency, swinishness, brainless elites, degraded masses. (Cæsaire, 1972: 21)

ENLIGHTENED RETRIBUTION AND UTILITARIANISM

The Enlightenment came about to challenge the privilege of divine right as well as the ideology of revealed knowledge among Europeans while denying that the colonised had the rational faculty to reason about what is just and what is cruel. In the place of divine right, moral philosophers like Hobbes (1650), Locke (1690), Rousseau (1762), Kant, Hegel and others insisted that a social contract was the best possible foundation for civil democratic rule, which must be informed by rational principles rather than by unverifiable claims of revelation. Yet under the slave trade and colonialism, democracy was completely denied, the social contract was nonexistent and whole populations were treated as criminals without human rights. Cesare Beccaria's (1804) publication is credited with laying the foundation of the classicist school of criminology by synthesising the principles of the (Hobbesian) social contract, which referred to political rule in general, and applying them directly to crime and punishment. According to him, men have the right to use punishment to deter one another from wrecking the social contract into which they have freely entered. Again, the emphasis is on the power of European men to punish others but, given that the enslaved and the colonised did not freely enter into any social contract, what was being administered to them is better understood as victimisation, especially when they were completely innocent.

According to Beccaria, punishment is justifiable only if it is not arbitrary (and it was certainly arbitrary under slavery and colonialism), if it is calculable (the pain caused by colonialism is beyond calculation though slave law often tried to calculate the quantity of torture that could be imposed at a time; see James, 1980), if it is applied to all offenders equally, irrespective of their social circumstances (slavery and colonialism punished the innocent as though they were offenders), and if it is proportional to the amount of pain caused by the crime. What sort of punishment would be proportional to the crimes of slavery and colonialism for which people of African descent are deservedly demanding reparations?

The French Revolutionary Penal Code of 1791 was apparently based on these Beccarian principles of inflexible rationality yet Napoleon refused to recognise the Haitian revolution of that year until his army was defeated by Haitian forces led by Toussaint l'Ouverture (James, 1980). Then Napoleon tricked this leader of the Black Jacobins, as James called them, to Paris for a peace treaty only to kidnap him and torture him in prison until his death. The impractical nature of the inflexible Penal Code resulted in neoclassical revisions to the Code in 1810 and 1819 to make allowance for the mitigating circumstances of age and premeditation, but still without recognising slavery as a crime against humanity. (That declaration waited almost 200 years until the World Congress against Racism in 2001, a conference that was boycotted by America and threatened by Europe because the issue of reparations for the crimes of slavery and colonialism was tabled for discussion along with the injustice of Israeli colonisation of Palestinian territories.) In England, insanity was added as a defence following the case of McNaughten who was charged in 1843 with the murder of Mr Drummond, secretary to the Prime Minister, Robert Peel (who organised the first professional police force). McNaughten claimed that it was Peel that he intended to kill because God had asked him to do so on the ground that the Prime Minister worshipped the devil and that he was running a government of Evil Tories. The fact that McNaughten was a political activist in the Chartist movement against the alienation of labour by the industrial revolution was ignored by the prosecution (Pfohl, 1994). Given his Irish name, he could have been an anti-imperialist too but the jury was satisfied with the insanity plea.

Before these neoclassicist reforms, Jeremy Bentham had found the archaic state of eighteenth-century English common law repugnant in the same way that Beccaria found the continuation of harsh demonic control in Europe repulsive. In his books, Bentham (1789) closely followed Beccaria in attempting to find an answer to the Hobbesian question of why society is possible in spite (but also because) of the love of private pleasure and dislike of personal pain (except when it is the sadistic pain inflicted on others under slavery and colonialism). Although Bentham and Beccaria are in agreement with Hobbes that European men are basically hedonistic bastards, they differ in the sense that Beccaria would want punishment to serve the purpose of retribution, whereas Bentham would add the utilitarian principle of deterrence to the purpose of punishment.

A review of the philosophy of punishment shows that the punishment of the innocent (the colonised, for instance) is treated as a fantastic tale found only in fiction and analogies. For example, a strong objection to the Benthamite utilitarian philosophy of punishment by Beccarian retributivist philosophers is that utilitarians would permit and even encourage the punishment of the innocent if this could be seen to have the utility of promoting order (a common colonial tactic). For example, if a white woman is allegedly raped by a black man in a colonial situation, the hypothetical example goes, it would be utilitarian to punish any black man, even if he is innocent, in order to satisfy the public desire for revenge and avert a race riot in which many more black people might be attacked and killed. Note that there is no hesitation on the part of this hypothesis that the rapist was a black man for, under the colonial situation, the native is synonymous with the offender.

Rawls (1969) attempted to solve this hypothetical case (without doubting whether the allegation that the rapist was black is true or false) by assuming that:

1. The punishment of the innocent in such a circumstance would not promote law and order and therefore would not be utilitarian, especially if it is known that the person punished was innocent. So,
2. Such a punishment can work only if it remains a secret and for it to remain a secret, there must be a special institution for 'telishment' whose job it would be to manipulate the public and control information about telished individuals and cases. In this sense, the punishment of the innocent would not be punishment but telishment and because the conditions for the establishment of institutions for telishment are impossible, telishment can only be hypothesised but never practised.

Rawls's assumptions are flawed by the fact that knowledge of innocence is never universal and collective, but often sectional and partisan. Under the colonial situation, people who are known by many to be innocent could remain under 'punishment' (Nelson Mandela, for instance) if the people who believe them to be innocent lack the power to effect or secure their acquittal. On the other hand, people who are widely known to be guilty could escape punishment because the people who know of their guilt lack the will or the power to prove their guilt and effect or secure their punishment. In other words, the sophisticated attempt to define conditions for telishment is an unnecessary diversion from the fact that existing institutions do 'punish' the innocent and attempt to conceal their innocence or even with public knowledge of their innocence, without having to rely on a philosophical institution for telishment.

Anthony Quinton (1969) comes close to recognising that 'punishing the innocent' is not only a logical contradiction or hypothetical hair-splitting, but also a historical problem that faces real people. Among moral philosophers, he is one of the few who agree that suffering can be inflicted on innocent people, but he insists that this cannot be called punishment. According to Quinton, such suffering should properly be described as 'judicial terrorism' or 'social surgery'. As he puts it, 'If we inflict suffering on an innocent man and try to pass it off as punishment, we are guilty of lying since we make a lying imputation that he is guilty and responsible for an offence' (Quinton, 1969: 58–9).

Quinton is right in observing that the punishment of the innocent is not punishment, but judicial terrorism. However, by making judicial terrorism equivalent to social surgery, he seems willing to let the judicial terrorists off too lightly by suggesting that their actions are equivalent to surgical life-saving operations. By saying that those who inflict suffering on the innocent are guilty simply of lying or perjury, he trivialises the problem of victimisation as mere punishment (VAMP) by suggesting that it is no more than a logical problem of imputation.

This book will show that the preoccupation with the punishment of offenders (POO) is only partly valid when applied to class, race and gender relations, especially under colonialism. It is not the case that punishment is proof of an offence, nor that all offenders are punished. However, since punishment is usually conceptualised as a predict of the offender, it is necessary to develop a different vocabulary for the phenomenon of the 'punishment' of the innocent (POTI). It is necessary to go beyond descriptive vocabulary to show the nature which such victimisation assumes in its impact on people with variable power and material resources corresponding to class, race and gender relations. It is not enough to explain this away as a pitfall along the penal paths of progress, or as irrationalities within largely rational bureaucratic systems, or as mistakes to be corrected with the payment of financial compensations, or simply as repressive fetishes for domination and exploitation (Agozino, 1997a).

I am convinced (and you are welcome to disagree) that the judicial process does not only punish offenders and protect 'victims'. The system sometimes also criminally victimises. A classic example of such systematic victimisation is the Dreyfus Affair which occurred in France at the end of the nineteenth century. (See Finkelstein (2001) for an account of what he calls 'the classic case of miscarriage of justice ... a full understanding of the triviality, the prejudice, the casual cruelty and the clannishness which sent a wholly innocent man to isolation on a Caribbean rock, kept him there for five years, and with a lack of scruple and a tenacity worthy of a better cause checked every move to re-open the case.') Douglas Porch (1995) contends that the case was insignificant in itself, but became prominent because it could be used to clarify ideological boundaries in the revolutionary and counter-revolutionary struggles of the time and the role of the French secret service in imperialist wars since then.

The anti-Semitism that was widespread in France, as in other European countries, at that time was expressed by the opponents of Alfred Dreyfus, who was framed as a spy and who was nearly lynched after his conviction. However, the notoriety of this individual case should not blind us to the fact that it was one among many that may or may not be well known today. For example, King Ja Ja of Opobo, Nigeria, was not even offered a trial by the British Merchant Navy, which deported him to slave labour in the Caribbean for opposing European domination of trade in the Niger Delta. Moreover, many other cases did not involve single individuals but whole groups and categories of people, as can be seen in the history of the judicial process under slavery, colonialism, fascism and authoritarian populism (Hall, 1988; Hillyard, 1993). In other words, what Stuart Hall calls the perspective of articulation is useful for understanding how punishment, victimisation and welfare practices are relatively articulated, disarticulated and rearticulated like race–gender–class articulation. This also suggests that the judicial process is articulated with other criminal/civil justice processes in such a way that the analysis of one benefits from a comparative reference to the others.

The principles of classicism are recognised by Taylor et al. (1973), Gouldner (1971) and many others as polemics by the rising bourgeois class against the privileges of the landed aristocracy. These same principles have equally been criticised for advocating formal equality between men without also advocating substantive equality, without which the former would be more or less empty words. The Enlightenment has also been criticised for concentrating on the rights of man and the rationality of man, with the underlying assumption that women are irrational and therefore undeserving of equal justice. This is recognised by many as an extension of critical race studies which have challenged the presumption that rationality is exclusively possessed by Europeans and that 'other cultures' are still ruled by tyrannical nature (Kingdom, 1992; Gilroy, 1993). The Enlightenment can therefore be likened to gangster philosophy – the idea that the people robbed, raped and murdered by the mob are fall guys, mugs and fools, while the Mafia are the wise guys or good fellas. Hence, Soyinka (1988) suggested to the Nobel Institute that works by the Enlightenment philosophers should carry a health warning to African readers: 'BEWARE, THIS WORK CAN DAMAGE YOUR RACIAL SELF-ESTEEM.'

These are valid claims, except that Enlightenment philosophy was prescriptive rather than descriptive. Kant (1964) would say that it was the Age of Enlightenment rather than the Enlightened Age. In other words, the universal man, equality before the law, individual freedom and even rationality were not decreed into existence by the Enlightenment, but were proclaimed as worthy goals of the movement towards increasing happiness. For example, the Enlightenment called for rationality and science, but the Enlightenment philosophers were not scientists themselves, they were philosophers offering what West (1993) calls 'prophetic thoughts' on the need for scientific knowledge of ways to improve human conditions. The problem with the conventional versions of positivism is that there is nothing positive or progressive about their reactionary, repressive ideology. It is for this reason that critical thinkers distance themselves from August Comte and his idiosyncratic version of positivism as social engineering. Apart from the assumption that eliminating people who are different from the white supremacist, patriarchal imperialists would make society more positive or better or happier, positivism wrongly assumed that only empiricism is acceptable as a scientific method. As a consequence, anything that is not observable, like surplus labour, the square root of minus one (the unknown 'X' in mathematics which Malcolm X adopted to replace the name imposed on his family during slavery) or race–class–gender relations would be ruled out of analysis by empiricist positivism.

The Enlightenment was not simply prescriptive, it was also descriptive in the sense that it too easily idealised the existing hierarchies of race, class and gender and represented these inequalities in power relations as evidence of the survival of the fittest. Apart from the fact that the Enlightenment philosophers described their own studies of history, philosophy, law, arts and language as 'scientific' in the sense of being rational and objective, the Enlightenment denied rationality to the poor, women and people of other cultures who were supposedly still ruled by nature and instincts rather than by reason and (Christian) civilisation. Similarly, the Enlightenment was too confident of the goodness of rationality, as if anything that is reasonable (to a white, middle-class man) is necessarily good. Uncritical faith in science and rationality is what distinguishes the Enlightenment, which was largely blind to enslavement, from a postmodern world which is conscious of the crimes of Nazism and apartheid as the collective victimisation of mostly innocent people, a collective victimisation that was articulated as a penalty for the subaltern 'offender' by the dominant collective offender. The ethic of collective responsibility exposes the ethic of individual responsibility as another prophecy of the Enlightenment that has not been religiously fulfilled.

Many writers, such as Emile Durkheim (1965), Max Weber (1905), Karl Marx (1980) and more recently Peter Fitzpatrick (1992), have pointed out that the demographic explosion in Europe in the eighteenth century, the burgeoning in scholarship initiated by the reformation of the Church and developed by improved means of communication, the French Revolution and the rise of modern states, the decline of feudal economy, the rise of mercantilist capitalism and the industrial revolution did not completely destroy the fatalism of the Middle Ages. Rather, the rituals and discourse of demonology, such as swearing on the Bible to tell the truth in court, remained an aspect of the judicial process. At a deeper level, the traditions of adjudication which were developed under feudalism, such as the jury system and the inquisitorial versus the adversarial systems of adjudication, were retained by the various European jurisdictions and transplanted to non-European cultures through conquest and trade.

THE RATIONAL IDEAL TYPE AND ORIENTALISM

Max Weber (1979) provides an account of these contrasting models of the judicial process in the language of the Enlightenment. His ideal types of judicial administration are effectively two models of the judicial process – the bureaucratic or 'rational' (Enlightenment) model and the traditional or 'irrational' (pre-modern) administration of justice. The bureaucratic model is more successful, according to Weber, because of its technical superiority. It has precision, economy, consistency, co-ordination and speed. It executes justice in a 'professional' way because cases are decided 'without regard to persons'. If this bureaucratic authority is applied consistently, it would level out social differences, but this is not always the case because bureaucracy is diverse in form and context. Modern bureaucracy differs from medieval attempts at bureaucratisation due to the relative 'calculability of its rules'. Needless to add that the bureaucratisation of justice was the primary goal of every colonial administration as it codified the law and tried to appear neutral in the adjudication of cases between European exploiters and the victimised.

In the Middle Ages, according to Weber, the reception of Roman law proceeded with the bureaucratisation of juridical administration. Adjudication by rationally trained specialists took the place of tradition or irrational presupposition. Weber contrasted rational adjudication on the basis of rigorously formal legal concepts with adjudication based on sacred traditions without any clear basis for concrete decisions. In the latter, cases are decided either on the basis of 'charismatic justice' – revelations by oracles – or as Khadi justice, which is non-formalistic and value-laden (Islamic law), or as empirical justice, which is formalistic but based on 'precedents' (English common law). According to Weber, contemporary England still has a broad substratum of the legal system which is similar to Khadi justice – untrained Justices of the Peace, for example. Continental jury systems operate similarly in practice, according to Weber, because jurors are not trained experts who understand the rational rules of an ideal bureaucracy. Democratic principles of adjudication are not necessarily the same as rational principles, according to Weber, because a democracy might lack the precision of formalistic adjudication. American and British courts are still largely empirical, even though they are not less democratic than continental European jurisdictions with a codified law, according to him. It is not clear how much of this is a sign that Weber was a patriotic German who believed that his country's system was the best and how much of it could be attributed to what Edward Said called Orientalism, or the idea that everything non-western is inferior.

Centrally organised lawyers' guilds, according to Weber, resisted codification in England and rejected Roman law because they produced judges from their ranks, kept privileged legal education in their hands as highly developed empirical technique and fought off the threats of ecclesiastical courts and university legal theorists to codify the laws of England and Wales. This instance of English resistance to legal imperialism is completely absent in the history of colonial criminology, probably because decolonisation resulted in the orderly replacement of colonialism with neocolonialism. Capitalism succeeded in England (and in the colonies by extension), Weber contends, largely because the courts and trial procedure denied justice to the poor (and the colonised). Modern judges are not vending machines of justice, however; they are still biased to some extent, especially under colonialism. Public opinion and popular justice still impinge on the rational administration of justice (but not necessarily the public opinion of the colonised, which is completely ignored). Weber's contribution was intended as a corrective to the traditional study of law, the study of 'dogmatics' or exegesis – the interpretation of statutes. Rational/irrational ideal types are, however, misleading because Weber must have meant regular/irregular. But even so, the rule that an oracle should decide is just as regular as the rule that the appeal court should decide.

Bauman (1989) has pointed out that there is nothing in Weber's theory of rationality to prevent the emergence of a phenomenon like Nazism (and colonialism, we might add). Such a phenomenon does not appear simply as irrational traditional forms of the administration of justice, but represents the application of science, legal rationality, medicine and the industrial revolution systematically to enslave or eliminate innocent people. In fact, Weber pointed out that rationality does not necessarily guarantee democracy, but he had no doubt that rationality was superior to judicial processes that took personal circumstances and the background of the actors into consideration in adjudication.

Weber's modernist sociology of law appears to be a defence of the principles of the Enlightenment at a time when they were increasingly coming under sustained attack. At the time the moral philosophers were developing their theories of social control, the French philosopher August Comte was already calling for progress beyond philosophy to what he called a positive science of society. According to him, such a science would be the queen of all the sciences and the practitioners would serve as the high priests of society by finding solutions to the social problems that plagued society. One of the earliest criminological writers to take this call for positivism seriously was the Belgian astronomer Adolphe Quetlet, who argued that the reason why crime is regular in frequency from place to place and from time to time has nothing to do with free will. Rather, according to him, crime is determined by forces such as socio-economic conditions and environmental factors. By implication, better social organisation would result in eliminating social ills such as crime. He was writing in the 1820s at a time when middle-class fear of the 'dangerous classes', or what Victor Hugo called *les misérables*, was so high that the state was developing statistics as a way of keeping the people under surveillance. Quetelet argued that social reform was what was needed to tackle what he called the social mechanism of crime not classicism, with its unverifiable emphasis on free will.

The expansion of prisons and the methods of statistical record-keeping by the state helped to constitute a specialised discipline for criminologists in Europe. If Quetelet and the criminologists that followed him had extended their focus to slavery and colonialism, they would have exposed the basic fact that crime control is not the principal aim of widening the net of social control. In this book, I am not arguing that criminologists deliberately tried to serve colonialism with their knowledge; rather, *Counter-Colonial Criminology* will show the extent to which criminology was underdeveloped due to its lack of awareness of colonial criminology.

One of those who followed the positivism of Quetelet was the Italian prison physician Lombroso, who shifted in the 1860s from the sociological determinism of the former to advance what has come to be known as biological determinism. According to Lombroso and his followers, those who are critical of Quetelet for expressing scepticism about free will miss the point that some people are biologically predisposed to criminality as a result of their low level of evolution. Applying Darwin's theory of natural selection to moral conduct, Lombroso observed that his experiments on dead criminals revealed that their skulls were deformed like the skulls of rodents. He concluded that criminals were atavistic throwbacks to an earlier stage of evolution and, much like Quetelet, concluded that rather than punish them under the ideology of free will, they should be treated for their deformities. He went on to say that born criminals can be easily identified by physical stigmata which made 'criminals, savages, and apes' stand out (Lombroso, 1911). The difficulty for him was that his list of stigmata mirrored the characteristics of dark-skinned Sicilians, who were racially profiled in the popular imagination and in official social control as the main sources of criminality in Italy.

Although Lombroso later revised this crude biologism, his views agreed with commonsensical notions of pure blood and nobility and so he remained influential, especially because he was the first to conduct a 'scientific' experiment in criminology. This 'father' of scientific criminology later influenced people such as Charles Goring, who observed in eugenic terms that the English convict in 1913 appeared to inherit criminality because crime ran in families. Quetelet could have offered an environmental explanation to such family crime records, but it was the view of Lombroso that supported the practice of transporting habitual criminals to the British colonies to prevent them from marrying and reproducing their type among the master race at the height of empire. This crude ideology was later to influence the Nazi propaganda that Jews were an inferior race that must be exterminated to save the master race from genetic pollution.

WHOSE CONSCIENCE IS THE COLLECTIVE CONSCIENCE UNDER COLONIALISM?

Underlying Weber's theory, like that of Emile Durkheim (1973), and in fact underlying all theories of the Punishment Of Offenders (POO), is the assumption that it is only offenders who are punished and so the history of Victimisation As Mere Punishment (VAMP) remains relatively untheorised, perhaps due to the blindness to slavery and colonialism in criminological theory. Even in victimology, VAMP is unrecognised because the sub-field follows the individualist Enlightenment criminological framework of POO theories to conceptualise the victimised as an *individual* 'victim' (Agozino, 1997a).

Durkheim was anxious to distance sociology from the atomistic explanations of biology and psychology by returning to the Comtean call for a social science *sui generis*, as attempted by Quetelet. According to Durkheim, the answer to the Hobbesian question of order is that every society has a collective conscience which regulates morality to ensure that social control is not too strong and deviance not too common, otherwise anomie would result. Just as Weber divided society into a dual typology of the rational and the irrational, Durkheim, at about the same time, divided society into mechanical and organic types of solidarity. He argued that the division of labour within society is what leads to increased specialisation and increased differentiation of roles but also to increased integration of the differentiated units and upgraded adaptation of the society that is evolving from pre-industrial mechanical solidarity to modern organic solidarity. He observed that one way to study the evolution of any society is by focusing on the system of punishment in that society. According to him, 'quantitative change' is identifiable in the history of penal justice because penal intensity is greater, the closer a society approximates mechanical solidarity – and the more absolute power is. 'Qualitative changes' are characterised by varying terms of imprisonment which, depending on the seriousness of the offence, become the only normal means of social control.

Durkheim recognises that absolutism, or unlimited governmental power over citizens who have no rights and who are treated like private property, could result in obstructions to the qualitative dynamic (though he failed to use colonial policies to illustrate this). Nevertheless, he argued that imprisonment is impractical under the ethic of collective responsibility of mechanical types of solidarity and that prisons ensured certainty of penalty for individual offenders in organic-type solidarities. (Again he failed to speculate on whether this was why European colonial administrations preferred to use genocide as a penal policy against largely innocent people who were presumed guilty by association.) According to him, increasing sympathy for and sensitivity towards human suffering cannot explain the qualitative dynamic towards imprisonment simply because such a humanism could also lead in the opposite direction of increasing intensity in punishment (especially under the colonial situation where the life of one European was judged superior to the lives of millions of natives). Durkheim impoverished his theory by failing to utilise the resources available to him through the French Colonial Office and relied instead on inaccurate travellers' tales about South Pacific societies which were presumably under mechanical solidarity. Consequently, he arrived at a less than satisfactory theory that argues that the evolution of criminal law tautologically causes penal evolution by becoming less sacred. The rational principle in operation, according to Durkheim, is that it would be contradictory to punish offences against human dignity in the victim by violating the self-same human dignity in the offender and so deviance increasingly demands less severe penalty (although the reverse was the case in the colonies). The historical inaccuracies in Durkheim's theory have been well summarised by Garland and there is no need to rehearse them here, except to say that even Garland (1990) was silent on the colonial dimensions.

Colonialism proves that repressive sanction is also characteristic of organic forms of solidarity. The examples of slavery, apartheid and fascism illustrate further that whole groups of people have been rationally repressed as if they were guilty of unspecified crimes – rational because it was in the interest of Europeans to do so. The crimes of fascism were internationally judged and punished, notably at Nuremberg, and yet some of those crimes may have been initially committed while carrying out orders to discipline and punish the Other. Moreover, what Durkheim saw as a more humane qualitative change could now be seen to be more quantitative in terms of the lengths of imprisonment rather than simplistically as more humane alternatives to imprisonment. Similarly, what he saw as quantitative change could be said to be qualitative in terms of the severity of punishment which is more difficult to quantify than prison sentences.

Durkheim's collective conscience is more like a hegemonic moral order in the sense that Antonio Gramsci used the term. According to Gramsci (1971), hegemony is the intellectual and moral leadership of a class which makes it possible for that class to rule not only by force and not without force at all, but also with coerced consent. This class hegemony has since been applied to race and gender hegemony by many writers. It is the rationalist conceptualisation of the most individual of attributes, conscience, in terms of the collective society, that prevented Durkheim from interrogating the dysfunctional aspects of penal justice. However, his emphasis on the popular, emotional dynamics of punishment provides an insight into why punishment is popular and why politicians are able to mobilise public opinion around issues of law and order, even under colonialism. Durkheim's call for the energy of the collective conscience to be kept at a moderate level in order to allow both good and evil geniuses to emerge and flourish in any normal society can also be seen as part of the campaign for liberatory social policy which the Enlightenment thinkers advocated, but which was under threat from biological and psychological positivists who were unwittingly calling for the final solution to the problems of difference, deviance and defiance.

Liberal sociologists in America, including Robert Parks (former personal assistant to Booker T. Washington) and his colleague at the University of Chicago, Anthony Burgess, borrowed the social structural theory of Durkheim and moved away from the anthropological criminology of the Italian School. According to the Chicago School, crime is not caused by the nature of individuals but by the social environment in which they live. They observed that crime was concentrated in inner city areas of Chicago even though different waves of immigrants from different cultural backgrounds moved into the poor housing available in the inner city and then moved to the suburbs while crime remained relatively high in this zone. Their students, including Shaw and Mckay, applied this ecological theory to juvenile delinquency and concluded that the cause of delinquency is social disorganisation, which happens to be more pronounced in inner city areas. Although these liberal scholars were well intentioned in their attempt to persuade policy-makers to tackle the dreadful poverty that poor immigrants are forced to endure, their emphasis on the crimes of the poor and their lack of interest in the crimes of the powerful resulted in racial–class–gender profiling of inner city youth.

The Durkheimian emphasis on individual freedom was continued in America by Robert K. Merton, who used the concept of anomie to explain why crime is prevalent in a liberal society. According to Merton (1938), a liberal capitalist society like America lays emphasis on the American Dream, according to which anyone can succeed if they work hard. However, according to Merton, anomie arises when there is a lack of fit (or unequal emphases) between cultural goals – the American Dream – and the legitimate means of achieving those goals – equal opportunities. As a result of the unequal emphases, individuals adapt in five main ways to their perception of relative deprivation of access to the legitimate means to the cultural goals.

The good guys, according to Merton, are the conformists – those who succeed by using the legitimate means of hard work to achieve the American Dream (Bill Gates, for example).

The rebels are those who reject the cultural goal of the American Dream and substitute their own dream of total liberation from capitalism while rejecting the institutionalised means of achieving the American Dream, substituting the Malcolm X philosophy of 'by any means necessary' (for example, the Black Panther Party of the 1970s).

The ritualists are those who know that by working hard they will not achieve the American Dream, but they work hard anyway (the masses of American citizens who work from 9 a.m. to 5 p.m. and sometimes work at two jobs to make ends meet).

Then come the retreatists, who reject the American Dream and the legitimate means of hard work, but fail to replace them with goals of their own or means of their own. The Hippies of the 1960s are an example, though they had their own goals of universal love and their own means of permanent partying.

Finally, Merton identified individuals he called the innovators. These are the clever ones who believe in the American Dream but are aware that working from 9 to 5 will not get them to the Promised Land. These individuals adapt to anomie by adopting their own means to the goal of the American Dream. According to Merton, these are the individuals who are more likely to adopt criminal means. The Mafia are an example of innovative individuals.

Merton's emphasis on liberty and individualism is what makes his theory very popular in postcolonial locations, where few writers call for equal opportunities as a way of stemming the epidemic of crime in societies where inequalities are simply scandalous. However, Merton has been severely critiqued for assuming that the modes of adaptation are individual whereas most forms of adaptation, criminal and otherwise, happen to be group activities. The more powerful critique of Merton, however, comes from the counter-colonial theory of Steven Box (1983), who states that the facts do not fit the Mertonian assumption that the poor are those most likely to become criminal due to their relative deprivation. In the colonial situation, for example, the conformists could be mass murderers who massacre whole villages, especially when there is organised resistance to forced labour and forced seizure of surplus produce and forced taxation without representation. Although the nationalists could fit into the category of innovators, they are treated as conformists under the colonial situation and this is probably prophetic since bourgeois nationalists accepted the cultural goal of colonialism – the domination of their own people – and the colonial means of force, except that their own is a neocolonial means of exploitation. Yet the genuine rebels who rejected the colonial goal and the colonial means and substituted their own genuine nationalist goals and nationalist means (Ho Chi Ming, Frantz Fanon, Kwame Nkrumah, Amilcar Cabral, Samora Machel, Agostino Neto, to name but a few) cannot be classified as common criminals following Merton's theory. The problem is that this was hardly what Merton meant by rebellion since these men were revolutionaries and not simply domesticated rebels without a cause. Box's theory is instructive for *Counter-Colonial Criminology* because of its convincing assumption that it is power, not poverty, that explains most crimes, be they the crimes of the rich or the crimes of the poor. If it is relative deprivation that causes criminality, why is it that top government officials, multinational corporations, dictators and wealthy drug barons continue to commit crimes despite their incredible privileges? The answer is that, like the criminal organisations that ran colonial empires, they have the power to do as they wish and, as Box, following Lord Acton, states: power corrupts and absolute power corrupts absolutely. This same theory of power or relative power rather than relative deprivation explains why some poor desperadoes offend against other poor people – because, as one disco record repeats monotonously, they've got the power.

Merton was severely criticised by Cloward and Ohlin (1960) who observed that unequal opportunities also exist in illegitimate activities and so it does not follow that anyone who cannot go to college automatically qualifies as a gang leader. Their theory of social disorganisation and delinquent subcultures, however, retained the Mertonian prejudice against the working poor. Edwin Sutherland (1949) tried to correct some of these blind spots in criminological theory by advancing the view that criminal behaviour is learned in the same way that lawful behaviour is learned. He observed that white-collar crime should not be ignored by criminologists and that his theory of differential association offered a satisfactory explanation for all types of crime, although he too focused on individuals' crimes and ignored imperialist crimes.

In an address to the Ghana National Assembly on 22 March 1965, Kwame Nkrumah analysed white-collar crime in the colonial situation with specific reference to the Congo:

In the five years preceding independence, the net outflow of capital to Belgium alone was four hundred and sixty-four million pounds.

When Lumumba assumed power, so much capital was taken out of the Congo that there was a national deficit of forty million pounds.

Tshombe is now told the Congo has an external debt of nine hundred million dollars. This is a completely arbitrary figure – it amounts to open exploitation based on naked colonialism. Nine hundred million dollars ($900,0000,000) is supposed to be owed to United States and Belgium monopolies after they have raped the Congo of sums of 2,500 million pounds, 464 million pounds, and 40 million pounds .... But the tragic-comedy continues .... To prop up Tshombe, the monopolies decided that of this invented debt of $900 million, only $250 million has to be paid. How generous, indeed! ... The monopolies further announce a fraudulent programme to liquidate so-called Congolese external debts of 100 million pounds. Upon announcing this, they declare Congo is to be responsible for a further internal debt of 200 million pounds .... Despite political independence, the Congo remains a victim of imperialism and neo-colonialism ... [but] the economic and financial control of the Congo by foreign interests is not limited to the Congo alone. The developing countries of Africa are all subject to this unhealthy influence in one way or another. (Nkrumah, 1967: 198–200)

While Nkrumah is right that these fraudulent practices continue with impunity, there is very little criminological interest in the phenomenon. As chapter 9 will show, African novelists are more likely than criminologists to explore the crimes of the powerful. Historians and general social theorists are more likely than criminologists to express interest in such events. For example, Adam Hochschild (1998), a literary theorist, catalogued the genocidal crimes of Belgian colonial officials in the Congo in the way that creative writers such as Mark Twain did when the crimes were being committed. Only dependency theorists like Offiong (1980: 163–4) come close to this issue by critiquing apologists of imperialism who assert that the French domination of Burkina Faso today and the US involvement in the assassination of Patrice Lumumba are part of the politics of 'containing communism'. Offiong argues that there are exploitative economic interests involved in imperialist domination and that it is not domination for the sake of domination. He goes on to analyse how the American multinational company ITT and the CIA plotted the overthrow and assassination of Salvador Allende in Chile in the early 1970s.

Third World criminologists who have studied fraud concentrate on desperate individuals in the Third World who try to con greedy people in the West. The unhealthy influence that Nkrumah referred to can therefore be extended to criminological influences by which western experts and ambassadors are invited to prescribe solutions to the presumed crime-proneness of the poor while saying absolutely nothing about imperialist crimes. Criminologists might object to this analysis and maintain that they are interested only in knowledge for the sake of knowledge, but critical criminologists would accept that knowledge and power serve each other intimately. However, Nkrumah has been criticised by Rodney (1974) for expelling critical members from his ruling party and surrounding himself with sycophants until he was overthrown by the bourgeois army, like Lumumba before him. C.L.R. James also criticised Nkrumah for sacking the country's Chief Justice for passing a judgement that Nkrumah did not agree with (James, 1982), warning that such an error could pave the way for fascist rule in Africa.

Aimé Cæsaire (1972: 10) stated that 'Colonialists may kill in Indochina, torture in Madagascar, imprison in Black Africa, crack down in the West Indies. Henceforth the colonised know that they have an advantage over them. They know that their temporary 'masters' are lying ... [colonialism is not] an attempt to extend the rule of law'. To drive home the point, Cæsaire quotes a white supremacist passage which reads like something from Hitler's *Mein Kampf*. But it was actually written by a certain Renan, a 'liberal' French intellectual who was interested in moral and intellectual reformation following the second imperialist world war which should have taught the French better about the injustice of fascism:

> The regeneration of the inferior or degenerate races by the superior races is part of the providential order of things for humanity. With us, the common man is nearly always a *déclassé* nobleman, his heavy hand is better suited to handling the sword than the menial tool. Rather than work, he chooses to fight, that is, he returns to his first estate. *Regere imperio populos*, that is our vocation. Pour forth this all-consuming activity onto countries which, like China, are crying aloud for foreign conquest. Turn the adventurers who disturb European society into a *ver sacrum*, a horde like those of the Franks, the Lombards, or the Normans, and every man will be in his right role. Nature has made a race of workers, the Chinese race, who have wonderful manual dexterity and almost no sense of honor; govern them with justice, levying from them, in return for the blessing of such a government, an ample allowance for the conquering race, and they will be satisfied; a race of tillers of the soil, the Negro; treat him with kindness and humanity, and all will be as it should; a race of masters and soldiers, the European race. Reduce this noble race to working in the *ergastulum* like Negroes and Chinese, and they rebel. In Europe, every rebel is, more or less, a soldier who has missed his calling, a creature made for the heroic life, before whom you are setting *a task that is contrary to his race* – a poor worker, too good a soldier. But the life at which our workers rebel would make a Chinese or a fellah happy, as they are not military creatures in the least. *Let each one do what he is made for, and all will be well.* (quoted in Cæsaire, 1972: 16)

Such imperialist reasoning might be dismissed by criminologists as having nothing to do with their scientific discipline, but in the early years of the discipline, this was the type of propaganda that criminologists produced in the service of imperialism. Initially, it was known as criminal anthropology and was well respected until the Holocaust dealt it the most effective critique by following it to its logical conclusion. However, before the Nazis came to power, anthropologists such as Ernest Albert Hooton were looking for the biological basis of criminality in the 1930s. Following Lombroso's theory of the born criminal, while trying to improve the measurement tools of anthropometry which he believed to be more advanced compared to the research of Lombroso, Hooton (1939) measured 17,000 people in the US to determine whether they had any of the 125 characteristics that supposedly disposed people to criminality. In conclusion, Hooton recommended that it is desirable to control 'the progress of human evolution by breeding better types and by the ruthless elimination of inferior types, if only we are willing to found and to practice a science of human genetics' (quoted in Barkan, 1992: 106–7). Needless to add that the Nazis were more than willing, and many states in America, with the support of the Supreme Court, forcibly sterilised tens of thousands of citizens who were deemed feeble-minded.

In 2001, a decorated Vietnam war veteran and former US Senator, Bob Kerry, confessed that the troops under his command massacred innocent civilians during the war, but pleaded that it was a mistake in the heat of battle rather than a deliberate war crime. This started a national debate on the extent of the culpability not just of Bob Kerry, but of the whole of the US in the crimes committed against the people of Vietnam. As usual, criminologists have not had a word to say about this controversy, leaving journalists such as Chang (1997) to be the best criminologists on similar questions about Japanese imperialist crimes in China. Richard Falk (2001), a professor of international law at Princeton University, analysed the controversy in *The Nation*. According to him, the US would contribute more to the promotion of international law if the crimes against the Vietnamese people were no longer denied or excused but acknowledged and reparations paid. He draws an analogy between the Nuremberg War Crimes tribunal and the war crimes committed in the name of America. Instead of condemning the war crimes simply because the war was not won, as the popular media tended to do, Falk urged more honesty and the admission of guilt. Instead of continuing with the arrogant spirit of denial and ridicule that greeted the Vietnam war crimes tribunal headed by Bertrand Russell in 1967, Falk recommended implicitly that America should negotiate a plea bargain. He suggested that an admission of guilt should be extended to the crimes committed against African Americans during the centuries of slavery. Meanwhile, criminologists have continued to bury their heads in the sand of administrative criminology, completely ignoring the relevance of such debates to the development of theoretical criminology.

Similar criminological work was abandoned to Edward Herman, a professor of finance, and Noam Chomsky, a professor of linguistics, who came very close to developing a theory of crimes of the state, with the propagandist mass media as accomplices, in their book *Manufacturing Consent* (1988). As they put it: 'A propaganda system will consistently portray people abused in enemy states as worthy victims, whereas those treated with equal or greater severity by its own government or clients will be unworthy' (Herman and Chomsky, 1988: 37). This charge applies to the imperialist logic of conventional criminology which ignores imperialist crimes. The mass media report events with obvious ideological biases, but criminologists are yet to summon the courage to address the imperialist crimes committed in Biafra, Vietnam, Laos, Cambodia, El Salvador, Nicaragua, the Middle East, Rwanda and South Africa, to mention but a few examples. Following the 11 September 2001 attack on the World Trade Center and the Pentagon, as well as the plane that crashed in Pennsylvania on its way to further attacks, criminologists are falling over each other to develop courses on terrorism. Only a few criminologists are addressing the forces that have resulted in the globalisation of terrorism (Onwudiwe, 2000). Some criminology departments even advertise on the internet that crime is now the leading social problem and so there are many more employment opportunities for criminology graduates.

FROM THE MICRO-PHYSICS OF POWER TO THE BIFURCATION THESIS

The long quotation from the imperialist ideologue Renan, cited above, reminds criminologists of the policy of transportation through which Europe shipped its prisoners to the colonies to act as the conquering hordes of imperialism. Today, the prisons of Europe, Australia and North America are exploding with surplus populations that cannot be off-loaded to a penal colony. Yet, the prisons resemble the slave plantations and the penal colonies given the increasing disproportionate warehousing of minority individuals behind their walls. At the same time, criminologists continue to write like the apologists of imperialism by pretending that all they seek in their research is the truth, the whole truth and nothing but the truth, refusing to recognise the fascist uses that criminological knowledge serves in unequal societies.

Exceptions include Foucault (1977) and his followers, who strongly argue that there is a knowledge–power axis in every discipline but who remain silent about the outrageous foundation of criminology on the bloody soil of imperialism. Every knowledge gained is gained in a power relationship and every knowledge relevant is exercised in specific power relationships. What distinguishes one knowledge from another is not truth or falsehood as such, but the varying power resources available to those who possess and exercise them in varying degrees and those who contest them relatively. However, Foucault shares with Durkheim a focus on the individual offender, on what he called the 'micro-physics of power', and the puzzling silence on imperialist power to punish and the consequent resistance (although Durkheim tried to avoid the atomisation of what he saw as social facts). We will see in this book that criminological modernity is not always concerned with the micro-physics of power but with the macro-physics of intergroup power relations and how these are juridistically represented – especially under colonialism.

Mathiessen (1983) has analysed a contested piece of law reform in Norway to show that in the future whole groups and categories could come under the disciplinary power of the judiciary. However, he also noted that the proposal was dropped, along with the originating minister, and so it was not put into practice. In this book, we will come across instances of such net-widening within the judiciary itself as a reality rather than as a future prospect. This is in agreement with the Foucauldian dispersal thesis of Cohen (1985), who identified the imminent reversal of the tendency towards individualisation which Foucault had identified as a feature of modern exercises of disciplinary knowledge and power. According to Cohen, the following processes are taking place in penal policy (although he could have used the well-documented history of colonialism to illustrate his points more clearly and correct the false assumption that all these things are happening mainly to offenders):

1. a blurring of the boundary between institutional and non-institutional penalty;
2. a widening of the net to include those who would escape judicial power previously;
3. a thinning of the mesh, greater intervention in the community to discipline more offenders; and
4. penetration of more informal networks by state agents.

Bottoms (1983) has argued, with his bifurcation thesis, that an exclusive focus on discipline, repression and oppression when looking at the criminal justice system is misleading. He applied Durkheim's second law of penal evolution, 'the law of quality', and found that punishment is not always disciplinary, although punishment for serious or violent crimes takes the form of disciplinary punishment – prison and supervised probation, for example. Non-disciplinary penalties – fines, suspended sentences and compensation orders – are given for less serious offences. The bifurcation thesis contradicts Durkheim's second law because imprisonment is falling at the expense of the fine, community service and the growth of compensation and related matters, whereas Durkheim predicted that the deprivation of liberty and liberty alone would become increasingly the main penal form under organic types of solidarity. It is difficult to know if all of the penal forks identified by Bottoms are exclusively disciplinary; it could more easily be said that they are all disciplinary to some extent. Moreover, the assumption is that it is penal policy that is bifurcating into disciplinary and non-disciplinary penalties, that it is penalty that is bifurcating into itself. It seems more convincing to say that what is bifurcating is criminal justice policy as a whole and not just penal policy.

Social enquiry reports help to diagnose and differentiate individual offenders according to their social circumstances. While this is a challenge to Weber's impersonal bureaucratic rationality, it seems to derive from the sociological positivism of Durkheim. In a similar way, the adoption of psychiatric detention orders and expert witnesses could be said to be the result of theories of individual positivism, which Lombroso (1876) pioneered. Apart from these two policy implications, positivism seems to have had little impact on the Weberian bureaucratic administration of justice. This field is dominated by classicism and neoclassicism, which supply the ideologies of individual responsibility, just deserts, free will rationality with a few exceptions and punishment as a duty different from the treatment that positivistic determinism recommends in the area of sociological research where it remains the dominant framework. This synthesis of classicist and positivistic principles in the administration of justice results in the penal welfare strategies identified by Garland (1985). The penal welfare strategies in turn reflect Bottoms' bifurcation thesis. However, Garland (2001) returned to Foucault for an explanation of why European and American penal policies have moved away from welfarism and seem to be reversing the process of civilisation that was notable in the past. He found European social theories incapable of explaining the history of present penal policies, but failed to consult the Third World theories of Fanon, Cæsaire, Nkrumah, Cabral, Rodney, Soyinka, Ngugi, Achebe, James, Hall, Said and others, who have interpreted these processes as being closer to the theories of imperialism that Foucault ignored.

Becky Tatum (1996) has argued that the 'colonial model can be used as a theoretical explanation for the over-representation of African Americans in crime, victimization and delinquency statistics'. She applies Fanon and other theorists to explain the marginalisation and alienation of African Americans in terms of their domination by another racial group that reaps huge material benefits from the colonial type of relationship. The frustration of African Americans is expressed in Mertonian terms of mimicry by some, misplaced aggression by others and resistance by yet others. However, she concludes that internal colonialism is a better explanation of the political, economic and social domination of African Americans and their behavioural adaptation (Mertonian) to such subjugation due to the elimination of the foreign element of colonial domination in American society. In a different context, I used internal colonialism theories to go beyond the bifurcation thesis and move towards a trifurcation thesis by recognising victimisation as a neglected feature of penal policy, especially with reference to black women and to the need to decolonise victimisation (Agozino, 1997a).

A Japanese colleague, Minoru Yokoyoma, agreed with the thrust of my argument at a session of the American Society of Criminology in San Francisco, November 2000. He added that western criminology has since colonised Japanese criminology by relatively monopolising the training of young criminologists who return to Japan to apply western theories uncritically. However, the Orient has a unique contribution to make to criminological theory which has only recently been recognised by western criminologists. This is the concept of criminology as peace-making, which is influenced by Buddhism among other spiritual, feminist and critical ideas opposed to imperialist war-mindedness (Pepinsky and Quinney, 1991). The limitation of the peace-making approach is that it focuses on the relationship between one individual victim and an individual offender. It is not clear how to make peace with imperialism or with a criminal state at the individual level without capitulating to imperialist reason. It is also true that peace is something that imperialists love – colonial peace treaties remind us of the fact that cowboys smoked peace pipes with the Indians before massacring them to steal their land. Peace and justice, but is there room for love in criminology? Is it possible to have real peace and justice while institutionalising white supremacist, patriarchal, imperialist hatred and intolerance of multiculturalism? Ho Chi Minh (1924) stated, almost echoing the African American classic of Ida B. Wells-Barnet (1892), what the Chicago School conveniently ignored in their obsession with broken windows in the inner cities:

It is well known that the black race is the most oppressed and most exploited of the human family ... What everyone does not perhaps know, is that after sixty-five years of the so-called emancipation, American Negroes still endure atrocious moral and material sufferings of which the most cruel and horrible is the custom of lynching. (Ho Chi Minh, 1924)

How satisfactory are the accounts of these theoretical perspectives in explaining how the judicial process has worked in the history of postcolonial countries?

2. From Determinism to Meaning: The Emergence of the Labelling Perspective

Deviance, like beauty, is in the eyes of the beholder. There is nothing inherently deviant in any human act, something is deviant only because some people have been successful in labelling it so. (J.L. Simmons, 1969)

The defeat of fascist Italian imperialism in Ethiopia in the 1930s followed the American war of independence against British rule 150 years earlier and the independence of the Irish Republic in the 1920s. These were followed by the war against Nazism in which colonised people played a crucial role to ensure victory for the allied forces. If these victories did not shatter belief in Emile Durkheim's idea of a 'collective conscience' as the answer to the question posed by Thomas Hobbes ('How society is possible', given what Hobbes saw as the selfish nature of human beings), the independence of India after the war helped to drive home the fact that, in a colonial situation, there is no single collective conscience. Then, in 1957, Kwame Nkrumah emerged from prison to assume office as Prime Minister of Ghana. This pattern was repeated in Cuba with the socialist revolution led by a former detainee, Fidel Castro; in Algeria with the victory of the nationalist forces, many of whom were tortured in jail; in Kenya with the election of the formerly jailed Jomo Kenyatta following the Mau Mau uprising; in Zambia with the election of Kenneth Kaunda who had been in detention; the success of the civil rights movement, even with leaders like Martin Luther King Junior in and out of jail; the victory of Vietnamese people over the joint armies of the superpowers; the defeat of colonialism in Mozambique, Guinea, Angola and Zimbabwe under the leadership of former political prisoners, and more recently in Namibia and South Africa with the election of the hitherto demonised Sam Nujoma and Nelson Mandela, respectively; in the Middle East with the achievement of limited power by the Palestine Liberation Organisation and the sharing of power with Sinn Féin in Northern Ireland. This incredible history, which saw colonised people formerly defined as criminals or terrorists redefined as heroes and political leaders around the world, must have forced some criminologists to question the positivistic assumption that there is a clear line dividing normality and pathology under a mythically consensual collective conscience.

Behaviours are never weird, bad, sick, deviant, sinful or criminal in themselves. They are simply censured or criminalised by the collective conscience (dominant conscience, *à la* Garland), according to Durkheim. The labelling perspective, or the perspective of societal reaction, agrees that deviance is socially constructed. However, instead of talking about a dehumanised collective conscience, the labelling theorists took stock of the civil rights movement, student uprisings, the anti-Vietnam war protests, the Cuban missile crisis, apartheid South Africa and the anti-colonial struggles in Africa and Asia. They concluded that social order is not based on the consensual picture painted by structural functionalism. They recognised social conflict and the inequality of power as being operative in the social construction of deviance. Their emphasis was on the people who have the power to label others deviant.

As Becker put it, 'Deviance is not a quality of the act the person commits, but rather a consequence of the application of rules and sanctions to an "offender".' The deviant is one to whom the label has successfully been applied; deviant behaviour is behaviour that people so label (1963, p. 9).

Do you find this statement true or slightly exaggerated? Are there not certain types of behaviour that are naturally deviant in every society? What about rape, homicide and genocide?

According to Stephen Pfohl (1994), the labelling perspective is not exaggerated; what is universal about deviance is not the content of the acts but the process by which definitions of acts and persons as deviant are socially generated and applied. As Kitsuse (1975) put it:

> the distinctive character of the societal reaction perspective ... leads ... to a consideration of how deviants come to be differentiated by imputations made about them by others, how these imputations activate systems of social control, and how these control activities become legitimated as institution responses to deviance.

THEORETICAL AND HISTORICAL BACKGROUND

The societal reaction perspective has been called variously labelling theory, the interactionist perspective and the social constructionist perspective. However, the adherents themselves have emphasised that it is not a theory as such, but a common approach or perspective. The theorists have collectively pursued three goals:

1. the social-historical development of deviant labels;
2. the application of labels to certain types of people in specific times; and
3. the symbolic and practical consequences of the labelling process.

Although the perspective emerged in the 1960s, it can be traced back to an essay written in 1918 (the end of the first imperialist world war) by George Herbert Mead, 'The Psychology of Punitive Justice', in which he followed the functionalist perspective to identify the positive contributions of labelling in awakening the conscience of law-abiding citizens. However, Mead went beyond functionalism by focusing on scapegoating and on the rituals of interaction which result in people seeing themselves in the way that others see them.

Edwin Lemert (1951) elaborated on Mead's thesis. He was critical of the pathological, disorganisational, functionalist, anomie and learning perspectives because these apparently take deviance for granted. Sumner (1994) summarises the main points of Lemert as follows:

1. There was little scientific support for the claim that people could be divided into the normal and the pathological.
2. Most deviation was inconsequential because it is inevitable in conflicted, multicultural, pluralistic society that some people will deviate some of the time.
3. Systematic social deviation depends on the individual's adoption of deviant identity.
4. Social control creates as much deviance as it deters.
5. The labelling of deviance is independent and not necessarily linked to the deviant act. It is more clearly linked to moral reformation, political/economic interests.
6. The above five points do not add up to a theory of deviant behaviour but remain a useful orientation or perspective for specific analysis.

This perspective flourished in the 1960s even though similar perspectives can be found as far back as early nineteenth-century England, according to Sumner (perhaps reflecting doubts about universalism raised by the successful American war of independence). What made the labelling perspective fashionable in the 1960s was not the originality of the claims made in its name, but the fact that it challenged the post-war consensus that proclaimed the end of ideology in the emergence of the welfare state. The labelling perspective reactivated Lemert's liberalism by renewing old debates.

What was it about the early 1960s that made sociologists in the United States particularly ripe for the societal reaction viewpoint? During this period, college students and some professors joined African-American civil rights advocates and protested against the Vietnam War. In the true sense of participant observation, sociologists experienced tear gas, arrests, surveillance, stigmatisation and intimidation as though they were common criminals. In the ensuing conflict, what is 'justifiable homicide' and what is murder, what is realism and what is paranoia, the dedicated and the misfit, were easily reversible and reversed. Some of those who did not experience these conflicts but who studied them, according to Becker, were forced to adopt what Pfohl (1994) called an 'unconventional senti-mentality' by sympathising with the viewpoints of the underdogs contrary to the conventional *hierarchy of credibility* that Becker (1966) analysed. According to Becker, sociologists who adopt the viewpoints of the superordinates are never accused of bias even though powerful officials are more likely to lie given that 'They do not perform as society would like them to. Hospitals do not cure people; prisons do not rehabilitate prisoners; schools do not educate students' (Becker 1966–67: 242–3). As Becker put it in his Presidential Address to the Society for the Study of Social Problems, Miami Beach, August 1966:

> In the course of our work and for who knows what reasons, we fall into deep sympathy with the people we are studying, so that while the rest of society views them as unfit in one or another respect for the deference ordinarily accorded a fellow citizen, we believe that they are at least as good as anyone else, more sinned against than sinning. (Becker 1966–67: 240)

Most of the early labelling perspectivists received their graduate education in the Department of Sociology at the University of Chicago. There, they were exposed to the Chicago School of symbolic interactionism, which states that the way we see ourselves is dependent in part on the way others see us. They were also taught the research method of participant observation. Many of the graduates were attracted to the universities of California which were expanding on land stolen from massacred Native American tribes in the previous two centuries. The new universities had more diverse staff and students (especially Hispanic students and African American students) compared to the older institutions. That was also when Ronald Reagan (the actor who made a name for himself playing cowboys who participated in the massacre of Native Americans, or what Mirandé (1987), described as 'Gringo justice') won the governorship of California with a perceived mandate to stem the spread of what he called 'tenured radical' ideas in the state university system.

SYMBOLIC INTERACTIONISM

The term symbolic interactionism was coined by Herbert Blumer to identify the teachings of his professor, G. H. Mead, according to whom people interpret the actions of others rather than simply reacting to them. Symbolic interactionists view society as a process of intersubjectively meaningful action in the way that Weber defined social action. Like social action, the self is also a process of interpretive interaction with significant others. These ideas are reflected in the emphases placed on meaning and interaction processes by the societal reaction perspective.

Becker argued that we should not regard any act as deviant simply because it is commonly regarded as such. *Was the anti-colonial struggle a crime or were Native Americans criminals for defending their land and heritage?* Rather we should try to understand 'the process by which the common definition [of crime] arises ... the process of labelling'. For this purpose, he distinguished between:

1. the concrete interaction;
2. the historical construction of the label;
3. formal/informal labelling processes; and
4. pure and secret deviants.

Becker concluded from his study of the Marijuana Stamp Tax Act of 1937 that the motive force for the origin and development of deviant labels is the role of 'moral entrepreneurs' who campaign to transform sectional interests into being perceived as general interests.

The law that made marijuana illegal came about after the prohibition of alcohol was lifted in the 1920s. The Drugs Enforcement Administration then saw a threat to its budget and turned to marijuana as a new area of responsibility. Surprisingly, due to the opposition of the big businesses that used hemp products, the Act was amended to require that those who sold marijuana had to pay taxes on what they sold. However, since it was difficult to tax marijuana because people could grow their own, the law was changed to make the growing, possession or supply of marijuana illegal, even though doctors and scientists stated repeatedly that it is much safer than alcohol and tobacco, legally available drugs that yield huge revenues in taxes and make big profits for multinational companies.

According to the labelling perspective, deviance develops in sequences in line with whatever factors appear significant to certain individuals. Becker illustrated this by the sequence of becoming a drug addict, which explains why some people experiencing the factors that lead to addiction do not become drug addicts when others do, depending mostly on the reactions of others.

PHENOMENOLOGY AND LABELLING

The labelling perspective borrowed heavily from the phenomenology of Alfred Shutz (1962) via the symbolic interactionism of G.H. Mead. Shutz was one of the first to move away from a macro-sociology to a micro-sociology of everyday interaction. Shutz observed that social experience is structured through 'typification', or the typical meanings associated with significant symbols. Phenomenology advocated that the goal of sociology is to understand the common sense of members of a community rather than trying to find universal explanations. The labelling perspective agrees.

Ethnomethodology extends the phenomenological perspective by focusing on the methods by which people commonsensically construct structured interaction. They do not agree with symbolic interactionists that a shared meaning is essential for ordered social interaction. They argue instead that what is shared is a body of interpretive skills with which to decode symbolic phenomena.

The labelling perspective borrows the concept of *indexicality* from ethnomethodology and applies it to the fact that interpretation is dependent on content. David Sudnow (1965) reported that the office of the public prosecutor was pressurised by overcrowding and under-staffing when deciding who was a 'normal criminal' to be locked away and who could plea bargain. As a result, they developed an index of normality which could be applied to everyone in order to simplify the problem of classification whereas a different public prosecutor with a different range of case loads might classify a normal criminal as an accidental offender.

Reflexivity is another concept that the labelling perspective borrowed from ethnomethodology. This means that who we are affects the way significant others see us. If the four New York Police Department officers who fired 41 shots and killed Amadou Diallo, an immigrant from Guinea, had been ordinary citizens pleading self-defence in court, no jury would have agreed that they had a right to say that they thought that a wallet was a gun, especially if they had been four black men who had executed an innocent white man. Harold Garfinkel (1974) combines indexicality and reflexivity in reporting that juries are often unaware that they are trying to justify their verdict after the fact of having acquitted or convicted a defendant and reflecting the pressures of public opinion.

THE POWER TO NAME AS A FOCUS

The societal reaction perspective focuses on who has the power to label another as a deviant. This is an issue that was not addressed by the collective conscience of Durkheim and the individual modes of adaptation to anomie, according to Merton. However, the question that Becker raised was never explicitly answered by the labelling perspective. Who makes the rules of what Sumner calls the rigged fruit machine? Who collects the profits?

The societal reaction perspective avoided answering the question directly and focused instead on the critique of official statistics as the tool of social research. The perspective called for the statistics to be studied in order to explain how they are produced rather than relying on them for answers to the question of crime causation.

In an attempt to explain the unreliability of official statistics, Aaron Cicourel (1969) reports two years' participant observation in police and probation agencies. He found that black boys were more readily perceived as frightening by officers than white boys. This is because of stereotypical common sense, which results in *perceptual bias by control agents*. This bias goes beyond the racial appearance of the boys to reflect their class backgrounds. Compare this with Gelsthorpe (1986), who claims that police officers do not discriminate against boys and in favour of girls because, according to the officers, girls are more likely to apologise and be cautioned, whereas boys are more likely to be confrontational and are therefore more likely to be charged with an offence. *Can a study based on juvenile boys alone be generalised to juvenile girls?*

Furthermore, the societal reaction perspective explores the 'situational dynamics of labelling'. The situation in which labelling occurs and the dynamics (power) of who is doing the labelling determine whether the act will be officially recorded as deviance.

Differential visibility of different groups adds to the unreliability of official statistics. In addition, the bureaucratic organisations that provide official statistics have variable codes and change coding with variable priorities from area to area.

Finally, the societal reaction perspective emphasises that official statistics are *political* in character. They are produced by agents who have something at stake in the image that the public has of them.

The programme of reforms advocated by the societal reaction perspective includes the following suggestive warnings, which imply the need to decriminalise *victimless crimes* such as abortion, prostitution, drug-taking, gambling, etc.:

1. Laws prohibiting consensual deviant exchanges may increase secondary deviance.
2. Such laws are costly to enforce.
3. Such laws support organised crime.
4. Such laws damage public respect for law.

These warnings are implicit in Becker's *Outsiders* (1963) and in Goffman's *Asylum* (1961) among other texts like Scott's *The Making of Blind Men* (1969).

To what extent can these warnings be applied in support of the *Independence on Sunday* campaign for the legalisation of cannabis in Britain?

AN ASSESSMENT OF THE LABELLING PERSPECTIVE

This perspective has contributed the notion that there is no such thing as a born deviant. Methodologically, the perspective's focus on the meaning of labels drew attention to the fact that official statistics should be the subject of research rather than the tool of research. The insights of the labelling perspective are attractive to researchers in the Third World because they expose the hypocrisy of administrative criminology that supports the imprisonment of human rights campaigners and innocent poor people while powerful criminals get away with murder. The adoption of this perspective should warn scholars that just because someone ends up in prison it does not necessarily mean that he/she is a criminal.

In spite of these influential (at least in the 1960s) contributions, the labelling perspective has been subjected to severe criticism, which led Sumner (1994) to write an epitaph in a comical obituary of the sociology of deviance. The criticisms are as follows (Pfohl, 1994):

1. *The causal critique.* Many right-wing critics allege that the labelling perspective suggests that labelling causes crime. They acknowledge that this could be the case only in *secondary deviance* but not in *primary deviance.*

2. *The normative critique* suggests that labelling perspective runs the risk of labelling innocent people deviant by assuming that they are what Becker called *secret deviants.*

3. *The empirical critique* asks whether race–class–gender indexicality-reflexivity alone account for higher proportions of labelled people in a group or whether their actual behaviours are the main factors and whether labelled persons are more likely to be secondary deviants.

4. The situated knowledge critique argues that the labelling perspective allows sociologists to examine the social construction of commonsensical reality while taking for granted the social situation of sociological knowledge. It is as if sociology can only study but cannot be studied to expose the knowledge–power axis underlying its claims, as Foucault suggested.

5. The structural critique of the labelling perspective is made by critical criminologists, who point out that societal reaction theory is evasive of the state and such macro-processes of power as imperialism, the state and the nature of the economy. Moreover, they largely ignore resistance to the extent that, according to Gouldner, the underdog is presented in the labelling perspective as the underdog on its back rather than the underdog fighting back.

6. Finally, the gender critique of the labelling perspective comes from many feminist scholars, who point out that the labelling perspective completely ignored the symbolism of gender and so failed to offer adequate explanations for women's fear of masculinist violence. The neglect of gender also resulted in an

inadequate understanding of deviant men. Becker came close to this when looking at the roles of the wives of jazz musicians, but he only adopted the commonsensical view that women are conformists who try to make their deviant husbands comply with societal expectations (see Heidensohn (1986), Stanko (1992) and many others).

These critical comments about the labelling perspective show that even though the social movements of the 1960s served as the catalyst that produced new thinking in criminology, the thinkers did not follow this stimulation to a logical conclusion. For example, the efforts by the civil rights movement were not simply phenomenological ones of understanding the source of the label of white supremacy, but a struggle to end racism and sexism in American society. While some of the assumptions of labelling perspective can be interpreted to support anti-racism and anti-sexism in the administration of justice, there is no indication of how to extend this perspective to racist and sexist assumptions in criminological theory. Moreover, the adherents of the labelling perspective mentioned the poor as underdogs, but did not highlight the role of the state in the fight against poverty or in the struggle by the privileged to maintain poverty.

Criminologists who are interested in increasing social justice have since moved beyond the labelling perspective to consider the role of the state and the role of big business in defining legality. Subsequent chapters will evaluate the radical perspectives in criminology and point out how even they have remained overwhelmingly Eurocentric in their conception of state power. In Africa, Asia and South America, criminology has significantly failed to be established either because of the irrelevance of Eurocentric theories to Third World realities or because of the suspicion by dictatorships in these regions that such a discipline would discover, sooner or later, that crimes of the state constitute the major crime problem, requiring different theories of social control. The analysis in the rest of the book will highlight the importance of race–class–gender articulation in the analysis of social control anywhere in the world.

3. From Societal Reaction to Questions of Power: From Labelling to Radical Criminology

The liberal perspective of labelling emerged by shifting the focus of analysis from deviant behaviour to the meaning, origin and impacts of deviant symbols. The perspective raised important questions of power by asking: 'Who has the power to successfully label whom?' Becker tried to answer this indirectly with his concept of a *hierarchy of credibility*, but he could have saved himself a lot of explanation if he had made even a cursory reference to colonialism.

According to him, people usually look to those in authority for the most credible view of the meanings of conventional symbols. He asked sociologists, 'whose side are we on?' and suggested that we should be on the side of the underdog. This is because, according to Becker, the perspective of the underdog is likely to be more truthful than the perspective of the superordinates, who rely more on power than on truth for the legitimisation of the conventional hierarchy of credibility. On the other hand, the goal of changing an unjust structure of interaction makes the leaders of the underdogs more careful with truth and facts since embarrassing errors of fact might erode further the little power that they have attained.

FROM THE SYMBOLIC TO THE STRUCTURAL

Becker made the call for sociologists to take sides apparently in support of Gouldner's critique of the myth of value-free sociology. Gouldner (1970) later attacked Becker for misinterpreting him by suggesting that support for the underdog is mandated by the greater truth-value of their claims. This means, according to Gouldner, that the myth of value-free sociology ran the risk of being replaced by the myth of the unsentimental sociologist, who is taking sides for the sake of truth alone. Gouldner agreed that sociologists should adopt the perspectives of the underdog, not necessarily because it is likely to be more truthful than the perspective of the top dog, but because they are likely to be less well known precisely because they are marginalised.

The major criticism from the more radical perspectives is that although Becker talked about elites, ruling classes, bosses, adults, men and whites as the superordinates, they were never really the focus of his research and he never mentioned colonialism. What is more, there is no mention of the state, especially the imperialist state. Matza (1964) came close to this when he talked about a 'Leviathan', which is very much like Lemert's idea of 'the societal control culture', but these abstractions sound hollow without reference to the absurdity of European colonialism.

This type of talk appeared liberal only in comparison with Durkheim's normal versus pathological forms of social solidarity, or in contrast to Weber's ideal typical market nationality of the law under the spirit of capitalism. Many students and sociologists ended up with the question 'So what?' when the labelling perspective repeated that the fruit machine of social control is rigged. Like Gouldner, they became increasingly dissatisfied with a picture of the underdog on its back and started looking for the underdog fighting back. They moved beyond elites to focus on the state and the political economy of social control culture. Who put the fruit machine there, who takes the profits and who gets ripped off? These were the burning questions of the late 1960s and early 1970s but, sadly, hardly any of these European beneficiaries of colonialism had the courage to use their criminology to critique the inherently unjust system of power.

BACK TO CLASSICAL MARXISM

None of these questions was new. As Greenberg (1993: 1) pointed out: 'ours, of course, is not the first generation to have drawn on radical critiques of existing social arrangements in writing about crime'. He went on to state that nineteenth-century utopian socialists, anarchists and Marxists all discussed crime and punishment in ways similar to critical scholarship today. Marx had identified a class, the lumpenproletariat, a parasitic class (caricatured in Charles Murray's (1984) right-wing concept of the 'underclass') whose crimes paled into insignificance compared to the crimes of colonialism and the crimes necessary for the primitive accumulation of capital. However, Marx, in *Contribution to the Critique of Political Economy* (1904) used an architectural metaphor to describe the law as an epiphenomenon or superstructure. Engels (1958) analysed the poor and the demoralising effects of capitalist exploitation and oppression in his 1848 classic *The Condition of the Working Class in England*. He stated that this condition leads to a social war of each against all, emphasising that it is not only the poor who are predisposed to criminality under capitalism. These classical views of Marx and Engels were revived even before the 1960s but became increasingly fashionable among theorists from different conflict perspectives who emphasised different aspects of the Marxist orthodoxy while almost completely ignoring Marx's devastating critique of imperialism.

The plurality of the criminological perspectives that draw from Marxism is evident in the fact that conflict theorists, radical multicultural thought, critical feminists, lesbian and gay scholars, poststructuralists, postmodernists and anarchists all draw to some extent from Marxism without identifying themselves as Marxists, unlike some critical criminologists. However, all these different perspectives were united in their call for openly partisan scholarship which must be organically linked to political struggles, as Gramsci recommended. Sadly, few criminologists who subscribe to Marxism extended their analysis to the political struggle against imperialism.

One of the responses to this new trend was the *New Criminology* of Taylor, Walton and Young (1973), who promised to offer a fully social analysis of deviance and social control. They called for the abolition of the inequalities of wealth and power. They set out to answer the question that Becker posed, but failed to ponder directly: who makes the rules? They dismissed the correctional type of criminology for being 'empirical emasculation of theory' under the ideology of pragmatism. They emphasised that there is a 'material necessity and material incentive' for crime which suggests the possibility of a crime-free, control-free anarchist utopia. Surprisingly, they were mute on imperialist crimes and how to eliminate such crimes from the world.

Paul Hirst (1975) critically reviewed the arguments for a *New Criminology* and pointed out that such arguments cannot be said to be Marxist. He emphasised that what Marx and Engels wrote about and struggled against were unjust social relations of production and not specifically the law, crime and morality which they often mentioned in passing.

Hirst has been criticised for assuming that Marx and Engels defined the limits of Marxism by the subject matter that they analysed. Following Louis Althusser (1971), who argued that Marx and Lenin did not discover a new philosophy but a new philosophical method, Bankowski et al. (1977) point out that it is not possible to have a radical criminology unless what is meant by that is the training of criminologists who are radical. All these are potentially useful ideas for the ideological struggles against imperialism, but it is amazing that these critical scholars could not see beyond postcolonial Europe.

The claim by Hirst that there cannot be a direct application of the Marxist method of historical materialism in criminology is denied by the evidence of varieties of Marxist-oriented theories. *Instrumentalist* conflict criminology is the type of view shared by Richard Quinney and others in the 1970s, who saw the law as an instrument of the ruling class, pure and simple. According to Quinney (1974) capitalism rules by force. You do not have to be a Marxist to accept that there is conflict between labour and capital and so the instrumentalist view was not completely or even exclusively Marxist. What is baffling is that the conflict between the coloniser and the colonised was not analysed as a variant of the conflict between labour and capital, whereas Marx, Lenin, Nkrumah, Cabral and Rodney found this link to be basic, perhaps because they were not criminologists trained ideologically to service colonialism by focusing on the punishment of offenders.

Structuralist approaches to law from critical perspectives like those of Pashukanis (1980) follow Marx directly by identifying how the 'commodity fetishism' of capitalism influences the content if not the form of legal relations. Pashukanis argued that the superstructure is also part of the infrastructure in the sense that it is not only the economy that determines the law; sometimes the law determines economic relations to the extent that they will break down without what E.P. Thompson (1975) called an 'unqualified human good' – the rule of law. However, Pashukanis overemphasised the extent to which law is characteristic only of capitalism and followed the Communist Party line by predicting the withering away of the law along with the state under communism without analysing what might be called the Asiatic mode of law or pre-capitalist law, which suggests the possibility of post-capitalist law.

Individualist approaches to the state are exemplified by Ralph Miliband (1969), who emphasised the similar class backgrounds of members of the ruling class – they all went to Oxbridge, Harvard or Yale. The danger in this type of individualism is that it completely ignores the fact that, like Marx and Engels, most criminologists are white, middle-class men. Yet, like them, their backgrounds did not prevent many of them from adopting the perspectives of the working class, ethnic minorities and women. Likewise, most of the heroes of the anti-colonial struggle were petty bourgeois elements who committed what Cabral (1982) called a class suicide by taking the side of the people against imperialism. However, the Eurocentric criminologists failed to understand this.

Another variant of the Marxist influence in criminology is that of Sol Picciotto (1982) and others who emphasise that capitalism works according to a certain logic which results in everything being reduced to economic force, not absolutely but relatively and eventually, in the final analysis. The problem is that the final analysis never comes to pass, especially under the colonial situation, due to the metamorphosis of colonialism into neocolonialism, partly because ideological formations are sometimes more determinant than economic formations alone.

After reviewing these variants, Hall and Scraton (1981) opted for Gramsci's perspective on class hegemony. What distinguishes this perspective from the others is that it focuses on the oppressed with a view to supporting their struggle for power; it is not simply a negative call for struggles against the powers that be. Gramsci wondered why the oppressed often willingly collaborate with the ruling class instead of fighting a class war. For example, why did working-class soldiers guard him in jail instead of aiding his escape to fight fascism in Italy? He found the answer in what he called the 'ethical and educative' roles of the state (through education, religion, the family, mass media and marketing). He called this process hegemony, which he defined as the 'moral and intellectual leadership of a class' and pointed out that when successful, hegemony encourages forced consent. Accordingly, the hegemonic class does not rule by force alone but not without force at all; the ruling class rules through consent as well. He emphasised that hegemony relies more on consent than on coercion, even though at times of hegemonic crisis the balance between coercion and consent is likely to shift towards what Stuart Hall (1979, 1988) called authoritarian populism. This perspective influenced the analysis of what Hall et al. (1978) called policing the crisis, which is still recognised as one of the most systematic applications of a Marxist perspective to the law and order debate. Why did it take a scholar who is not trained in criminology and who grew up in a former colony (Jamaica) to point this out to European criminologists?

PRACTICAL IMPLICATIONS

According to Pfohl (1994), 'critical perspectives [note the plural] challenge sociologists, to make connections between the ritual construction of our everyday lives and the historical organisation of power'. According to him, this means that sociologists must recognise the extent to which they are part of the landscape of deviance and social control that they study. It is part of the argument of this book that criminologists have failed, or refused, to interrogate how much they are implicated by their discipline in imperialist reason. Similarly, critical poststructuralists recognise the centrality of language as a ritual force that affects all knowledge claims, but they are notorious for their conspiratorial silence on their cultural debts to colonialism. Dominant forms of knowledge are never free of the 'deviant' forms they exclude and so critical criminologists should begin to acknowledge their debts to European colonialism and global imperialism.

Dominant forms of knowledge are forever dependent on policing the boundaries between what is hegemonic and what threatens the reproduction of hierarchical power. By paying careful attention to such 'epistemological police work', critical poststructuralism subverts hierarchies of knowledge that are otherwise taken for granted even by the labelling perspective.

As Foucault put this: 'Power and knowledge directly imply one another. There is no relation without the correlative constitution of a field of knowledge, nor any knowledge that does not presuppose and constitute at the same time power relations' (1977: 27).

The policy implications of the critical perspective, according to Pfohl, are as follows:

1. Refuse the legitimacy of efforts to secure 'public safety' unless such efforts simultaneously aim at the realization of social and economic justice.
2. Refuse all uses of sexist, racist, homophobic, xenophobic and other culturally degrading languages, including visual languages, signs, gestures and icons.
3. Refuse to do business with business that support social injustice.
4. Refuse ignorance of history and of other people's cultures.
5. Refuse the commonsensical character of all authority.

Pfohl also advocates four 'strategic power-reflexive affirmations' that would go beyond the above refusals:

1. Affirm counter-hegemonic forms of community.
2. Affirm popular and unpopular cultural subversions.

3. Affirm theoretically informed activism.
4. Affirm the construction of alternative social institutions.

Compare these policy positions with those of the labelling perspective in terms of whom they are respectively directed at for action.

A CRITIQUE OF CRITICAL CRIMINOLOGY

One of the most important critiques of critical criminology comes from feminist scholars like Carol Smart (1990), who emphasise that the 'fully social theory of deviance' promised by the New Criminologists was blind to the issue of gender just like the labelling theorists that they criticised for being insufficiently structuralist. This critique has been taken on board by many critical criminologists, who now start almost every discussion by emphasising the need to take into consideration race–class–gender articulation. Few of them, though, have wised up to their colonialist blindness (Hall, 1988).

The second type of criticism comes from David Downes (1966) and others who believe in the labelling perspective and disagree that critical criminology has offered any real alternatives. According to Downes, critical criminologists talk a lot about a new, crime-free society, implying socialism, but fail to specify how such a society will differ from capitalist society, how such a society will be brought about and how such a society will necessarily eliminate crime.

This type of criticism echoes the common critique that David Garland makes against Marxist criminology. The perspectives that draw from Marxism tend to be economically deterministic without taking into consideration the issue of conscience, which Durkheim strongly analysed. A similar critique was made against Paul Hirst by Jock Young for completely ruling out the possibility of a Marxist criminology. Partly in response to this type of criticism, Hall and others have developed critical cultural studies while Young and others have adopted what they call left realism.

'Left realist criminology', as Jock Young and Roger Matthews put it in 'Questioning Left Realism'), emerged in the mid-1980s from the debates within critical criminology in the mid-1970s. It differs from old realism, which flowered in America and elsewhere, mainly due to the critique of official crime statistics by adherents of the labelling perspective. Most of the realist researchers of the 1960s attempted to discover 'real' crime by interviewing individuals to see if they would self-report their involvement in criminality which may not have come to the attention of the police. Such self-report studies suggested that crime was more widespread than was previously assumed. Later, the realist criminologists adopted victim surveys in an effort to go beyond the recognition that crime has 'dark figures' and attempted to illuminate these dark figures by estimating the volume of crimes not known to the police. New left realism, as some of the adherents call the perspective, borrowed the victim survey method from old realism and localised it in early 1980s Britain, mainly as a response to Thatcherite populism based on law and order claims. However, the self-professed left realists emphasise the uniqueness of their 'geographically focused' surveys which go beyond victimisation to ask for self-reported criminality and the evaluation of agents of law enforcement. The question that Hughes (1991) and many others ask is, what is new about new realism and what is left in left realism?

WHAT IS NEW ABOUT NEW REALISM?

Self-professed left realism does not seek to break from existing criminological perspectives completely but to synthesise the 'kernels of truth' that its adherents eclectically borrow from competing and conflicting perspectives. According to left realism, crime involves a dyad: (1) the relationship between social action and reaction, and (2) the interaction between victim and offender. Other perspectives, according to Young and Matthews (1992), focus on only one of these two and are therefore insufficient rather than being completely wrong.

Left realists, like positivist criminologists, are interested in finding out why people commit crimes. Labelling perspective rejected any such focus as misplaced and focused on societal reactions to crime. Left realists want a 'full-blown criminology' that would be interested in why people commit crimes and how society reacts to criminal behaviour. This project of 'criminological synthesis' was originated by the *New Criminology* of Taylor et al. (1973), but the left realists now want to accomplish the project by renewing their commitment to sub-cultural theories of crime causation.

The 1980s created a favourable atmosphere for left realism because it was the era of right realism. The new right concentrated on what should be done about broken windows in the inner cities while the old left was still focusing on what should be done about oppressive state power and white-collar crime. The left realists saw a link between the electability of the Conservative Party and Thatcher's emphasis on the need to be tough on criminals. The left realists wanted to compete with the new right in the field of policy instead of abandoning this completely by focusing on a critique of the state, as the old left did. Eventually, local councils controlled by the Labour Party supported the local crime surveys that variously proved: (1) that crime disproportionately affects the vulnerable and the marginalised; (2) that fear of crime or anger against criminals is widespread in working-class communities; (3) that the huge increases in crime control budgets and the deployment of officers have not prevented huge increases in reported crime and fewer crimes being solved by the police. They decided that in the interest of working-class victims of crime and working-class unity, it is necessary to take crime seriously at the level of the working class. The Labour Party soon adopted the slogan of left realism by proclaiming that Labour is the true law and order party because it takes crime seriously and it takes the causes of crime seriously.

Scraton (1990) has argued convincingly that a lot of what is sometimes dismissed by left realists as left idealist criminology is not idealist but materialist in the true sense of the word. Young (1992) has argued further that criminology cannot do without a healthy dose of idealism anyway. Critical legal scholars in Australia have denied that their work could be said to be simply idealist because they have always aligned themselves to the practical concerns of community legal centres and prison movements. However, the critical realists in Australia make a point of distancing themselves from the essentialist tendencies in the overemphasis on relative deprivation as a source of criminality by left realists (see Brown and Hogg, 1992). Similarly, radical criminology in South Africa has retained a healthy dose of idealism even while being more closely involved in the formulation of policies for the new South Africa through an alliance with the ANC. Perhaps due to their influence, South Africa conceded the right to vote to prisoners before the first democratic election, but unlike the left realist advocacy of net-widening, South Africa has experimented with a Truth and Reconciliation Commission while also trying to decriminalise the juvenile justice system in addition to abolishing the death penalty.

REALISM, NEOCLASSICISM AND SOCIOLOGICAL DETERMINISM

In response to some of these criticisms, British left realism tries to overcome its identity crisis by agreeing with neoclassicism that coercive state intervention to control crime through the police, courts and prisons is necessary, but unlike neoclassicism it emphasises that repression is not enough. In addition to state intervention through various agencies, left realists emphasise the roles of structural causes, community involvement and victim support in preventing crime. They see the emphasis as bridging the gap between those who advocate repressive law enforcement and those who advocate the transformation of the 'structural' conditions of poverty and patriarchy which left realists consider more important than the issue of discrimination in the administration of justice (this implies racism). This differs from right realism, the new right or neoclassicism by:

1. Denying that law enforcement is the major deterrent to crime given that it could be counterproductive in certain situations and completely ineffective in others, suggesting that the official definition of crime should not be accepted as given.
2. Agreeing that procedural equality is important as the new right believes, but is less important than the fact 'that poor people (and hence blacks) are under greater pressure to commit the crimes which are at present the main focus of the criminal justice system and prisonization' (Young and Matthews, 1992: 5).
3. Accepting, as liberal neoclassicism and the labelling perspective do, that victimless crime should not be criminalised, but making an exception for hard drugs, which left realists still want the state to regulate through repressive policing of the 'black market' and the medicalisation of the addicts.
4. Advocating the widening of the net of repressive social control to areas including racist attacks, domestic violence and child molestation which, according to the realists, is largely ignored by the police; but not a word on imperialism.

Left realists deny the allegation that with their acceptance of empiricist methodology they have returned to positivism. Unlike positivism, which sees crime as a Durkheimian 'social fact' waiting to be measured, left realists argue, along with the labelling perspective, that crime is socially defined by actors in interaction. According to sociological positivism, crime increases when poverty increases because poverty unquestionably causes crime. Left realists modify this hypothesis by observing that what causes crime is not necessarily absolute poverty but differential association (Sutherland) and relative deprivation (Merton), depending on the interpretation of the social situation by the potential offender as just or unjust and the individual adaptation to the defined situation.

On the other hand, left realism distances itself from what it calls idealism, which, unlike the earlier categories, has not been adopted by any known criminologist but is identified by self-professed left realists to be made up of left idealism, the labelling perspective, social constructionism, moral panic theories, abolitionism, postmodernism, etc., which are lumped together as avoiding any need to face the problem of crime while focusing exclusively on crime control.

Left realism also differentiates itself from various forms of idealism by taking the fear of crime to be real rather than a manufactured myth propagated by the media and politicians, as some idealists suggest. Left realists accept that they are pragmatic in the sense that they actively seek reforms that could work rather than dismissing all reform short of revolution as ineffective. According to them, post-modernist critiques of the idea of progress too easily lead to the 'ideology of impossibilism' or the idea that nothing works.

THE EXAMPLES OF COUNTER-COLONIAL CRIMINOLOGY

If we read classical anti-colonial literature from Ireland, Africa, the Caribbean, Asia, South America, Australia and Aboriginal sources, we find echoes of the analysis of colonialism as a criminal enterprise that is sustained with organised crime-type activities. Kwame Nkrumah (1968) should be required reading in classes that deal with white-collar crime, but hardly merits a footnote in relevant literature of bourgeois criminology. The book details the fraudulent ways that imperialism is sustained even after formal political independence has been granted to the petty bourgeoisie in neocolonial locations. Similarly, Nkrumah's book on the Congo (1967), with its emphasis on the imperialist-instigated plot to murder Patrice Lumumba, is a classic study in organised crime, but conventional criminology does not get it. At the same time, even criminologists who call themselves left realists have abandoned realism by excluding the punishment of the innocent or victimisation as mere punishment from their focus, due partly to their ignorance of the crimes of imperialism.

All the books written by Frantz Fanon should be read by students majoring in criminology but, unfortunately, most criminology students and even professors would ask, Frantz who? From *Black Skin White Masks* to *The Wretched of the Earth* and the collections of essays between the two, *A Dying Colonialism* and *Towards the African*

Revolution, Fanon makes it clear that imperialism is a criminological problem of vast proportions and outlines the structural penology through which the offended societies go about redressing the crimes of imperialism.

Similarly, the works of Walter Rodney (*History of the Upper Guinea Coast, Groundings with my Brothers, How Europe Underdeveloped Africa* and *A History of the Guyanese Working Class*) emphasise that slavery was a crime against humanity which is continued today in the form of imperialism. The same is true of the work of Amilcar Cabral as is clear from the collection of his speeches and essays: *Unity and Struggle* (1979) and *A Return to the Source* (1972). To these we can add the literature of the anti-apartheid struggle which is more familiar to many due in part to the immense popularity of icons like Nelson Mandela. However, even apartheid is seen as a historical event that ended in 1994 instead of being analysed as part of the resources for the construction of criminological theory. We can go on multiplying the examples by highlighting anti-colonial literature from regions of the world apart from Africa, but the point has already been made. Criminology has been relatively underdeveloped – especially in underdeveloped countries – by being aligned with imperialism instead of being made relevant to the daily struggles of the masses for social justice. The following chapters will highlight how critical criminologists came close to developing a criminology that is sensitive to social justice and how much more critical criminologists need to do before their discipline will appeal to the millions of people who are suffering daily injustice at the hands of white supremacist, sexist imperialism with apparent impunity.

The following chapters illustrate the potential uses of the decolonisation model in criminology. Chapters 4 and 5 critically review the contributions and shortcomings of feminist perspectives. Chapters 6 and 7 dwell on the potential contributions of poststructuralist perspectives to the project of decolonisation while highlighting the inherent shortcomings. Finally, chapters 8 and 9 use radical African literature to illustrate the potential for the decolonisation of criminology. The theory of executive lawlessness as outlined in chapters 8 and 9 is further illustrated through the creative works of African writers. The works of Ngugi, Iyayi and Fatunde were used to indicate to criminologists the potential growth in their discipline should they develop the decolonisation imagination reflected in the creative radical work coming out of Africa.

Consider the story that Chinua Achebe (2000: 63–7) tells from Jomo Kenyatta's anthropological dissertation, *Facing Mount Kenya*, regarding the elephant that asked a farmer for shelter from the rain. The kind farmer obliged and the elephant took over the hut, destroying it in the process. When the farmer complained, King Lion set up a public enquiry with the elephant's cabinet colleagues, the rhinoceros, the hippopotamus and the crocodile as members. They concluded that the farmer's complaint had no merit because, when the elephant arrived, the farmer had no history of residence in the area. The moral here is that imperialist reason is like gangster philosophy: it will take more than arguments to bring justice to the victimised, as the Mau Mau demonstrated in Kenya under the leadership of Dedan Kimathi.

The farmer went on to build more houses and each was claimed by the Right Honourables Crocodile, Hippopotamus and even King Lion in turn, and each new panel of enquiry ruled against the farmer. Finally, he resolved that you can fool some people some of the time but that you cannot fool all the people all the time and that no beast is too big to be trapped. He went on to build the most magnificient house of all and no sooner did he complete the building than the Right Honourable beasts rushed in and started scrambling over who would claim it just as the Europeans scrambled for Africa. While they were arguing over who should claim the mansion, the farmer quietly set the house on fire and burnt it down, Right Honourable beasts and all. The man went home saying: 'Peace is costly, but it is worth the expense', and he lived happily ever after.

4. Feminist Perspectives and Critical Criminology

We came across the position of Hirst (1975) on the impossibility of Marxist criminology given what he saw as the preoccupation of Marxism – the class struggle, modes of production, relations of production, revolution and not reform – whereas criminology is concerned with deviance, crime and punishment. Similar questions are being asked about critical criminologists by feminist writers who do not wish to be identified as criminologists.

Carol Smart (1990) addresses this issue. She is a professor of sociology, even though her publications are criminological, indicating the desire on her part to go beyond criminology. According to Smart, the ultimate questions of conventional criminology are: what causes crime and what should be done about criminals? Thus, criminology tends to be conservative, always intervening on the side of the state and the powerful. This type of criminology has been rejected by the labelling perspective and, more emphatically, by the critical perspectives in criminology. Any criminology that was interested in discovering ultimate causes was dismissed in the 1960s and 1970s as positivistic, and positivism was supposed to represent everything bad in research methodology and epistemology. Smart asks how far critical criminologists and especially left realists are from those they condemn as positivists. She argues that if positivism is defined as the search for ultimate truth or for exact causes, then there could be left-wing positivism and right-wing positivism.

In the previous chapter we heard the clarion call by the left realists that we should take crime seriously, compete in policies and in the search for the causes of crime, instead of concentrating on what is seen by 'idealists' to be impossible under capitalism – justice. It is the direct linkage between theory and policy that left realists make that Smart finds positivistic, even when these same left realists lambast positivism. It is a version of the old Enlightenment ideology that science has the answers for increased human happiness which is found in biological, psychological and conservative sociological positivism. Left realists defend the search for causes and indicate that mainstream as well as critical criminology have abandoned the search for causes. The former became administrative by concentrating on how to make control more effective and more efficient, while the 'idealists' concentrated on the oppressive consequences of the control culture. The distinction between left realism and the rest ignores the fact that the search for ultimate causes has a more conservative legacy and that such universalising theories are being resisted by marginalised groups and thoughts, including varieties of feminist thought: *feminist empiricism, standpoint feminism* and *postmodern feminism*, based on the typology proposed by Harding (1986; 1987). Unfortunately, few feminist writers are sensitive to the crimes of imperialism and the struggles of colonised women and men against imperialist reason.

FEMINIST EMPIRICISM

Within this category are feminist writers who have concentrated on showing that what passed for objective knowledge was sexist and was based on the knowledge of men only. This critique suggests that women should be brought into the perspective in order to guarantee its objectivity. This suggests that there is no problem with empiricism as a methodological or epistemological approach to knowledge. According to Harding, Smart and many others, bringing women into the focus of conventional criminology without questioning its key assumptions would be to imply that the only error in the objectivity of empiricism is that it is not empirical enough; in other words, it is an error of omission rather than of foundation. This type of critique is often necessary and effective in that, by focusing on violence against women rather than on delinquent women, feminist scholars have broadened the scope of criminological subject matter and agenda. The work of Pat Carlen, Frances Heidensohn, Mary Eaton, Gelsthorpe and Morris, Kathleen Daly, Naffine, Mackinnon, the Dobashes and many others is significant, even though Carlen's work concentrates on 'criminal women'.

However, empirical research is not synonymous with empiricist research. Empiricism implies the search for ultimate explanations which may be empirical, theoretical or philosophical. Empirical research, on the other hand, may not be empiricist at all if it is not interested in universalising explanations but only in documenting the lives of women in the interest of broader knowledge and struggles. The early feminist empiricists in criminology did not only challenge the claim to objective truth in criminology; they also challenged the idea that the criminal justice system is just and objective. This question is important to feminist empiricist critiques because women have been largely ignored in 'objective' conventional criminology. Many writers have pointed out the error of using only men to construct something like Lombroso's positivist theory of crime causation. Others have criticised Otto Pollak (1950) for arguing that the criminal justice system is guided by the chivalry thesis, according to which women are given preferential and more lenient treatment by male officials, who associate them with their sisters, wives, daughters or mothers.

Official statistics were used to show that men were more likely to be given custodial sentences, but Farrington and Morris (1983) found that this had more to do with the profile of male offenders than with the fact that they were male. According to them, the relatively low gravity of the offences committed by women, and the fact that they were more likely to be first-time offenders, meant that they were less likely to be sent to prison than men, and that men who had similar profiles to the women were not likely to be given custodial sentences. Gelsthorpe (1986) supports this with the observation that police officers are more likely to caution girls than boys because the boys are less likely to be apologetic than the girls. Gelsthorpe suggested that this might have to do with the way boys and girls are socialised, but she did not say whether the police officers act as agents of social-isation by reinforcing how boys and girls are expected to behave and by questioning them in different ways.

The claim that serious cases are treated equally seriously by the courts irrespective of whether it is a man or a woman that is involved is challenged by Allen (1987), who states that violent women are consistently portrayed as harmless in psychiatric reports in court. In a survey of 200 cases in which courts called for a psychiatric report, she found that women were more likely to be remanded for a report due to lesbianism, sexual promiscuity, truancy and occasional acts of violence, whereas men were remanded for more violent offences. Allen argues that her evidence reveals that violent women are being rendered harmless, but her evidence seems to suggest that harmless women are being rendered harmful. Is a lesbian harmful, to whom and why?

Heidensohn (1986) points out that what is unsatisfactory about the law is that it operates under the 'Portia' model. The ideals of Portia are justice, revenge, punishment, control, order, just deserts, etc. This is the male model of law, according to Heidensohn. The female model, in contrast, is that of Persephone the blindfolded Greek goddess, holding the scale of justice and a sword. The ideals of the female model are caring, support, sympathy, dialogue, sharing, equality and fairness. Heidensohn does not call for Portia to be discarded; she only demands that there should be room for Persephone in order to produce a balanced justice system. She concludes that adding the female voice to the male voice in law would be impossible without addressing the gender inequality that makes a woman unequal to a man even before they appear before the law. However, is it all women that are seen as unequal to all men, irrespective of race–class–gender–generation differences? Can it not be said that the voice of care is not completely outside the law as it exists? In any case, what is it that makes caring essentially feminine?

Empiricist feminism has been criticised for assuming that the male model is the standard of justice which should then be extended to women in order to make it more just. Mackinnon, Smart, Harding and many others argue that comparing men and women always assumes that men are the standard and that women are the 'Other'. The danger in setting up false standards, as Cain (1990) warns, is that if you demand that women should be treated better when they come out of a comparison badly, you will be forced to demand that women should be treated less favourably in comparisons where they are better than the norm. In this connection Carlen (1992) warns that it is wrong to see female prisons as holiday camps compared to male prisons because that would be a denial of female imprisonment. bell hooks (1984) also argues that the demand for equality without demanding for an end to sexism, racism and imperialism is to demand inclusion in the white, male, middle-class norm, but it could also result in treating women like poor black males or what Barak et al. (2001) call 'equality with a vengeance'. The call by Marcia Rice (1990) for criminological research to be extended to the crimes of black women is an example of the call for inclusion without a clear critique of what includes.

STANDPOINT FEMINISM

Harding identifies standpoint feminism as that which emphasises that those who feel it know it, that experience is the best teacher and that the best experience is gained in the struggle against oppressive, hegemonic standpoints. This type of feminism emphasises the superiority of women's knowledge based on the fact that it is subjugated knowledge. Standpoint feminism starts with assumptions of a universal sisterhood, which was strongly influenced by Simone de Beauvoir's *Second Sex*, Mary Daly's *Gyn/Ecology* and Germaine Greer's *The Female Eunuch*. All these texts assume that women's experience is universal. The closest representative in criminology is Mackinnon (1993a), who seems to argue that being raped, being afraid of being raped and campaigning against rape and pornography are essentially female concerns. Standpoint feminists argue for research on women to be done by women in the interest of women.

Universal sisterhood soon gave way to multicultural feminist standpoints and realist standpoints. The former is representative of the work of writers like Amina Mama and Patricia Hill Collins, who claim to be writing about the experience of black women from a black or Africanist feminist standpoint. Mama (1989) documents and analyses little-known cases of domestic violence against black women, whom she defines politically as women who have been subjected to white imperialism and racism. Collins (1990) elaborates this perspective beyond criminology and demands that black feminist thinkers become more knowledgeable about certain things because they have been 'outsiders within'. She calls for them and people who are like them to be brought in from the cold – not as an act of charity, but because they have unique contributions to make to scholarship.

While defending 'realist standpoint epistemologies', Cain (1990) criticises the essentialist implications of claims to universal sisterhood. She, however, calls for women to be compared with other women because women are diverse and because comparisons with men often lead to the setting of false standards. This suggests that the problem is not with the comparative method as such, but with the setting of false standards. If women are compared with other women, the problem of false standards does not disappear because white, middle-class women might easily become standards against which poor black women are compared for evidence of racism and sexism. Cain also questions the assumption that women's knowledge is better or more true, simply because it is subjugated knowledge. This is similar to Becker's suggestion that we should take sides with the underdog because the underdog standpoint is likely to be more credible because it does not depend as much on power for its validation as does the standpoint of those conventionally placed at the top of the credibility hierarchy. Gouldner, in response to Becker, states that it is important to take the side of the underdog, but not simply because it is more likely to be truthful, as Becker suggested. Rather, we should adopt the perspective of the underdog because it is likely to be less well known by reason of being marginalised. Cain's response is similar to essentialist standpoint feminism. According to Cain, to claim that the perspective of women is better simply because it is a perspective from below is to argue that women must remain below, lest they lose their clearer view of reality. Cain prefers a realist standpoint which recognises that one speaker can move into different standpoints at different times by speaking sometimes as a woman or as a black woman, or as a working-class woman. Of course, people often speak from different standpoints at the same time, but what matters is what standpoint they wish to emphasise at any given time.

This means that standpoint feminism has very little to say about criminals and about masculinities given that these are not characteristic of the feminist standpoint. Moreover, experience is never the only teacher. We do not have to die before 'knowing' what it means to be dead. It does not follow that any woman who has never been raped or who has never been afraid of being raped or who is not preoccupied with the campaign against rape is not woman enough. In other words, even women who have experienced violence will need to study the experience in order to reach a deeper understanding of it.

I had no hesitation in recommending Linda Smith's indigenous standpoint text, *Decolonizing Methodologies* (1999), as a required text for my course, Criminological Research Methods, for junior undergraduate students of criminology. The problem is that hardly any of my students is an indigenous researcher, even though my university is in a town called Indiana, without any Indians. They had been massacred two hundred years earlier. A minor problem for my class was that the book is not about criminology. I found myself questioning why the book is addressed primarily to indigenous people whereas there is nothing in the book that is exclusively applicable to indigenous people. Some might even argue that everyone is indigenous somewhere on earth.

Linda Smith would reject this globalisation of indigenousness and reserve the term for those she called the victims of colonialism. I have my doubts about this usage of the term and its repetition as a mantra throughout the book. Few African or Asian or Eastern European researchers will refer to themselves as indigenous especially if they come from areas without settler colonialism. This is because, as in the term native informant, used by writers like Gayatri Spivak

(1999) to critique colonial anthropology, the word 'indigenous' tends to be used pejoratively in the colonial discourse of the civilising mission. Otherwise, why do we not hear about native or indigenous European researchers?

To resolve this problem of who is indigenous and who is not, I introduced Smith's book to my American students as a text open to debate around the issue of what makes for good research or poor research according to whether the researcher is indigenous or Other. I think that the central issue Linda Smith addresses is precisely what makes for effective research strategies, the issue of indigenousness being tangential rather than central. In other words, any researcher, indigenous or otherwise, could benefit from reading this book in a critical rather than a religious manner. The author herself borrowed widely from 'non-indigenous' writers like Foucault and even reserved some of her most critical comments for indigenous writers like Fanon.

Given the homage to western theorists in her book, my hunch that the tag 'indigenous' is only a front appears to be justified. The second question is: what relevance does a research manifesto for indigenous people have to criminology? This is the easier question to deal with, given how Foucauldian her analysis is. By a simple substitution of the word 'prisoner' for the word 'indigenous', we find that Smith's book is relevant to criminology in the abstract way that Foucault's work is. A lot of what the author has to say about indigenous people and power relationships between them and colonial researchers is even more true of criminologists and prisoners.

The dominant assumption in criminology is that prisoners are not normal people, they are pathological and barbaric and prison conditions are equally inhumane – rightly or wrongly. Some believe that prisoners are born criminals; it is in their genes or in their psychology or sociology to be deviant, and so they should be controlled, incapacitated or even killed because they are beyond redemption. Once this substitution is made, the rest of the programme outlined for indigenous research can easily be carried out with slight adaptations by criminology students.

In contrast to the fan club veneration of European theorists in the book, Smith dismisses an 'indigenous researcher' like Frantz Fanon unfairly by asserting that Fanon essentialised the 'nature' of the colonised, that he took the binary categories of western thought for granted, that he accepted arguments of cultural relativity and that he simply inverted the coloniser/colonised categories without reference to power relations! Which Fanon is she talking about? The author of *Black Skin White Masks* or the author of *A Dying Colonialism* and *Towards the African Revolution* or the author of *The Wretched of the Earth*? No reference is made to any of Fanon's work to justify such rubbishing commentary on page 26 of Smith's book. When Fanon is directly cited, you wonder if the author read him a long time ago and has forgotten what she read. For example, we are told that because Fanon was educated in France, he, and people like him, 'are the group most closely aligned to the colonizers in terms of their class interests, their values and their ways of thinking' (p. 69).

When it comes to Foucault, a man who is notorious for analysing power relations without saying a single word about colonial power relations even though he chose to rent the former residence of the colonial governor in Tunisia while writing the book, we find the author of *Decolonizing Methodologies* most deferential. We are told early on that 'the French philosopher Foucault' recognised that travellers' tales contributed to Europe's knowledge of itself as much 'as has the scientific gathering of scientific data' (p. 2). The truth of what Foucault claimed is not contested at all as Fanon was, or seen as a threat to Smith's claim to originality. Foucault appears again on page 44 as a theorist of how little the West understands the 'rules' of archiving that the colonised can describe and understand because they have experienced them. Finally, Foucault's focus on the micro-physics of power or the disciplining of the body of the individual in different institutional settings is offered on page 68 as a theory of imperialism, whereas imperialism is a macro-physics of power and not a micro-one, as Said (1993) pointed out in his critique of Foucault and Habermas.

This practice of what Spivak (1999) would call 'epistemic violence' towards intellectuals of African descent is continued in Jacobs et al. (2000), in which Teboho Maitse – a political adviser to female parliamentarians in South Africa (in conjunction with Jen Marchbank) – accused Steve Biko of being sexist simply because he observed that African culture is 'man-centered'. The fact that Biko was using 'man' here in the relatively non-feminist early 1970s as a generic term for human beings was not explained, nor was any reference made to the observation of Donald Woods that the Black Consciousness Movement contributed immensely to the radicalisation of South African women in the gender politics of resistance to apartheid. Instead, the authors challenge African women to contest the strategic essentialism (as Spivak would put it) of heroes like Biko.

On the next page (p. 203) these authors again attack Fanon irrationally by asserting, without a shred of evidence, that he 'maintained that violence against "others" is liberatory' and that Fanon approved the use of violence against one's own. Before the reader starts doubting his or her own reading of Fanon, the authors admit in the next sentence that 'Fanon did not say so but ...' This is a misleading interpretation of *The Wretched of the Earth* where Fanon analyses why the colonised are forced to adopt violent means of resistance to the violent means of domination they experience. Fanon was not saying why the colonised should adopt violent means of struggle; he was only explaining the conditions that made such means of resistance inevitable. And when he commented on violence against one's own, he saw it as a psychological problem that afflicted the colonial torture officer who went home to torture his wife and family; as well as the nationalist who succumbed to the pitfalls of cultural nationalism to the extent of seeking those who are deemed to be culturally impure.

While these two icons of African resistance to violence are mis-represented in chapter 11 as sexist enemies of women to be discredited, you will find the usual reverence reserved for European theorists of modernity and postmodernity like Habermas and Foucault, who are uncritically invoked throughout the book. African writers are very familiar with the hierarchies of prestige in intellectual work that follow racialised ideologies in denigrating contributions from Africa while praising Eurocentric perspectives. I am not saying that African intellectuals should be above criticism, but when that criticism is unfair while Europeans are uncritically adopted, we risk recolonising Africa in the intellectual field. This should serve as a challenge to African readers in particular to return to the sources of our classics and familiarise ourselves with them, especially when we find them being dismissed in preference to relatively irrelevant Eurocentric jingoism.

Having sounded that note of caution, it is important to point out that like the book *Decolonizing Methodologies*, *States of Conflict* makes interesting reading. The second book tends towards treating gender analysis as the analysis of women's experiences by focusing on violence in general and sexual violence in particular. However, the contributors also point out that violence affects men adversely too, even though men as a group are responsible for most acts of violence. They also point out that women are increasingly being involved in violent actions, especially as members of the armed forces throughout the world, and that privileged women may commit violence against men in subordinate race–class positions. However, while critical of the essentialist view of women as carers, the authors are cautious not to focus too much on female violence because such a focus could mask male violence.

The most important insight in the book comes from the chapter by Lee-Anne Broadhead in which it is argued that the report of the Commission on Global Governance, 'Our Global Neighbourhood', is superficial because it fails to address the underlying causes of violence, such as poverty and environmental degradation. Evidence for this is found in industrialised economies where the poor are trapped in cycles of violence, as well as in underdeveloped societies in which environmental degradation and poverty make violence commonplace. This is reflected in the other chapters in the book, with examples from Uganda, Rwanda, China, Northern Ireland and South Africa, where it is shown that the women most likely to suffer violence, especially state-sponsored violence, are poor women, just as poor men are relatively vulnerable to violence. Liz Kelley adds to this theme of poverty as the underlying cause of victimisation the issue of *machismo*, or the ideology in militarised states that men should not be challenged, and where there is no respect for the lives of women and children as violence becomes recreation.

What is relatively lacking in the book is a focus on racist violence. The only chapter that attempts this with reference to South Africa mistakenly focusesd on the violence of the victims of Apartheid, thereby relatively masking white supremacist violence. This oversight could have been avoided if the authors had not completely and inexcusably ignored the works of feminist theorists of African descent such as bell hooks, Angela Davis, Ifi Amadiume, Patricia Hill Collins and Ama Ata Aidoo, to mention but a few.

POSTMODERN FEMINISM

Postmodernism is traditionally based in the philosophy of the arts and movements in the arts questioning truth-claims rather than seeking to tell truths. In feminism, by contrast, the postmodernist movement started in political practice where universal sisterhood quickly bowed out to the notion of different sisterhoods. At the same time, critical scholarship accepted that the oppressed come in various forms and not simply in the form of the working class, and that even among the working class, there is a plurality of identities.

This is the way feminists started questioning claims to universal truth. Like the standpoint feminist perspective outlined above, the postmodern perspective exposes the partiality of claims to universal truth by masculinist thought. Unlike standpoint feminism, however, postmodern feminism does not seek to establish an alternative universal claim based on sisterhood, or anything like it. The aim of postmodern feminism is to challenge the knowledge and power based on claims of truth. This is what Carol Smart calls for. She suggests that criminology is too small for the potentials of feminism to be fully realised within the scope of its major questions. Postmodern feminism looks beyond crime and punishment to focus on knowledge and power more generally, as Foucault does.

Alison Young's *Femininity in Dissent* (1990) is an example of a postmodern feminist account of the Greenham Common anti-nuclear protest. The book analyses how the women protested, how they protested against men joining the protests, and how they were portrayed in the press as dirty and threatening. What does not come across is how the women represented themselves by themselves and how they represented the authorities. Greenham Common women were known to have run their own newspapers, but this is not reflected in Young's book. This contrasts with Penny Green's *The Enemy Within* on the policing of the miners' strike which reflects the views of the workers adequately from the perspective of critical criminology or the feminist working-class standpoint.

This indicates the commonest problem that feminist and critical scholars have with postmodern feminism. The latter is suspected of trying to substitute textual politics for the practical politics of everyday struggles. Postmodern feminism is influenced by the post-structuralism of Foucault, but many feminists, while agreeing with Foucault that the discourse of the body should be interrogated, emphasise that there is something that lies outside discourse, something that is pre-discursive. An example is the body. It does not depend on discourse for its existence; the social construction of its image does not mean that the reality of its existence is in any doubt. There is more in the next chapter about how poststructuralism deals with the scepticism regarding its call for universal scepticism about everything. In the next chapter too, the contributions of feminist perspectives to poststructuralism will be highlighted and, at the same time, critiques of its Eurocentric focus that denied it the opportunity to revolutionise theory by learning from the struggle for decolonisa-tion in the Third World. The next chapter challenges homophobic patriarchal scholars to realise that their dominant metaphor in the discourse of international relations is a lesbian metaphor. The chapter also challenges feminist thinkers to go beyond body politics and confront the sexualised violence to which the majority of people on earth are subjected by white supremacist, imperialist patriarchy. More on postmodern feminism, especially the work of Mary Joe Frugg, in chapter 6, on poststructural criminology.

5. Lesbian Rape: Maternal Metaphors for the Patriarchal State and International Conflict Resolution

This chapter analyses the appropriation of the metaphor of rape and its representation in the iconography of international conflict, spatial conquest, exploitation and imperialism. This chapter questions the appropriateness of the metaphor within the masculinist discourse of international conflicts. Furthermore, it compares and contrasts images of motherland or mother earth with the patriarchal rape of real women by men and sometimes by other women. Such a comparative analysis raises the question of whether the discourse of spatial rape in works like *The Rape of Britain* by Colin Amery and Dan Cruickshank, *The Rape of Europa* by Lynn Nicholas, *The Rape of the Wild* by Andrée Collard et al., and *Rape and Plunder of Shankhill in Belfast* by Ron Wiener, for example, are consistent in their assumption that nation-states, nature and the earth are feminine or whether they perform a transvestite operation for the rapist state or agents of rape as essentially male. If the feminine identity is retained by all nation-states in international conflict situations and rape is acceptable as a metaphor for international plunder, is it a heterosexual rape or a lesbian rape that is assumed? The chapter concludes by looking at how much the international community has prioritised the prevention/punishment of actual rape of mostly women by mostly male invading troops and the extent to which this real 'fate worse than death' is marginalised in patriarchal peace negotiations and sanctions against the rape of the motherland.

This chapter was banned from an international conference on feminist perspectives in international relations because the organisers found the language 'most offensive'. I have since presented the same chapter to succeeding classes of my students in the module 'Law and Popular Culture', with this health warning and an appeal to them to point out the offensive aspects, if any. The only offensive aspect that they have pointed out so far is the passage about chainsaws, which was not in the original paper that was accepted and circulated internationally before being banned. Feedback on the offensiveness of the chapter will be welcome for its improvement, since the intention of the author is not to cause offence.

When we say, see or hear the phrase 'lesbian rape', what do we imagine? One possibility is the scene in Spike Lee's *She's Gotta Have It*, where Nora Darling says that she is curious about what it feels like to make love to another woman and finds herself misunderstood by her lesbian friend who wants to initiate sex, ignoring the refusal of Nora, the curious, until she pushes her off (see hooks, 1989). Such an image will be less than rape considering the brutal way that curious Nora was given 'it' by her possessive ex-stalker lover, Jamie, who hollered while doing it, 'Whose pussy is this?' 'Yours, your pussy', she answered, as if he was a man with a pussy of his own, or as if he was so depraved that he could not tell the pussy from the anus that he seemed to be attacking from behind, his anus being his very own pussy. This question of pussy-ownership must have been on the mind of the London police officer who raped a Nigerian woman anally under the intimidation that if she did not comply, she would be deported. She later won damages for the rape (IRR, 1987).

Have you ever peeped at your anus to find out what colour it is? That is a childish question we used to ask in rhetorical answer to impossible questions. The anal is present in analogy – the study of the anal – analysis, analyse, analyst – it exposes the hidden because it is the hidden. You cannot see your behind without a mirror. That is why you need analysis, a mirror with which to reveal the hidden fact that even though the ex-stalker pussy-owning lover-man raped her anally in order to own her, the lesbian kisser attempted a similar franchising of her body through more subtle means of care for her when she was ill (see hooks, 1989). However, the lesbian was not invited to the lovers' dinner of mutual jealousy, suggesting that Nora did not consider her to be one of her darlings.

Another image conjured by the icon of lesbian rape is that of the atavistic man, the throwback to phallic nature proclaiming the universalism of his manhood. 'Lesbians rape too' could be seen on a banner in a Men's Movement rally. It could be a way of saying that to rape is natural: birds do it, bees do it, even educated fleas do it (to paraphrase Old Blue Eyes). It has nothing to do with being a man. However, if lesbian rape universalises rape, does it justify it?

Is lesbian rape a travesty of the real thing, or is it real in itself? Is it 'artificial' rape, as in rape with a bottle, which Mackinnon (1993a: 18–19) demystified and recognised as real rape? What is real rape anyway: video-taped rape, rape-and-murder as in snuff movies, or murder-and-rape as in Dracula, bloody infectious rape as in the film *kids*, in which a teenage black girl is shown saying how much she preferred 'fucking' to making love, demonstrating with her hand the forceful style she meant before adding the expression, 'boy!' to drive home her point; statutory rape, date rape, gang rape, international rape, ecological rape, rape seed plant or rape seed oil, the rape of Europa, the rape of the Sabines, the rape of Lucretia, the rape of Africa, *le viol*, to seize, possess, take, violate, force, subjugate, win, conquer, humiliate the other by force or threat of force?

The chances are that rape itself is ecstatically empty of meaning, as Baudrillard (1990) would say in his *Fatal Strategies*. Perhaps, the scepticism about the reality principle should be suspended when it comes to rape because it is not a simple question of meaning but also of feeling, feeling hurt, really feeling pain that is not empty of meaning. The aim in this chapter is not to discover the true meaning of rape, to fill the void of its (dis)contents, but to empty out the patriarchal metaphor of rape in international relations and still call the spade with which to carry out the emptying a spade; the metaphor of rape as a spade with which to excavate violence.

This is probably similar to what Foucault (1988: 200) told a seminar in 1977: 'When one punishes rape one should be punishing physical violence and nothing but that. And to say that it is nothing more than an act of aggression: that there is no difference, in principle, between sticking one's fist into someone's face or one's penis into their sex.' Vicki Bell (1993: 161) is sympathetically critical of this 'desexualisation' of rape and links it to Foucault's understanding of the Women's Movement as a project of desexualisation of the female sex object. Foucault was challenged by two women present at the seminar who saw rape as something completely different compared to a punch in the face. In response, he asked them what was so special about the sexual organs that they should be subjected to closer surveillance, protection and repression than the rest of the body.

This style of thinking is common in Foucault's work. He argues (in *Discipline and Punish*) that judges judge something other than crime and that (in *Madness and Civilisation*) the rise of psychiatry had nothing to do with humanitarianism. This is intolerant of views that see rape as both a sexual and a violent offence. There are always two sides to a coin and so the Foucauldian style of either/or is very misleading. This chapter is using rape as a metaphorical spade with which to excavate international violence, but the aim is not to question whether rape is different from a kick in the arse. If it is not different 'in principle' (whose principle?), why is a kick in the arse not called rape, and vice versa? The aim here is to look beyond Foucault's micro-physics of power and focus on the macro-physics of imperialist power relations. Foucault talked about punching someone's face or putting 'one's penis into their sex', suggesting by this Freudian slip that it is not just the atomised raping of one woman or someone's sex that is involved, but a mass rape of 'their sex' that is most feasible in the mass rape that is imperialism or international violence. It is at this macro-level that Foucault's desire that rape should be punished as nothing more than violence is most feasible. Although the metaphor of rape is common in the discourse of international conflict, the connotations are (1) actual rape of women, children and prisoners of war; and (2) analogical rape of the land, country, environment, liberty, etc.

THE LITERATURE OF RAPE

Andrée Collard with (as if she was her spade, but using her because the author is truly dead and her book is posthumous) Joyce Contrucci (1988) traced the origin of rape back to nature in *Rape of the Wild*. The book, which was encouraged by the radical feminist Mary Daly, documents the patriarchal objectification of 'nature, animals and women' (are men and women not animals too?) who share the experience of being 'hunted, invaded, colonised, owned, consumed and forced to yield and to reproduce (or not)'. Reich (1970) linked the rise of fascism to this mystical sex-economy, which views the family as a corporation owned by patriarchs with strong vested interests in good breeding, rivalry and domination.

Rape as a patriarchal property is an enduring imagery even when it is the rape of nature or bestiality. Is such a patriarchal 'dick thing' (hooks, 1994) not being misrecognised by being called lesbian rape? Was it feminism that created the notion that rape is patriarchal, or is it a belief that is propagated by its chief founders who proclaim the rights of man and by the atavistic man of Carol Smart (1990)? Lesbian rape is not liberative from patriarchy but amplifies it.

It is only recently that lesbofeminists have found the courage to acknowledge a fact known to oppressed black people for centuries, that camaraderie does not spring from the colour of your hair or the bank of the river that you swim from. Susan Brownmiller (1975), in *Against our Will*, was reluctant to admit this fact. Although she analysed the homosexual rape of men who are feminised and even pimped by their attackers before and after being inside total institutions, she attributed the rape of girl inmates to the local boys whom the attacking girls recruited for the exclusively male job of penetrative rape.

Similarly, Brownmiller constructed the rape of black women during slavery and European women by white imperialist world warriors in the past tense while presenting in the anthropological present the immediate threat of the confession by Eldridge Cleaver (1969) that he regretted once viewing the rape of black women as target practice for the eventual retaliatory rape of white women, like Bigger (dick? Bigger John Thomas, Bigger Tom, bigger than the Tom in Harper Lee's *To Kill A Mocking Bird*?) Thomas in Richard Wright's 1972 novel, *Native Son*. The nativity of violence to aliens and rape as invasion necessarily suggest that the rapist is always the other man, the different man, the abnormal man, the loner, sick, mad or bad, or both (Bains, 1989).

This nativity play of words is not far-fetched because soon one man's personal confession is interpreted by a follower of Brownmiller to mean that rape was only politicised in America when 'the black Panther leader notoriously urged raping of white women as a tactic in the black struggle' (Porter, 1986: 218). No mention by Porter of the fact that the Black Panther leader later became a right-wing supporter of the Republican Party and that even before that he was speaking in the context of justifiable anger that nine young black men were jailed after being falsely accused by white men of gang-raping two white women who later issued statements exonerating their alleged attackers.

The dominant picture of the rapist is not simply a male, but the other male. To suggest that hegemonic masculinity could also be rapist is to suspect that there could be rape within marriage (the British legislated against it only in 1992 – six years after Caribbean women won legislation against it, according to Turner (1994); the Germans caught up only in 1996, as this chapter was being written). The law could be what Mackinnon (1993a) calls *Only Words*, especially if married women are still viewed as consenting to bondage rape, as in the 1992 prosecution by Trish Crawford against her husband in South Carolina.

A thirty-minute video of the 'alleged' assault was viewed in court, but Mr Crawford won the argument that cries of 'no' by his wife actually meant yes. His attorney asked the jury, 'Was that a cry of pain or a cry of pleasure?' There was evidence that he penetrated her with his penis and with objects, tied her hand and feet, gagged her mouth and blindfolded her with tape. Following the acquittal, the *Houston Chronicle* (18 April 1992), reported the event almost as if it was a masturbatory lesbian rape of herself: 'Acquittal of Husband Spurs Anger; Wife Accused (him?) of Raping Her' (Mackinnon, 1993a: 83).

If Mr Crawford had been black and Mrs Crawford white, would he have got off that easily? It would seem provocative to allege that victors and not only the vanquished are capable of war crimes. But if you look at the rockets of Hezbollah and the mortars of the Israeli army, or if you compare the Scud missiles of Sadam Hussein with the Patriot missiles and smart bombs of the US and her allies, they are all unmistakably phallic in shape. This is apart from biographical rape, but it is still conducted in the logic of universal rape. 'Fuck the Nazis' and 'Smash the Fascists' are graffiti familiar in English inner cities and they frequently jostle for position with other graffiti announcing the umbilical cord that joins the BNP (British National Party) and the GNP (Gross National Product). This indicates that the rapist and the anti-rapist might employ the same imagery for different purposes, just as Caliban learnt the language of Prospero but used it to demand decolonisation. Perhaps the journal *Living Marxism* has a point when it uses the subtitle, 'For men and women who have balls'. There is nothing wrong with having balls or with masculinity if it is used to stand up to rapists and bullies.

When Tawana disappeared for four days and was found in November 1987, she was silent and shocked, but her soiled body, the 'Nigger' and 'KKK' written on her bare torso and her apparent petrifaction on being shown a photo of a senior white police officer who later committed suicide, suggested that she had suffered at the hands of normal white men (Williams, 1993). Sister Tawana was typically the one on trial by the media, her credibility was doubted by the articulation of her class, race and gender, the harm done to her was evaluated in terms of whether it was her hair that was raped as in *The Rape of the Lock* by Menander, or whether it was the artificial extension to her hair that was cropped; whether she was silent because she was in shock and could not hear the doctors or whether she was just playing dumb; why she was taken into hiding by a black pop-culture preacher and was later initiated into the Nation of Islam;

why she shared in the laughter at a joke that was made at her expense in a Harlem community club.

No one was charged with raping Tawana and some news reports even speculated on the possibility of a masturbatory self-rape. The logical conclusion to the she-was-asking-for-it logic was that she did it to herself. When a white police officer was charged and convicted of raping a black woman in his patrol car, the evidence of a good character witness from the canteen cop culture and the fact that the victimised was a black woman won the appeal for the officer (Kennedy, 1992).

Mary Daly, Catherine Mackinnon and Andrea Dworkin have sustained the impression that rape is something that men do to women and they have the figures and anecdotes to prove it. The problem with their argument is that they do not acknowledge the fluidity of masculinities as relationships that could be oppressive or liberatory, shared by men and by iron ladies equally. Ifi Amadiume (1987) analyses the Igbo culture of Nigeria, where a barren woman is allowed to 'marry' another woman to bear her a son for her husband's family line. Without a son she would not have access to land after the death of her husband. Among the Igbo, to be male is to be successful, just as 'you are rich because you are white and you are white because you are rich' in a colonial situation (Fanon, 1967). 'You are a man' is a noncontradictory congratulatory message given to successful Igbo women, yet lesbian rape is unthinkable in such a society where respect for a woman comes through her husband. The 'male daughter' does not challenge patriarchy but sets up an ideal patriarchy that could be accessible to both men and women in con- tradistinction to the false standard of real men that is beyond the reach of most men, lesser men and many more women. Yet Igbo women know that men are the norm and often wish that they could be reincarnated as men.

This duality or gender duplicity was identified by Lyotard in the work of Rose Selary, alias Marcel Duchamp. According to him, a male viewer 'will notice that the body of the woman in *Given*' has a 'right breast and shoulder [that] are those of a man, and especially that between the vulva and the right of the groin, a swelling suggests the birth of a scrotum'. This would lead the male viewer to conclude 'that the right half of the body is male, the left half female' (*Duchamp's TRANS/formers*, pp. 9–10). This scepticism about sexual difference is developed further by Lyotard (1988: 20–1) when he states: 'of course there's masculinity in women as well as femininity in men'. According to him, this is the reason why people of the opposite sex are attracted to one another: they want to complement their mutual incompleteness, while hegemonic conceptions of gender purity want to keep them separate.

The problem is that Lyotard envisages a social contract in which heterosexual partners draw up contracts 'for purposes of common "enjoyment" of sexual difference itself'. The pleasure principle is dominant here and any sign of either party being hurt should lead to a suspending if not a breaking of the contract. It is not difficult to see that rape is a variation on this theme of incompleteness, except that there is nothing mutual about its pleasure, nothing contractual, and it is based on harm instead of being broken by the emergence of harm. The relevant point here is that masculinity and femininity are not fixed; they flow through men and women. If rape is essentially 'the male crime', as Madhubuti (1994) put it, women could also exercise this masculine act on other women with very similar consequences. For example, a woman raped by another woman or a country raped by another country could internalise the pain and blame herself for bringing about her victimisation. The only difference is the danger of pregnancy in patriarchal rape, a problem that is absent in lesbian rape and in international rape, making professionals doubt the allegation of rape as if rape is defined by the prospect of patriarchal impregnation. However, neocolonialism was conceived and born as a result of colonial rape.

THE SISTERS DO IT FOR THEMSELVES

> You cannot change your abuser's behaviour. You will have already noticed that it does not make any difference what you do to pacify her, she will continue to be violent or threatening. The only way for the abuser to change is for her to realise she has a problem and to seek help.

These are powerful 'affirmations' with which Joelle Taylor and Tracey Chandler (1995) open their pioneering *Lesbians Talk: Violent Relationships*. Whereas Ross Harrison (1986: 55) asserted unproblematically that, 'The only good sex would be lesbian sex among the sisterhood itself' (assuming that goodness has a fixed meaning and that sisterhood is singular). Taylor and Chandler argue that,

> Although according to the legal definition, a woman is incapable of raping another woman, we will refer to the sexual violation of

a woman by another woman as rape. Rape is not simply a physical act. It has long-term psychological consequences, whether it is committed by a man or a woman. When a woman is the rapist, the only missing element is the penis, and that is easily replaced by a fist, a dildo, or another object (a rocket, mortar bomb, missile, gun, knife, bottle?) ... rape is not defined by whether or not penetration occurred. It is simply the most powerful word available to describe the devastating experience of a woman being forced to have sex against her will ... As we have learned from research into sexual violence perpetrated by men, it is one of the most effective means of control. It has long been used as a weapon in war, though the emphasis here is on demoralising the male members of the enemy and by implication, the enemy nation. (Taylor and Chandler, 1975: 17–18)

Similar analysis can be found in the work of bell hooks (1994), where rape is connected to imperialism and white supremacist patriarchy. In response to Madonna's apparent betrayal of the hopes of those who saw her as a transgressor of conventional sexuality with her mimicry of hegemonic masculinity, hooks argues that women do not want to be 'dicks in drag', acting like a man, asking for a spanking, smiling at the camera in a rape me posture while being held by two black men in the book *Sex*. She calls for the empowerment of the pussy in its own right.

hooks craves the freedom to love a man or a woman without the pressure of pressurised rape. According to her, the meeting of Native Americans with the Africans who came before Columbus was fraternal without being homosexual, giving the impression that African men must have landed with their own women and that they had no intention of conquering and owning their hosts. When Columbus landed with his men, the landscape became sexualised and the encounter was marked by the rape of both the land and the women that lived on it. The explorers delivered the biological warfare syphilitic missiles and conquered the land for King and Country, in the Name of the Father and of the Son and the Holy Ghost, as Daly (1978) observed in *Gyn/ecology*, with reference to the witches massacred in Europe. In the words of one of the *conquistadors*:

I captured a very beautiful Carib woman whom the Lord Admiral [Columbus] gave me, and with whom, having taken her into my cabin, she being naked according to their custom, I conceived a desire to take pleasure [rape her]. I wanted to put my desire into execution but she did not want it and treated me with her finger nails in such a manner that I wished I had never begun ... I took a rope and thrashed her well, for which she raised such unheard of screams that you would not have believed your ears. (quoted in Turner, 1994: 25)

Note the discourse that places the woman on the level of a fruit tree whose nakedness is to blame for conceiving desire in the rapist. He captured her after all (just as the Lord Admiral 'discovered' America) and if his captive needed a good thrashing to tame her wild claws, the master race was at hand to deliver it. He was there to 'take' pleasure and give nothing in return except pain ('such unheard of screams'). Turner argues that this spirit of rebellion is still alive, especially in the New Rastafari which, according to her, is environmentally conscious, anti-racist, anti-sexist and anti-imperialist in line with the New Society envisaged by C.L.R. James.

The appointment of Clarence Thomas to the US Supreme Court was considered a relatively safe political appointment by George Bush Sr given that white voters would support him for being against affirmative action and black voters would support him for being a successful example of affirmative action and not for the official reason that 'he was the best qualified jurist' for the post. Manning Marable (1995) points out that Bush's calculation misfired mainly because he failed to look *Beyond Black and White* to see issues of gender and class, or what Stuart Hall (1988) would call the articulation, disarticulation and rearticulation of race–class–gender relations in societies structured in dominance. Anita Hill came up with the allegation of sexual harassment and divided the house into rainbow coalitions with radical white, black, men and women opposing Clarence Thomas on the principle that he was not the best for the post, while Thomas mobilised the imagery of false rape accusations against lynched black men. He alleged that he was being subjected to something more horrific than the assassin's bullet – 'high-tech lynching' by the media – because he was black. According to Marable, Thomas's nomination was narrowly approved mainly because of widespread support for him from a cross-section of the black community, including black women like Maya Angelou who was herself raped (though Thomas was not accused of rape) when she was a child and who suffered the humiliation of not being believed in court.

Since then, many more black intellectuals have been addressing the issue of rape in the black community (see Morrison, 1992). However, discussions that focus on intraracial rape in the African American communities tend to ignore the global rape of black people by imperialism. The exception is hooks (1994), West (1993) and Madhubuti (1994), who mention imperialism, although they apply the term restrictively to the internal colonisation of African Americans or people of colour. In the case of West, the focus is still exclusively on American institutions whenever he looks beyond interpersonal 'nihilism' to see 'institutionalised victimisation' against black people. Madhubuti includes information about the mass rape and murder of Kenyan schoolgirls by their fellow schoolboys allegedly for refusing to join an anti-government protest organised by the boys. Madhubuti includes information about the higher rate of rape especially for women in the military compared to women in the general population. This chapter attempts to address the global aspects of rape by abstracting from the local aspects.

Discussions of the 'taboo' subject of rape in the black-on-black rape debate, although guided by the need to develop the lesbian-like love of hated black flesh by self-loving black flesh outlined by Toni Morrison with her ever-poetic prose from *Beloved* (quoted by West), frequently leave the impression that only black men (especially those of them who love misogynist rap music rather than rap against rape), or at least individual men (who are suspected of buying into the phoney *machismo* of rap music), are a risk to individual women in the community. However, post-colonial cloning of concepts would suggest that nations are still raping nations, and nations are still addressed with feminine pronouns, which suggests that 'she raped her' is a taken-for-granted idea of unequal international relations.

The danger in focusing exclusively on black sexuality in an attempt to 'demythologise it', as Cornel West suggests, is that it is possible to perpetuate the myth of the black rapist and the black whore (contrary to analytical intentions), against which black people have struggled, without calling into question the institutionalised rapist practices over which individuals do not have a choice as individuals because they are structured as inverted mass rapes, the rape of the masses simultaneously (Davis, 1987: 28).

This intra-female international rape was prefigured by Fanon, who analysed the white folk's fear and fascination with the black people as objects of wild sexuality. In the conclusion to *The Wretched of the Earth*, Fanon writes:

Europe undertook the leadership of the world with ardour, cynicism and violence. Look at how the shadow of her palaces stretches out ever farther! Every one of her movements has burst the bounds of space and thought. Europe has declined all humility and all modesty; but she has also set her face against all solicitude and all tenderness. (Fanon, 1967: 251)

What is described here as international relations appears to be between women, but Fanon wrote in a masculinist style which suggests that the colonised was essentially the colonised man. He suggests a heterosexual raping of African men by the sadomasochistic 'Butch' and 'femme dykes' of Europe, who see the idea of 'lesbian rape' as a coded condemnation of 'butch-femme passion' (Taylor and Chandler, 1995: 45). The difference here is that heterosexual rape could not be a 'butch-femme passion', even by definition. Little (1995) provides a review of Cirque Archaos, the transgressive and controversial circus that was dogged by repressive controversies in Canada. One of the highlights was a scene in which

A young woman attacks a car with a chainsaw, slicing it down the middle. As the car splits in half, its three male occupants scatter across the stage in a frenzy. Suddenly, one of the men is seized by the others and dragged to an executioner's block, where the young woman gleefully decapitates him with her chainsaw. Then kneeling down and placing the severed head under her crotch, she rides her trophy to orgasm.

This scene is understandable only within the context that Archaos deliberately uses shock to mock conventional sexuality and its surveillance as spectacle to be consumed and at the same time subjected to health and safety inspection in the interest of public health. The chainsaw woman could not be said to be lesbian just as women are generally less likely to wield a chainsaw in real-life encounters. Rather than displaying transgression as Little suggests, the kneeling ride to orgasm on the severed head could be seen as a surrender to patriarchal power in the sense that even the severed head of a man was enough to bring a woman to orgasm. This suggests the immortality of masculinity, the continuity of its force even after the head had been divorced from the rest of the body. Perhaps international rape is more like this heterosexual rape in which the raping nation is always conceived as male while the raped is seen as the female from the point of view of the victims, although the rapist nations continue to see themselves as female (Britannia, Europa, etc.) while denying the humanity of the victims. Cirque Archaos challenges this accepted wisdom from the point of view of the victim by handing the chainsaw to the woman but without questioning heterosexuality. This is a bit like the eponymous heroines of *Thelma and Louise* who, despite their rebellion, remain in love with patriarchal sexuality and never show any sexual affection for each other to the annoyance of feminist reviewers.

However, when we listen to women who have suffered sexual abuse or rape in lesbian relationships, we see the emphasis placed by them on the need for decolonisation in interpersonal (and by extension, international) relationships.

Becky: She continually pressured me to be who she wanted me to be. I had to be princess and a whore. I had to mother her and be a wife as well. She wanted me to act refined in public but not in bed. 1 think she enjoyed treating me like I was disgusting. I didn't enjoy that. She'd force herself on me when I was in bed. I felt she was capable of rape and I was afraid of that too (as well as threats of murder). She'd continually invade my physical and sexual space since we'd been finished as lovers, whenever she was alone with me basically. She couldn't seem to see that each time it was a big crisis for me to have someone disregard my right to sexual autonomy, or how much it affected me even though I told her. It felt like constant assault.

Jo: I went on holiday for a week with a big group of lesbians. During this week I was sexually molested twice, by my lover and another woman I didn't know very well. My lover was being sexual with a number of women and one night she arrived in the communal bedroom where I was alone in the bed in the dark. She got on top of me and tried to make love but I pushed her off. I have to say she was easier to get off than the other woman. I was asleep when she landed on top of me. I came round with her trying to kiss me. I was not as strong as this one and also she took no notice of my protests and my trying to push her off. I probably also wanted to protect her feelings since I didn't want her. I think she was very upset because she felt no one fancied her. She apologised later in a letter but I was always afraid to be alone with this woman after that. The result of these assaults was that I felt it must be something to do with me. I felt I must be giving off victim vibes, or responsible in some way for leading women on without meaning to. The final straw with my lover came when she was abusing me verbally during hitchhiking. She said she hoped I'd be raped and murdered. Then she added, 'You'd probably enjoy it.' I never trusted her again after that.

Sue: She stopped me from caressing her, took total control of our love-making and hurt me. I figured I'd asked for sex so couldn't complain about what I got.

Aine: I think I could call it 'rape' as that's what I'd call it if a man did the same thing. It was from a lesbian I know slightly who was staying in the house I lived in and who talked me into letting her share my bed. This may sound really naive and stupid of me, but she said she was afraid to sleep alone, and as I'd heard from a mutual friend that she was an incest survivor and had terrible nightmares, I felt sorry for her. I can't cope with describing what actually happened ... It was complicated by the fact that after 'it', memories of incest began to surface for me, first of abuse by my father and then by my mother. This was especially difficult because feminists/lesbians tend to focus on male sexual violence so some women didn't believe me. Also what I remembered my mother doing to me was almost exactly the same as what this other lesbian did, it has been a really difficult three years – for two of them it has been impossible for me to form lesbian/love relationships or to be sexual with other women. (Taylor and Chandler, 1995: 19–21)

These women's stories raise many questions for a feminist perspective on international peace resolution. Each of the lesbians above resisted being raped in different ways but did not completely hate her attacker, showing that it is possible to love someone and still hate what they do and say to the extent that you do not wish to be close to them. This is similar to African and Mexican people who welcomed invading white men with great hospitality and generosity, who signed 'Treaties of Friendship and Protection', but ended up being pacified, parcelled out and owned by their ex-guests.

Like the colonised, these lesbians resisted being raped or attempted to discontinue a relationship that was based on rape. Like the colonised and the enslaved, the pain of being raped never really goes away due to the fear that it could happen again, that it never really ended, that justice will never be done because might is right. No one would believe the lesbian who alleges rape because there is no pregnancy expectation just as the ex-colony is emptied as a result of rape rather than being impregnated with meaning, neocolonialism notwithstanding.

To help us answer the six questions at the end of this chapter, let us consider briefly the incidence of real rape in international conflict. Brownmiller (1975) provides a detailed historical account of rape in times of war, revolution and peace, but that will not be rehashed here. The Romans raped the Sabines in order to forcibly acquire brides for the building of a Roman state, but Norman Bryson (1986) argues like a defence attorney that the Sabines were not really raped given the noble aim of the Romans and given the fact that the union was solemnised before being consummated. When the Sabine men whose honour it was that the Romans violated through the rape of 'their' women reorganised and returned for retribution, the women intervened with their children, pleading with their fathers and brothers not to kill their sons and husbands.

A similar view of Lucretia was taken by Saint Augustine, who was of the opinion that if Lucretia consented to sex in order not to be killed with her Negro slave, as if she was caught in the act with him before being killed by an angry member of the royal family, then she was not virtuous enough; she was at best an accomplice and not a heroine (Bryson, 1986). This thesis of complicity in oppression is an assumption that is often ascribed to the colonised, according to hooks (1994), in the sense that the new man who is not into the 'dick thing' is often suspected of being gay, as if women subconsciously crave a man who will take control of business in the bedroom.

Julia and Herman Schwendinger (1983) offer a structuralist account of rape as a symptom of unequal power relations which could result from actual inequality of strength or from intimidation and surprised attacks. Alice Walker (1988) narrates the difficult experience of trying to visit a black woman, Desire Woods, who was jailed in Georgia for defending herself against a white rapist. To the surprise of Walker, she was turned away and refused a visit, not by a white male prison officer but by a black female officer who looked identical to the visitor. This theme was later developed by her in *Possessing the Secret of Joy* (Walker, 1992) where Tashi was condemned to death by firing squad for the (lesbian?) murder of the old woman who had genitally mutilated her.

It is a myth, according to the Schwendingers, to say that rape is impossible if the woman is not consenting because even countries that resisted imperialist rape of their territories did not always succeed in decolonising by force. It is this myth of complicity that pollutes the raped woman beyond redemption in Cyprus and Bangladesh, for example.

The case of Cyprus (Roussou, 1987) and the more recent case of Bosnia (for which a token suspect was being tried by the International Court of Justice in the Hague at the time of writing this chapter) illustrate the point made by Amnesty International (1992) that rape is used by all sides as a weapon of war. The Cypriot women who were raped by the invading Turkish troops were too scared to press charges because if their husbands knew of their violation, they might be divorced or abandoned. A similar thing happened in Bangladesh, according to Brownmiller, during the war of independence from Pakistan which led to mass divorce of raped women after the war. As a reminder of how seriously the international community takes actual rape even when documented, let us end with a quotation from an American researcher of Bosnian-Croatian origin, bearing in mind that the atrocities perpetrated in that region were not done by only one party to the conflict, as even this partisan view recognises:

> Serbian forces have exterminated over 200,000 Croatians and Muslims thus far in an operation they've coined 'ethnic cleansing'. In this genocide, in Bosnia-Herzegovina alone over 30,000 Muslim and Croatian girls and women are pregnant from mass rape. Of the 100 Serbian-run concentration camps, about 20 are solely rape/death camps for Muslim and Croatian women and children ... [There are] news reports and pictures here of Serbian tanks plastered with pornography ... [and reports that those who] catch the eye of the men looking at the pornography are killed ... Some massacres in villages as well as rapes and/or executions in camps are being videotaped as they're happening. One Croatian woman described being tortured by electric shocks and gang-raped in a camp by Serbian men dressed in Croatian uniforms who filmed the rapes and forced her to 'confess' on film that Croatians raped her. In the streets of Zagreb, UN troops often ask local women how much they cost ... There are reports of refugee women being forced to sexually service them to receive aid ... Tomorrow I talk to two survivors of mass rape, thirty men per day for over three months ... The UN passed a resolution to collect evidence, a first step for a war crimes trial but it is said there is no precedent for trying sexual atrocities (quoted in Mackinnon, 1993b: 86–7)

1. *When rape is used as a weapon of war, are female troops accomplices only or sometimes also victims or even perpetrators of rape?*
2. *Do you think that the notion of lesbian rape diminishes or advances feminist critiques of and campaigns against patriarchal rape?*
3. *Do you think that only those who experience it will know it, or do you think that lesbian rape is worthy of study by all, including heterosexual men, who could use the concept to shield their own 'natural' inclination to rape? (See Agozino (1995) for a relevant debate).*
4. *What are the lessons that lesbian rape learnt from or teaches international conflict resolution?*
5. *Name any works of art, books, films or songs that could be used to illustrate the idea of lesbian rape in international relations.*
6. *Is lesbian rape in international relations real rape and is international ecological rape lesbian in any way?*

6. Poststructuralism and Positivism in Criminological Theory

Many of us are familiar with the influence of positivism in criminological theory. For those who are not, let us reiterate some of the points made in chapter 1. Bougeois criminologists certainly claim that empirical research in criminology originated with the development of the Lombrosian School and its measurement of individual characteristics. But there are other strands of nineteenth-century research such as those of Bonger which pre-date Lombroso. The word positivism is misused by reactionary criminologists as merely a metaphor or idealistic metaphysics. The Lombrosian School is 'positivistic' by analogy because it relies on Social Darwinist empirical strategy for quantifying criminal attributes to validate a priori theories of evolution and natural selection or 'progress'. Positivism is recognised as the dominant perspective in criminological research and its principles of rationality, empiricism, universal truth and objective scientific methodology are key features of modernity as advocated by the Enlightenment. Positivism may assume that sense-impressions are the only basis of knowledge, but Lombroso's theory is not 'positivistic' simply because it adopted operational definitions of causal attributes. Lombroso's claim to valid knowledge was not merely based on the appeal to immediate apprehensible measurements. It was based on ideological 'truths' derived from race–class–gender stereotypes and imperialist dogma.

Basically, modernity called for an end to the metaphysical belief in demonology or the belief that morality was ordained by God and that those who deviate from societal norms were breaking the ordinance of God under the influence of demonological possession. Such beliefs produced arbitrary administration of justice in the form of the Inquisition, witch hunts, trial by ordeal and trial by battle, all of which assumed that God would be on the side of the just and the righteous (see Mary Daly, 1978, for an analysis of the witch trials primarily against women in the name of the Father and of the Son. About nine million people, mostly women, were killed). However, as Fitzpatrick (1992) and many others have argued, the modernists did not completely abandon metaphysics, but merely replaced the mythology of God the Father with mythologies of the bourgeoisie as the class with the manifest destiny to rule over others.

Enlightenment philosophers posed the question that Hobbes formulated most simply, 'How is society possible?' This Hobbesian question of law and order was answered in different ways by different philosophers depending on what they saw as the character of 'man in the state of nature'. Those like Hobbes, who saw the character of man to be selfish and brutish, advocated authoritarian forms of government, but those like Locke and Rousseau, who saw man to be inherently good and rational, advocated more democratic forms of government. However, all the Enlightenment thinkers subscribed to the idea that the source of social order is a mythical social contract by which men in a state of nature willingly gave up some of their rights to a sovereign in return for protection of their fundamental rights. To Hobbes, the sovereign is an absolute monarch, but to Locke and Rousseau, the parliamentary form of government is preferable, with citizens retaining the right to remove incompetent or oppressive rulers from office.

Beccaria and Bentham followed Hobbes more closely by recommending ways of deterring crime through making punishment fit the offence, irrespective of who the offender was. This was a radical recommendation in hierarchical feudal Europe where status and class determined almost exclusively who got what type of penalty for what type of offence. This was later adopted by the French revolutionaries in the Penal Code of 1791 which specified fixed penalties for specific offences and to some extent proved unworkable, especially because there was no mitigation for young people and the mentally ill, who could not be assumed to possess the key attributes of Enlightenment – free will, rationality and liberty. The recognition of these exceptional circumstances modified classicism and resulted in neoclassicism, which remains the dominant philosophy of punishment in modern society (see Gilroy, 1993, for a critique of the universalism of the Enlightenment from the perspective of black people who built and yet remain outside the claims of progress).

Later Enlightenment philosophers like Kant and Saint Simon supported the call for rationality to be applied to social administration in order to arrive at increased human happiness. Saint Simon was the first to call for a 'positive science of society', or 'sociology' as he put it, a science that would be the 'queen of all sciences' (monarchical influences?), a science whose practitioners would function as the 'high priests of society' (demonological influences?). This call for a positive science of society aspired to reproduce Darwin's achievements in biology and resulted in organismic analogies as models of social organisation. The call for a positive science of society was not taken up by the Enlightenment philosophers themselves, but was first adopted by Lombroso who performed what is known as the first scientific (as opposed to philosophical) criminological analysis of crime causation by a chance discovery that the skull of one notorious brigand reminded him of the skulls of lower animals, such as rodents. Lombroso's hasty conclusion from what is now recognised as inadequate evidence has been criticised enough, but his examples of empirical observation, quantitative measurement and inferential conclusions remain the dominant examples of how to do criminological research.

Durkheim and sociological positivists adopted Lombroso's critique of the philosophy of free will, but also moved beyond Lombroso's focus on individual traits. To the sociological determinists, what mattered most were the features of crimogenic societies rather than the features of individual criminals. However, in spite of the critique of the philosophy of free will by the positivists of all shapes and shades, the assumption of the Enlightenment philosophers that social events are knowable and that fundamental truth is discoverable through the application of rational, objective scientific methods was accepted by all. The Enlightenment advocated scepticism towards all forms of received knowledge, especially religious knowledge or dogma, but the Enlightenment did not extend this scepticism to its own claims to truth, objectivity and knowledge. Likewise, positivism adopted a sceptical approach to the claim by the Enlightenment philosophers that human conduct was freely willed, but did not extend this scepticism to their own claim to be fulfilling the Enlightenment's promise of science, objectivity and verifiable truth as avenues to better social organisation.

Poststructuralism emerged in the postwar period as the main perspective that extended the Enlightenment tradition of scepticism to all claims to truth, all claims to knowledge and all claims to universality. The key formulation of the poststructuralist critique of objectivism was stated by Foucault in *Discipline and Punish* where he wrote: 'There is no power relation without the correlative constitution of a field of knowledge, nor any knowledge that does not presuppose and constitute at the same time power relations' (1977: 27). In his *Selected Interviews* (in *Power/Knowledge*, 1980) he clarified this further by stating: 'It's not a matter of emancipating truth from every system of power (which would be a chimera for truth is already power) but of detaching the power of truth from the forms of hegemony, social, economic and cultural, within which it operates at the present time' (p. 133). In other words, what Foucault argues is that those who claim to be objective are actually partisan because their claim to be objective is only a way for them to acquire and exercise power. Moreover, those who claim to be seeking knowledge in the interest of the less powerful cannot claim to be powerless because their claim to knowledge itself embodies power relations of some sort given that power belongs to those who oppose hegemony as well as to those who exercise hegemony, albeit unequally. In his 'What is Enlightenment?', he argues that we should abandon the wish to write a universal history of everything and concentrate on the history of the present. The idea of progress should not be accepted as a given, but should be interrogated from the point of view of whether it is a claim based on truth or a claim based on power.

This view that there is a knowledge–power axis from which all those who profess knowledge or power or both cannot escape reminds us of Smart's (1990) critique of positivism. The poststructuralist approach seeks to expose the ways that theorists try to exercise power through their use of language, through their gaze or observation, through their classification and through their programmes for the control of the bodies and the minds of individuals. In their essay 'Criminological Displacements: A Sociological Deconstruction' (1986) Stephen Pfohl and Avery Gordon argue that poststructuralism differs from both positivism, with its emphasis on objective truth, and humanism, with its emphasis on symbolic interactionism. This is because both perspectives assume that there is a 'reality' out there waiting to be discovered, whereas poststructuralism 'resists the temptation to forget that its own re-presentation of facts is an essential feature' of the rituals of authenticity which should not be privileged over any other representations on the basis of claims of truth and validity. Smart pointed out that this is one of the problems facing this perspective among feminists: if they claim that they know nothing about 'truth', masculinist criminologists will laugh and say that they have always suspected that they knew nothing about the 'Truth'.

Pfohl and Gordon try to avoid this type of objection to poststructuralism by re-presenting positivistic criminology as an enterprise based on three interrelated 'pleasures' instead of being the truthful discipline that it has always been assumed to be. These are:

1. 'The Pleasures of Sadism: Mastering the Facts of Crime as "Things"'. Here, the criminologist is depicted as a 'he' and the criminal is depicted as a 'she'. In the dramatic dialogues between the he and the she, it becomes clear that although this depiction of the criminal as a she flies in the face of conventional 'reality', what is suggested is that, like the woman, the criminal is treated by positivism as the 'Other' to be 'penetrated' in order to 'master' the causes of criminality. This is likened to the domineering ways that men gaze at women with a will to master them, penetrate them, lay them bare and control them. The authors argue that this sadism has nothing to do with rationality but everything to do with the pleasures of exercising power over others, which the Marquis de Sade was describing at the same time that criminology was emerging as a respected science. It is pleasure from the ability to inflict pain on others.

2. 'The Pleasure of Surveillance: The Eye upon Her' is the gaze that categorises the Other. The birth of positivism is regarded as the end of ideology because of the assumption that we can measure, differentiate and control the Other through close observation. The assumption here is that all those who adopt similar methods of observation will obtain the same results and thereby see if the claims of any theorist are reliable or otherwise.

3. 'The Pleasure of Truth: The Normal Subject and His Other'. This pleasure is reflected in the privileging of 'true confessions' which the social sciences seem to have borrowed from the demonology of pre-Enlightenment times. It is assumed by criminologists that when you interview victims or offenders, they are telling the truth and, if they are not telling the truth, they can be exposed with clever questioning. The same is true of police interviews of suspects and cross-examinations in courts or clinical consultation with medical personnel. The criminologist, the police officer, the judge, the psychiatrist, in turn, claim that their truth is superior because it is not the truth of an individual but the balanced, objective truth gleaned from all the individual truths told by interviewees. According to Foucault, this pleasure of truth found among positivist criminologists must be interrogated, not for the purpose of discovering a higher truth, but for the purpose of

exposing the will to power inherent in what seems to be a disinterested objective view.

The call by Foucault for greater scepticism regarding the expertise of criminology has been applied by many criminologists to Foucault himself. Many feminists have criticised Foucault for failing to analyse gender even though he wrote a lot about the body and sexuality. Colin Sumner (1990), argues that in spite of Foucault's silence on gender, his analysis of knowledge and power over sexuality offers a potential opportunity for a Marxist-feminist perspective in criminology. According to Sumner, what Foucault demonstrated is that 'attempts to mark off the deviant, the pathological, the dangerous and the criminal from the moral and the good' are attempts to exercise moral and political power rather than simply a value-neutral search for truth relying on objective scientific methods. According to him, if these moral categories are reversed and applied to people in authority, it will become clear that there is nothing inherently deviant about them and that they are partial, superficial and morally selective 'censures'. What Foucault offers, according to Sumner, is an opportunity to analyse the extent to which masculinity affects men adversely, especially if they are men who subscribe to subordinate masculinities. Following Foucault and Gramsci, he argues that the law displays a hegemonic masculinity that affects subordinate femininity and subordinate masculinity adversely, a point that many feminists are yet to acknowledge.

Adrian Howe (1994) agrees and argues that 'the deconstruction of modernist ideas such as "truth" and "reason" has led to a questioning of the very idea of a politics founded on notions of justice or equality and the announcement of the death of the subject urges transgression of 70s feminism'. This is because the category 'woman' or even 'women' will no longer be adequate as a taken-for-granted basis for feminist politics, given what Foucault has argued about the social construction of identity and categorisation. Alison Young (1990), adopts Sumner's concept of moral censures to describe the representation of the 'unusual deployment of the body' in the Greenham Common women's anti-nuclear protest. To Young (1990: 14), this illustrates the Foucauldian idea that the body is 'the object of the operation of technologies of power and control, while simultaneously remaining the site for potential strategies of resistance'. According to Young, the press treated filth as a commodity, not because their reports were truthful or objective, but because they would sell more copies by subjecting the women to 'defilement through the language and images of revulsion and disgust which equate them with excrement, dirt, blood and disease'.

Many feminists argue that Foucault should be read with a lot more scepticism than postmodern feminists attempt. For example, many contributions to *Up Against Foucault* (Ramazanoglu, 1993) outline what Foucault can and what he cannot contribute to feminism (Maureen Cain). One of the things that Foucault cannot contribute is what it feels like to be at the receiving end of disciplinary power without this being expressed in discourse because it belongs to repressed knowledge which lies outside politics. Cain recognised that there is something which Foucault called the pre-discursive, something that lies outside discourse or something that exists before discourse commences. As Cain (1993: 74) put it:

the realist position which I and others have developed denies the strong postmodern position that social life derives in its entirety from a play of communications resulting sometimes in temporal sedimentations of meaning. Such a view gives ontological primacy to discourse, it being impossible to 'have' a relationship which is not expressible in, and ultimately constituted by, some discourse or other. I argue instead ... that whereas such transitive relations obviously exist ... other relations exist which have not, or have not as yet, been formulated in discourse.

An example Cain gives is the relatively unknown finding by Kelly that virtually all women have suffered a form of sexual violence along the continuum from pressurised sex, through coerced sex, to rape. Foucault concentrated on the critique of the knowledge–power relations involved in every discourse, but said little or nothing about what it feels like to be at the receiving end except by recognising that pain is administered for the pleasure of hegemonic groups and not simply in the name of truth and justice, as is often claimed. Other feminists are sceptical about Foucault's rejection of the reality principle especially with reference to the body. They argue that the acceptance by Foucault that the body is the site of power struggles should lead to an unquestionable acceptance that the body is real and that this reality does not depend on the course of the power struggle over the body.

Mary Joe Frug's unfinished draft, 'Postmodern Feminist Legal Manifesto', acknowledges the existence of this reality that lies outside discourse. For example, it is true that men and women differ in their bodies but this does not mean, according to Frug, that the differences between the role and status of men and women are natural. Those differences are still discursively constructed and the task of postmodern legal feminism would be to render more visible the ways that the law operates to sustain or help construct these images of the female body. She identifies three ways that the law does this: terror-isation, maternalisation and sexualization of the female body. Terrorisation of the female body in legal rules is the discourse that advises women to seek protection from terror and thereby recognises that the female body is the body in terror, the body that cringes, the body that submits to the protection of an other. Often, the assumption is that the threat is from an alien, whereas Elizabeth Stanko and many others have identified the terrorist who pays the rent, the fact that women are more likely to be terrorised by people they know and people they are expected to submit to under patriarchal authority.

Maternalisation operates by rewarding women who assume respon-sibility for child-rearing within a married relationship while women who are either single or childless by choice or by circumstances are repressed for not conforming to the image of the real woman. Similarly, working mothers are frowned upon in court while housewives are more readily given mitigation even for serious offences.

Sexualisation operates in legal rules by blaming a rape victim for her victimisation if she is known to be sexually promiscuous, if the alleged attacker is her lawfully married husband, if she dressed 'provocatively', if she is a whore or if she is a poor black woman complaining about a middle-class white man. These go to emphasise the imagery that is legally available through advertisements and pornography, that the female body is there for the sexual pleasure of men. Women who exhibit signs of lesbianism would be repressed and even subjected to psychiatric reports because they seem unnatural, as Allen reported.

What terrorisation, maternalisation and sexualisation demonstrate is that the female body is not naturally given because the body of a terrified married mother is never the same as the body of a drug-taking, independent prostitute in the eyes of the law. This is why radical feminists are opposed to the call by prostitutes that sex work should be legalised. People like Dworkin and Mackinnon suspect that such a reform would serve only to legalise the terrorisation, maternalisation and sexualisation of the female body in the interest of men. Frug suggests that the role of postmodern legal feminism is not to support the radicals or to support the liberal prostitutes who demand legalisation, but to render more visible the ways that the law colludes in this politics of patriarchal domination of women.

A broader application of poststructuralism comes from Henry and Milovanivic (1994). According to them, crime is conventionally defined as a social fact *sui generis*, but a look at the way categories of crime are constituted will reveal that there is nothing inherently criminal about criminal categories, a point that the labelling perspective made in the 1960s. Henry and Milovanovic argue that policy is also assumed to be a course of action rationally or deliberately taken. But in the criminal justice system, this is not the case because policies do not follow any single programme of action. According to them, criminal justice policy is often represented as a series of proposals aimed at eliminating crime but this is contradictory given that opposition to crime would result in more criminal categories being constituted by policy-makers. As they put it: 'Social control agents in their practice of criminal justice policy both produce and sustain deviant categories, and they tacitly frame coherent narratives on "what happened", hence objectifying interactive experience.' This sounds almost identical to the societal reaction perspective, but Henry and Milovanovic move beyond that perspective by calling for criminal justice policy to be directed at all the processes that constitute and contribute to crime. Whereas the labelling perspective focused on interaction between individual deviants and individual officials, Henry and Milovanovic state that 'criminology and its implied criminal justice policy must begin with global economy since it is with global economy that power, however directed by particular nation states, is most widely constituted'.

This call is probably evidence of scepticism on their part regarding Foucault's preoccupation with what he called the 'micro-physics of power', i.e. what is done to the body of the individual and what the individual does to his or her own body as an expression of knowledge and the will to power to control the body. This global focus is found in postcolonial scholarship which, like postmodernism, is more common in the arts and the humanities than in the social sciences. An example of this can be found in Bhabha (1992). According to Bhabha, 'It is one of the salutary features of postmodern theory to suggest that it is the disjunctive, fragmented, displaced agency of those who have suffered the sentence of history – subjugation, domination, diaspora, displacement – that forces one to think outside the certainty of the sententious.' He argues that there is emphasis in postmodern thought on the fact that meaning is temporal, on the political struggles around the meaning of truth rather than on the scholarly objectivity of truth claims. He illustrates this type of theorising by quoting Toni Morrison's novel *Beloved*, which opens with the number '124', an address that meant everything to previously enslaved African Americans who had never had their own addresses until emancipation. The book narrates how the ghost of 'Beloved' haunts the address where her mother now lives long after cutting her throat as a mercy killing rather than allow her to grow up and experience the indignity of being a black woman in slavery. This raises the question of what crime is and what justice is in a society structured in dominance (see Hall, 1980, 1988, 1996 on the articulation thesis).

This story might be dismissed by criminologists as fictional, no matter how historically based it might be. However, Bhabha quickly illustrates that the issue of crime and punishment in literature is not always a matter for literary theorists alone. Sometimes, it is literally dealt with like any common criminality. This was the case with the imposition of a Fatwa on Salman Rushdie for making what many Muslims regard as offensive remarks about the person of the Prophet in his *Satanic Verses*. What is postmodern here is the fact that the sentence on Rushdie was pronounced without trial in a distant Third World country and had immediate repercussions in Europe where the author was taken into virtual protective 'custody'. What is more, those who defend the right of Rushdie to write what he likes, according to Bhabha, are as fundamentalist as those who condemn him because neither side seems to have read the book. The lesson here is that western criminologists must take cultural studies seriously and go beyond Europe and North America to examine the relationships between North and South in law and in culture. Bhabha cites Fanon as a good example for the postmodern theorist of guilt and authority to follow. According to Fanon: 'The native's guilt [under imperialism] is never a guilt which he accepts; it is rather a kind of curse, a sword of Damocles ... He is overpowered but not tamed' (Fanon 1963: 53).

This concern with global power relations was addressed by Derrida (1994), who argues that the unequal exchanges between the North and the South are enduring issues which remain to be tackled and so it is ridiculous for Francis Fukuyama and others to start celebrating the end of history. Jacques Derrida recognises that the intellectual debt owed to Marx must be repaid in full by returning to interrogate the spectres of Marx just as Hamlet interrogated his father's ghost. The second type of debt, owed to the North by the South, cannot be repaid and should therefore be cancelled. People of African descent, as the Trans-Atlantic Slavery Gallery documents (see also Ekwe-Ekwe, 1993), have recognised a third type of debt owed to them by Europe as a result of the crimes of slavery and imperialism. They now call for reparation along the same lines as the payments made by Germany to survivors of the Nazi Holocaust. As in the case of the Holocaust, many of the crimes against the enslaved were executed as 'punishment' for 'offences' committed by the relatively powerless, but the fact that these categories have been reversed is an example of the claim by poststructuralism that what makes one point of view acceptable at any one time is not that it is more truthful than another but that it is backed by greater power resources at that particular time. For example, vast regions of Iraq had been declared 'No Fly Zones' after the Gulf War but they are the very regions over which US and UK war planes fly every day. Despite almost daily bombing of Iraqi targets for more than ten years by allied pilots, no one has reported that there was a war going on in Iraq. Jean Baudrillard (1995) predicted this when he wrote before the Gulf War that all the talk of war in the media was hyper-real and that a real war would not happen because the reality principle had been replaced by the principle of evil in public discourse. The question was no longer who was telling the truth and who was lying but who was good and who was evil? After the war, critics challenged Baudrillard to see if he would eat his words and admit that his prediction was dead wrong because there was indeed a war in which more than 100,000 people were killed. On the contrary, he defended his thesis by asserting that the Gulf War did not take place. 'Does the guy not watch CNN?' A Doctoral candidate who was not familiar with Baudrillard asked when he heard of this unusual thesis; and that was exactly the point of Baudrillard – only a simulacrum of a war, like video games, would be programmed, edited and censored for primetime viewing on television screens since a real war would not be televised. Baudrillard has been severely criticised by Cohen (1993) and Norris (1992) on this issue for taking postmodernism too far by apparently trivialising the death of more than 100,000 people. However, I believe that what Baudrillard was calling attention to is identical with the concern of Cohen regarding the silence of criminologists on human rights crimes. Baudrillard was pointing out the difference between premeditated mass murder and a war. You may call the Gulf War a Turkey Shoot or gunboat criminology but was it really a war? More on Baudrillard's ideas in the next chapter.

7. Social Fiction *Sui Generis*: The Fairy Tale Structure of Criminological Theory

This chapter questions both poststructuralist criminological scepticism and the Durkheimian positivism of verifiable facts, not by defending the social factual basis of criminological claims, but by demonstrating the role of fiction, in itself, within the construction of criminological knowledge. The chapter questions the privileging of facts and values by Habermas (1996) and raises issues with Baudrillard's (1996) perfect-crime-as-no-crime thesis. The chapter ends with a review of criminological motifs in fairy tales and the mythological assumptions grounded in criminology. In conclusion, the chapter outlines the interdependence of fact and fiction in the social construction of knowledge along the 'constitutive criminology' lines suggested by Henry and Milovanovic (1996).

TENSIONS BETWEEN FACTICITY AND VALIDITY

In his *Between Facts and Norms* (1996), Habermas tries to answer the Hobbesian question of order, why society is possible given the selfishness of human beings in the state of nature. He argues that a review of Hobbes through the perspective of Kant will reveal him to be less the theoretician of the absolute monarch enforcing a social contract than 'a theoretician of bourgeois rule of law without democracy'. According to Habermas, Hobbes tried to resolve the tensions between facticity and validity by designing a social contract that would maintain an egoistic social order supported by all those involved. As Habermas put it: 'what appears as morally right and legitimate then issues spontaneously from the self-interested decisions of rational egoists or as Kant will put it, a "race of devils". This type of social order is justified on the ground of economic rationality or the idea that a system which 'makes as many people as possible well off for as long as possible ... bestows material justice on the sovereignty of a ruler who by definition can do nothing unlawful' (1996: 90–1).

Habermas followed Kant in disagreeing with Hobbes by arguing that a social contract is not the same thing as a contract in private law. Whereas individuals enter into a contract in order to achieve a determinate end, the social contract is empty of all content, and serves only as a container or framework into which to package the three principles of law, morality and democracy. According to Habermas, the tension between facticity and validity can be resolved by seeing law as the reverse side of the coin of democracy, instead of seeing it as the mid-point on a morality–democracy continuum.

Habermas returns to his earlier theory of communicative action by emphasising that society is possible because social actors follow what American pragmatists identified as the general structures of language that enable intersubjectively meaningful action whether or not the actors understand the rules of grammar. Communication requires that speakers should base their interactions on validity claims that are acceptable to their fellows. When there is a disagreement about a validity claim, this is resolved through an agreement about the meanings of the words being used, an assumption that all the participants are rationally accountable for their actions, and a belief that any consensus arrived at is beyond all reasonable doubts. Habermas concedes that such ideal situations do not always exist for communicative action especially when the issue at stake is ethical (one person's good can be another's evil) and so communicative action will enhance conflict resolution if the issues at stake are limited to broad moral issues (such as human rights) over which there is a broad consensus.

When actors resort to strategic reasoning with threats and promises, they are bargaining to get their own way in spite of opposition from other actors. This is what makes the law (as a system of communicative action and also a strategic system) essential for conflict resolution especially in pluralistic free market societies (1996: 24).

This is similar to Durkheim's thesis according to which societal evolution from mechanical types of solidarity to organic types of solidarity proceeds through increasing differentiatiation that paradoxically results in increased integration of the differentiated units by matching increased social density with increased moral density. Habermas also borrowed the Durkheimian concept of social facts to describe mutually intelligible communication. The slight difference here is that Habermas replaces what Durkheim called the collective conscience with what he called the counterfactual idealisation of norms broadly shared for the purpose of redeeming 'criticizable validity claims' in intersubjectively meaningful (Weberian) speech-acts (1996: 35). This is closer to structuralist conflict theories than to structural functionalism especially because Habermas is more interested in conflict resolution through meaningful dialogue. In this sense his theory of communicative action is relevant to views of criminology as peace-making, except that he sees dissension consistently as a 'risk' to communication, requiring the double binding of being circumscribed and being allowed unhindered play through the force of law (1996: 39).

In chapter 2, Habermas turned his attention to two opposite responses to the tension between facticity and validity: sociology of law and the philosophy of justice. He outlined the advantages and disadvantages of 'an objectivist disenchantment of law' in the systems theory of Niklas Luhmann (1995). Then he compared this with the abstract theory of justice advanced by John Rawls (1969). Enlightenment theories of the social contract presumed that the nature of commercial activity derived from the rational nature of social solidarity. In other words, the reason why individuals continue to draw up contracts in commercial transaction is because rational human beings realised that a social contract was the best way of evolving beyond the tyranny of nature. Marxist theories inverted this equation by placing the economy at the base and insisting that the idea of the social contract was derived from economic rationality in order to justify the self-reproduction of capital. According to Marx, this is the objective nature of how capitalist accumulation works and so this is what needs to be understood by those who wish to change society. It is only for the purpose of changing society that subjective views about the nature of capitalist exchange society become important; otherwise, that would be false consciousness, especially if the people disadvantaged by the system support the system.

Luhmann opted for a more objectivist perspective on systems theory by ignoring the subjectivist dimensions of individual consciousness and focusing exclusively on the self-reflexivity of the system. Drawing from mechanistic equilibrium models and biological homeostasis, early systems theory was developed largely by Talcott Parsons. Luhmann introduced from biology the organismic analogy of 'autopoesis' to underline the fact that the whole is more than the sum of its parts or that society is not made of the sum of individuals within it. This means that both economic and legal systems are autopoetic in the sense that they are 'operationally closed'; their nature is determined by their own operation even though influences from their environment could lead to their transformation, especially because the environment is part of the internal structure of the system. This suggests a pluralistic view that society is polycentric. It does not have a single collective conscience but a multiplicity of perspectives representing subsystems.

Habermas points out that autopoesis finds it difficult to account for inter-systemic communication without accepting a theory of communicative action. In other words, systems theory is mistaken in ignoring the everyday interaction between groups and individuals, while abstracting the individual organism and applying the model to the social system. He prefers to follow Weber and Parsons at the same time as a way of combining both intersubjectivity and system-atisation in his analysis of the tensions between facts and values. Of particular interest is his emphasis that the operation of law is not free from the exercise of economic and political power.

To advance the project of modernity instead of completely abandoning it, Habermas identifies the internal colonisation of juridical power in particular and life-worlds in general by monetary or economic power. He calls for deliberative democracy as a way of addressing the power imbalance that is evident in the law as a system of communicative action. He sees the problem of substantive and material equality before the law as something that goes beyond the law especially due to the internal colonisation of juridical power by economic power – a point that was missed by social contract theories of justice.

Habermas concludes that what is needed is a 'reconstructive legal theory' based on the idea that the 'counterfactual (that is, idealist as opposed to empirical) self-understanding of constitutional democracy' is a basic assumption presupposed by the relevant actors. For example, when constitution-makers declare 'We the people', they are fully aware that all the people are not equal in material terms but they are expressing an ideal that, in spite of material inequality, everyone should be given an equal chance of being heard and treated fairly. This implies that conflict is part of the social system given that societal complexity requires the exercise of criticism as well as that of consent, as people freely choose, act strategically and realise themselves. These competing interests are released and at the same time channelled through the compulsion of social norms over which the citizens reach an understanding through deliberative democratic procedures that enable the exercise of 'legally guaranteed commun-icative liberties' (1996: 462). As a result, the legitimate coercion of dissent, which appears as a risk to communication and social solidarity, becomes converted into the means of social integration.

This is a counterfactual or prescriptive account of the tensions between facticity and validity. The major problem with a counter-factual theory of facts is that of empirical tenability. Habermas should be commended for attempting to overcome the strongest critique of classicist criminological theories of equality before the law by looking at feminist politics of equality and considering the status of migrants from Eastern Europe and the South to affluent Western Europe. The major difficulty here is that his prescription of deliberative democracy as a panacea for the tensions between facticity and validity is more likely to work for feminist politics than for the politics of immigration, precisely because non-citizens will not be allowed to participate in the communicative speech-acts of deliberative democracy while the citizens are increasingly hostile to increasing immigration. Although Habermas called for post-national citizenship as a response to the problem of the Other, he does not mean global citizenship, but European citizenship, which would continue to be a fortress against non-Europeans.

Furthermore, a mythic, counterfactual formulation that privileges self-regulation gives the false impression that under deliberative democracy, individuals will be regulating themselves, but this is far from the case in actually existing constitutional states where party politics under the strong colonial influence of monetary power turns the self into the dehumanised self-regulation in Luhmann's theory of autopoesis.

If self-regulation means what it says, assuming agreement on the meaning of the words that Habermas premised his theory of communicative action on, then it will be a dangerously reductionist notion of the self. In a deliberative democracy, for example, how would self-regulation be applied to children, the mentally ill, convicted offenders and foreigners? Since these categories of the self will continue to be regulated by others, even in a deliberative democracy, the emphasis on communicative action and social facts in Habermas needs to be qualified.

Moreover, self-regulation is not always benevolent, even in the atomised sense of the self-interested individual actor. In fact, self-regulation is capable of being fascistic in the sense of seeking a final solution to the self through suicidal communicative actions. Durkheim would say that even suicide cannot be understood in atomistic terms but must be understood in broad sociological terms, especially when it is altruistic rather than egoistic suicide. Credit goes to Foucault for recognising that technologies of the self are the means for the exercise of power and control over the body by the individual and by others. Hence, the fact that self-regulation refers to the collective social self of the sovereign state needs to be underscored in order not to be confused with the atomistic self.

Finally, Habermas talks about the intrusion of economic power from the outside into law or what he called the internal colonisation of juridical power by economic power. Yet he failed to apply this to imperialist power relations where such intrusion is even more prominent because, in international law, power is more important than the facts and truth-claims which Habermas concerned himself with. Perhaps a look at the postmodernist work of Jean Baudrillard could help to provide answers to some of these doubts raised regarding the modernist work of Habermas.

THE MURDER OF REALITY

> *This is the story of a crime – of the murder of reality. And the exterm-*
> *ination of an illusion – the vital illusion, the radical illusion of the*
> *world. The real does not disappear into illusion; it is illusion that*
> *disappears into integral reality.*

That is how Baudrillard starts what appears to be a rejoinder to Habermas, without mentioning him in his *Perfect Crime* (1996). Whereas Habermas writes about the life-world as a social fact, Baudrillard starts from the opposite assumption that the world (not just the life-world) reveals itself only through appearances that are better seen as clues to its non-existence rather than proof of its being. He suggests that the world could have been a perfect crime – without a criminal, motive, victim or clue, were it not for the appearances that betray the secrets of the world. This sounds similar to what Habermas called the 'counterfactual' nature of social contract ideas for, according to Baudrillard, 'Just as we cannot plumb the first few seconds of the Big Bang, so we cannot locate those few seconds in which the original crime took place either' (1996: 2).

Baudrillard argues that even when truth-claims are made, it is like a Madonna striptease in which the promise is to reveal the truth by rendering it naked yet what the voyeurs get is only the appearance of nudity wrapped in secondary clothing that appears less erotic compared to the charm of the dress.

This is an indirect way of raising the question why Habermas preoccupied himself with truth-claims of validity without offering a theory of deception and falsehood. On the contrary, Baudrillard points out that 'Not to be sensitive to the degree of unreality and play, this degree of malice and ironic wit on the part of language and the world is, in effect, to be incapable of living.'

Baudrillard goes beyond the idea that the social contract is 'counterfactual' by arguing that it is a 'radical illusion' committed by an original crime that 'altered' the world from the beginning, rendering it unreal or never identical with its original self. Furthermore, contrary to the idea that self-regulation is a democratic requirement for communication in a plural society, he points out that the three-dimensional view of power (to make people do what you want, or to stop them from doing what they want, or to construct what they eventually say they want) could be seen as abusive (1996: 12).

From this critique of the classicist idea of free will, he questions the idea that communication is geared towards the production of meaning. He suggests that contrary to the view of communication being based on shared meanings, meaning is never fixed as the truth but always interfaces with illusion.

Having adopted a sceptical approach to notions of truth, reality and meaning, Baudrillard accords fictional accounts the same status as empirical or philosophical statements. He points out that Bertrand Russell based *The Analysis of Mind* on a fable or fiction in which the world was created only a few minutes ago but is peopled by individuals who remember a past that is in fact an illusion. This is clearly a critique of the social contract theories that Habermas paid such meticulous attention to in his work. Baudrillard equates philosophical faith in the idea of the social contract with an equally 'blind faith' among natural philosophers that even the evidence of biology and geology supporting evolution were simulated by God in order to protect the mystery of the creation of the universe from inquisitive scientists. In other words, Baudrillard thinks that it is a waste of time to dwell on the origin of the social contract when we could be discussing the ways that virtual reality is effectively replacing reality everywhere through modern technology (1996: 94–5).

Anticipating reaction to this provocative statement, Baudrillard points out that critics say that no one should discredit reality in the face of people who find it difficult to get by and who have a right to see their sufferings as real. He sees such resentment as coming from profound contempt for illusion, a contempt that, according to him, social theorists apply to themselves by 'reducing their own lives to an accumulation of facts and evidence, causes and effects' (1996: 97).

On the contrary, Baudrillard argues that the very nature of language makes it impossible to talk about the real since language can only deliver a virtual reality that is 'in its very materiality, deconstruction of what it signifies'. He concludes that fictional writing is not inferior to theoretical writing in terms of its approximation of reality because both genres are characterised by a void running beneath their surface: 'the illusion of meaning, the ironic dimensions of language, correlative with that of the facts themselves, which are never anything but what they are' (1996: 98).

Baudrillard has been subjected to severe criticism by many criminologists, along with postmodernists in general. Such criticism has been summarised by Stuart Russell (1997); a more sympathetic attempt to compare postmodern criminology with radical and conflict criminology has been provided by Arrigo and Bernard (1997). Without going into too much detail, Bernard and Arrigo compared six theoretical assertions in conflict criminology with variants in radical and postmodern criminology and concluded that although they are not identical, each strand offers something useful in our attempt to understand crime and social control.

Russell (1997) argues that postmodern criminology can be of little assistance to critical criminologists who are interested in social change and concludes that by dismissing metanarratives out of hand, postmodern criminology renders itself obsolete for the purpose of a critical understanding of crime and social control. He relies on others to prove that postmodernism prides itself with being the first to attempt to go beyond the modern, whereas such efforts are common in the history of criminology, and previous attempts remain more convincing precisely because the earlier theorists recognised the importance of policy-relevant theory while the postmodernists disdain both policy and metanarratives. Milovanovic (1997) found this 'old wine in new bottles' type of critique of postmodernism a failure. He presents both paradigms as locked in a duel. They are not (yet) structured in dominance to each other.

THE FICTIONAL CHARACTER OF CRIMINOLOGICAL THEORY

The critique of postmodernist thought notwithstanding, it is a fact that many criminological theorists make extensive use of analogy, myths and literary allusions in their construction of reality. However, even when such fiction is seen simply as an analogy with which to better explain complex reality, the role of fictional narratives in themselves are rarely recognised as an essential element in social thought. It was for this reason that this chapter focuses on social fiction *sui generis* as the obverse of Durkheim's social fact *sui generis*. Most critics of Baudrillard accuse him of denying the existence of reality but it is possible to read him as warning that reality is not everything. In other words, Baudrillard seems to be challenging criminologists to admit that works of fiction can tell us as much about society as works of abstract theory. He exemplifies this by citing novels, poetry, biographical narratives, films and television programmes alongside philosophical and theoretical writing.

Baudrillard is not alone in recognising the value of fiction in social theory. Almost every social theorist from the Greeks, through the Enlightenment philosophers to modernists and postmodernists make elaborate use of fictional material. What Baudrillard is challenging us to do now is to accept that social theory or law or morality is not simply a question of the tensions between facts and norms, or of telling the truth, the whole truth and nothing but the truth, but one of the coexistence of fact and fiction. Elsewhere, I have argued that this 'factional' use of fact and fiction is not restricted to social theory, given that all writing is creative writing and creative writers, so called, make extensive use of social theory in their fictional narratives (Agozino, 1995; see the next chapter in this book).

Henry and Milovanovic (1996) make similar claims when they endorse the sceptical postmodernist critique of the exaggeration of the truth-claims of criminology. At the same time, they disagree with postmodernist tendencies that ignore the practical meaning of discourse for real people. They prefer to label their style 'postmodernist realism' because they try to go beyond discourse to address the practical struggles of those interested in bringing about political and philosophical changes that would demarginalise the marginalised. However, their two-dimensional Mandelbrot set representing the hypothetical embezzler seems unrealistic when they interpret it as if blackness signifies deviance without reference to the practical struggles against this kind of colour coding: 'Area outlined in black represents convergence (those with law-breaking commitment profiles) and the area outside it in white represents divergence (those with law-abiding profiles or other forms of harm).' This sounds very much like fairy tales in which the big bad wolf is invariably black, in which the baddy is always represented as the

Other, an assumption that was carried over into many prominent criminological theories that rely on immigrants as a crime-prone category (Agozino, 2000). But even in fairy tales, it must not be forgotten that the Beast was a gentleman to Beauty, that all the frog prince wanted was a kiss, and that Goldilocks was the delinquent, not the victimised bears.

Tucker (1984) made a similar point in his review of Angela Carter's version of Red Riding Hood and Carey Harrison's Freud on television. He cites the demolition of the Grimm brothers' reputation by Ellis (1983), who argued that the Grimms were not disinterested folklorists but moral entrepreneurs. According to Ellis, the brothers retold German fairy tales to make them more palatable to the prudish bourgeois conscience whereas the original stories were full of incest, pornography and bloodletting. It is debatable whether the bourgeoisie were really more moral than the serfs or simply more pretentious and more hypocritical. Masson (1984) suggests that Freud assaulted the truth in the interest of bourgeois morality when he analysed fairy tales such as the Wolf-Man. Instead of believing children who complained of incestuous abuse from their bourgeois parents, Freud gave their stories a spin and represented them as the incestuous impulses of the children who wanted to kill their fathers and marry their mothers (the Oedipus complex) or kill their mothers and marry their fathers (the Electra complex). He claimed that little girls suffer from penis envy (some feminists joke that that means that Freud wished he had a bigger one).

Instead of dismissing the claim that the reality principle has given way to the principle of evil, according to Baudrillard, we should re-examine the truth-claims of criminological theory that we tend to take for granted. Such a review was recently conducted by Herman and Julia Schwendinger (1997), who found that citation analysis of the influence of criminologists is mistaken because it fails to say whether what is being cited profusely is necessarily true or grossly misleading. They argue that although reductionist neo-Freudian research on delinquent groups are cited more frequently than classical alternatives that are more convincing, the former are 'wrongly authenticated and largely fictitious "real science"'. It is not necessary to add that the Schwendingers are not postmodernists but the type of meta-narrators that postmodernists critique and yet they have reached a conclusion that is not remote from Baudrillard's.

Which of the two competing perspectives do you find more logically consistent, more empirically tenable and more efficacious in relation to the criminological problems facing African countries?

8. Executive Lawlessness and the Struggle for Democracy in Africa

> Everyone is talking about crime – crime
> Tell me who are the criminals.
> I really don't see them.
>
> (Peter Tosh, 1977)

Gani Fawehinmi, the Nigerian human rights lawyer and activist, coined the phrase 'executive lawlessness' to represent the widespread practice of ordinary law-breaking by people in office who behave as if they are above the law. This is a step ahead of the view that an Austinian emphasis on law and order without a stronger or, at least, equal emphasis on social justice has inevitably resulted in great injustice (Aguda, 1985). Executive lawlessness suggests that the politics of law and order is mainly rhetorical given the widespread disregard for the law by those who are empowered to uphold it in many parts of the world. This concept serves a warning to those who seek solutions to the hegemonic crisis through legalistic means alone. The democratic crisis in Africa is not the result of legal errors alone, even though executive lawlessness and the predatory survival of some poorer people contribute to the crisis as much as the crisis contributes to them. The major democratic crisis in Africa today is a crisis of hegemony or a situation where the ruling ethnic–gender classes have failed consistently to win the ideological struggle in the continent. Debate after debate at the international, national and local level has been won by the African masses. This is why hegemony in Africa has always been based more on force and fear than on consent, but never without some degree of consent or at least lethargy. The African experience differs from the 'authoritarian populism' which Hall (1980, 1988) identified as the modality of the law and order state in Britain under Margaret Thatcher. What we have always had in colonial and neocolonial Africa is authoritarian authoritarianism which shuns the populism of Thatcherism by executively breaking the law itself. This suggests that even if executive lawlessness is effectively checked, hegemonic groups will continue to be authoritarian rather than democratic in their exercise of power. This chapter suggests ways of looking beyond the law and the lawlessness of individual offenders in our analysis of the relationship between the politics of law and order and the struggle for democracy in Africa and in the wider world.

WHAT IS CRIME AND WHAT IS PUNISHMENT?

> I have a poo-poo theory
> Everybody has a poo-poo story to tell.
> 'Cause if you have a poo, you must go to potty.
> When you go to potty I beg you pull down panty.
> When you've done your best left hand wipe your butty.
> When you wipe it up you must wash both hands
> 'cause the poo-poo sickly.
> Everybody has a poo-poo story to tell.
> I bet your mummy and daddy told you
> that government has a poo-poo story too.
> They say if you take your doggy out for a walkie,
> remember to take the doggy baggy.
> When doggy mark territory with them poo-poo,
> you must scoop it up otherwise you could get fined
> 'cause the poo-poo messy.
> Everybody has a poo-poo story to tell.
> I bet your nanny never told you
> criminologists have poo-poo theory in short,
> they talk about punishment of offenders,
> how about the punishment of the innocent?
> Punishment Of Offenders – POO!
> Punishment Of The Innocent – POTI!
> So don't let nobody ever tell you
> that nobody has a poo-poo story to tell
> 'cause me say if you've got a poo-poo you must go to potty.
> When you go to potty I beg you pull down panty.
> When you've done your best left hand wipe your butty.
> When you wipe it clean you must wash both hands
> 'cause the poo-poo smelly.
> Everybody has a poo-poo story to tell.

I performed this poem in private for my toddler sons long before its first public performance. The first public performance was simultaneously broadcast 'live' on a local radio station in Liverpool City Centre as part of the Video Positive (Poetry Slam) Festival on 3 May 1995. There were more than 60 performing poets that night in the Bluecoat Gallery. This meant that each performer had little more than three minutes and so I had no time to give a theoretical background to the poem, which I introduced simply and suggestively as a poem for toddlers and potty-trainers. Nevertheless, many listeners recognised the deeper meanings beneath the symbolism of the poem and often bring up 'the poem about poo' in discussions with me. I got the chance for a proper theoretical introduction to the poem when I used it to preface the initial presentation of this chapter at an international conference in England where I met Stephen Pfohl for the first time and where he later blew me away with his multi-media performance on *Criminological Displacements*, which inspired me to complete this book.

The autobiographical background to the 'Poo Theory' is that I became a potty trainer while completing my PhD research in Edinburgh. My supervisor clearly saw the influence of parenthood on my choice of words for narrow criminological theory and tried to polish my cruder expressions to fit in with formalistic writing. However, the germinal idea for the concepts and for the poem itself refers to my own childhood 'potty-training' with emphasis on the different functionalism of the left and the right hand. I grew up knowing that it was rude to take food from the table with my left hand which wipes the butty or to accept a gift with that hand (ironically, I went to a boarding school where I was taught the exact opposite in the knife-and-fork duet). I also learnt the ethic of collective responsibility from an old African saying that when one finger picks oil, it rubs off on the rest. It is this folk wisdom that I brought with me to the taken-for-granted concepts of crime and punishment, and this made me question why someone should be fined when his or her dog fouls the pavement (a very serious concern of the residents of suburbia, I gather from letters to the editors of local newspapers in Britain). If the right hand does not also get into direct contact with the butty, why must it be sanitised as well?

To beg the question, it could be pointed out that many people do not bother to wash either of their hands most of the time and sometimes only the left hand washes itself, of course not as well as in a communal washing of hands. However, even when one hand is being washed, the assumption that the whole hand, rather than one finger or two, is soiled is challenging to a philosophy of individual responsibility. A more direct answer to the question of washing both hands would be the old African saying that when the right hand washes the left hand, the left hand also washes the right hand. This type of answer would have to admit the reality of shared interests in the washing of both hands by both hands. This may be seen narrowly as evidence of an individual's power over his or her body, but this chapter suggests that there is more to it than the body of the individual in terms of its rhetorical, theoretical and practical effects. The washing of every finger when one is suspected of being fouled is directly analogous to the collective victimisation of the marginalised by the state, among other actors. If the ethic of collective responsibility is still operative in the practice of punishment, why do many theorists carry on as if only individual offenders are punished?

Those who expect this chapter to recount the gory details of the violations of democracy and justice in Africa and elsewhere will be disappointed because what the chapter offers is a theoretical clarification that assumes a degree of familiarity with the history of popular struggles in Africa. *Review of African Political Economy* and *Africa World Review*, to name just two learned journals, have several special issues on democracy and justice in Africa and so this chapter will not be offering any new overviews. There is no attempt to offer a comprehensive description of actual histories of (in)justice in Africa, in the detailed way that Shivji (1995), for instance, focuses on hegemony and counter-hegemony in Tanzania. What is offered here is an attempt to abstract from such histories, theoretical lessons that have practical implications. Shivji ends his review with the recommendation that it 'is in the people's actually existing struggles and consciousness that elements of an alternative ideological and social project are to be found and need to be practically activated and ideologically interrogated' (Shivji, 1995: 169). This chapter contributes to the project of reconceptualisation, but without Shivji's rather essentialist dichotomisation of social thought into African theories and western theories. The chapter explores whether events in Africa and elsewhere could lead to a theory of punishment for what are now widely known as crimes of the state all over the world.

Crime is conventionally defined as the action or omission of an individual against the state (see Henry and Milovanovic, 1994, for a 'constitutive' critique of this conventional wisdom). Crimes of the state against society are called human rights violations. This chapter attempts to reconceptualise 'crime' to include the crimes of the state and 'criminal' to include the criminal state. The chapter argues that what is legal is not necessarily just or legitimate and thereby argues for a trans-legal definition of crime. However, since the state treats the criminal individual in such a way as to punish/rehabilitate the person or deter others, how does the society go about treating the criminal state? The chapter attempts to answer this question by exploring the avenues for redress open to a society under a criminal state and equates these with the severity of the crimes of the state. The chapter concludes by showing why the right to resist must be recognised as a fundamental human right. This conclusion seems unnecessary given that individualist practices of rights have been criticised for legitimating social injustice even as defenders of rights are not having an easy struggle (see Herman, 1993: 40, especially her convincing conclusion: 'To say that rights are difficult, complicated tools for social change does not mean that the struggle for their acquisition is doomed or that "real issues" are being obscured'). To add another fundamentalism to the politics of rights will neither guarantee rights that were recognised earlier nor guarantee that the right to rebel, even when recognised, would never be violated with impunity in the way that other fundamentalisms are violated in unequal power relations that operate with an obvious might-is-right logic. The calls for counter-hegemonic thought and practice to be legitimised may seem rhetorical and even tautological given that the people, rather than the state, are the actual legitimisers to whom the state must turn for this rare commodity (Shivji, 1995). If the state earns, deserves, wins, achieves legitimacy by appealing to the people, is it not theoretically possible for the state to earn, deserve, suffer, undergo punishment from the people in a criminal state?

The concept of crime has come a long way from the time of what is now known as 'personal justice' by which wronged individuals were assisted by kin or community group members to enforce retribution against the wrongdoer or his family (Reid, 1976: 4). This corresponded to a social arrangement by which property and privilege were collectively shared such that offences against the individual were treated as offences against the group to which the individual belonged and this often led to blood feuds between groups defending their respective members. With the emergence of different forms of private accumulation of property, personal interests overshadowed group sentiments, and the right to self-defence came to be increasingly emphasised. But to avoid an anarchic situation of each for himself, or herself, against all, the state emerged with the professionalisation and specialisation of force, to enforce order by recognising offences against individuals as offences against itself. Invoking the legal principle of *nullum crimen sine lege*, which simply says that crime cannot exist without being so defined by criminal law, Reid (1976: 18), argues that a legal definition of crime is inevitable because 'the system of criminal justice with which we are concerned is based on the legal approach'.

In apparent agreement with this philosophy of legal positivism, Edwin Sutherland and Donald Cressey submit that

> criminal behaviour is a behaviour in violation of the criminal law ... It is not a crime unless it is prohibited by the criminal law ... [which] is defined conventionally as a body of specific rules regarding human conduct which have been promulgated by political authority, which apply uniformly to all members of the classes to which the rules refer, and which are enforced by punishment administered by the state. (quoted in Senna and Siegel, 1984: 5)

Do Sutherland and Cressey mean that if the action or omission is not punished by the state, then it is not criminal? In other words, are statehood and penalty essential elements of the definition of criminality? What about stateless societies – were they by definition crimeless societies? We have many problems with the approach of the legal positivists to crime just as Reid (1976: 18) found it confusing. First, going by their philosophy, people should not be called criminals unless they have been tried and convicted, whereas the public, the police and the press call people who have not even been arrested criminals. Even when we call them suspected criminals, we are still not on safe grounds because people are often wrongly convicted and so are called criminals. Again, some people may break the law and get away with it, for various reasons. Moreover, there are many acts like the exploitation of workers by employers, which the public believe should be punished as crimes, but are not. On the other hand, some acts, like street trading, considered as crime, are not popularly known as such. Furthermore, people may safely act in ways that are not crimes today but may be punished for the same act tomorrow if a retroactive law is enacted.

We are opposed to a strictly legal definition of crime because what is legal is not necessarily legitimate or just. Apartheid, for example, was (im)properly grounded in law, yet we regard it as a crime against humanity for obvious reasons. The Nazi war criminals may have believed that they were serving their nation legally and with patriotism. This could be seen as an example of the nationalist developmentalist ideology, which Shivji (1995), to some extent following Amin (1987), Campbell (1986), Mamdani (1983) and many others, identified as the bourgeois rationalisation for extra-juridical coercion by the state in the periphery of the imperialist world economy. However, the Nazi Holocaust, Stalinism, Vietnam, apartheid, Northern Ireland, the wars in Eastern Europe and all the proxy wars in the Third World are indications that such national interests rationalisations are not the exclusive luxury of dictators in the periphery but an essential element of state forms of domination. Everywhere that the national interest is invoked as an ideology, it serves to justify arbitrary power as easily as it could serve to mobilise support against real/imaginary/fictional 'enemies' without and within. The national interest, of course, could also be invoked by counter-hegemonic thinkers and activists, but this is often in the form of the invocation of the assumed mandate of the amorphous masses, the popular masses, the working class and peasants, progressive forces or simply the people. Whoever 'the people' and the 'enemies' are, and whatever the national interests are, insurgent-hegemonic thoughts and struggles have historically demonstrated that the people perceive a lot of injustice in state–civil society exchanges. The fact that the state which formulates and professes to uphold the law also violates the rule of law requires that we should look beyond the law and the rule of law in our search for an organic penology for structural criminality.

Thorsten Sellin proposed that legal definitions of crime should be retained for administrative purposes while scientists should go beyond them to formulate non-legal definitions in order that the development of science should not be shackled by limitations of the criminal law. He went on to explain the origin and development of what he called 'conduct norms' which differ from group to group but are not necessarily codified in law. However, he did not offer an alternative to the legal definition, but only added that violations of conduct norms which are not illegal should be called abnormal conduct (Sellin, 1972). His efforts were thus limited by the fact that he was apparently searching for scientific knowledge for its sake without any political or social commitment to social justice – a position which, when shed of all the mystifications of value-free social science, is a disguise for the defence of the status quo and apathy to social injustice.

Sellin's limited attempt at reconceptualising crime needed to be transcended, and was by Herman and Julia Schwendinger, who insisted that the concept of crime should incorporate acts that violate basic human rights. Such acts, they suggested, should include sexism, racism and imperialism which satisfy all the legal requirements for criminality but are still treated as civil wrongs (Schwendinger and Schwendinger, 1970: 123–57; see also, Cohen, 1993). Fitzgerald (1990) has pointed out that all theories of the reconceptualisation of justice are not necessarily transgressive because many retain the form of law and only demand changes in its contents even, or especially, when popular justice is advanced as an alternative without recognising the temporality of popularity and the inevitability of routinisation (in the Weberian sense of rationalisation) as revolution passes into reconstruction. What the Schwendingers and Cohen advocate is not necessarily the alternative to formal justice, but the need to formalise the diffuse, spontaneous, popular responses to crimes of the state.

It is obvious that the state is conceived in the Enlightenment philosophy of justice and democracy as a rational and infallible organisation for the pursuit of the welfare of all. Hence crime is defined one-sidedly as the exclusive grief of the state unleashed by selfish individuals. However, it is accepted today that the state is run by groups of people who have interests to protect by force and that these interests may, and do, conflict with the interests of other groups in society. This is partly why Garland (1990) is right in reconceptualising the 'collective conscience' of Durkheim (1982) to mean nothing more than the 'dominant conscience'.

If individuals can offend against the state at their own peril, what is the basis for the dogma of the criminal infallibility of the state? We believe that the state often commits offences against the society by, for example, pursuing interests that are against the interests of the majority of the members of the society. Borrowing from legal jargon, it is not difficult to conceive of a state committing treasonable felony if it pursues policies that will inevitably lead to the subversion of the independence of the society, just as we can accuse a state of criminal negligence if it refuses to meet the basic needs of the people even though the society produces sufficient resources to meet these needs.

Now, it appears that we are confusing the individual and the societal levels of analysis by jumping from the crimes of the individual against the state to crimes of the state against society rather than against the individual. This apparent confusion disappears the moment we realise that 'the members of civil society are not *atoms*' (Marx, 1961: 225). It is true that the individual can act alone against the laws of the state, but the latter rarely act against the individual as though the individual is isolated. Even when the state isolates a single individual for the purposes of punishment or reward, it is meant to serve as an example to society as a whole. This is because individuals live and act as members of civil society and enjoy certain privileges and/or suffer certain disabilities due to the pattern of relationships within the society and between the society and others as enforced by the state. When the pattern of the relationships is exploitative or oppressive, we can say that the society is a victim of state crimes. Thus it is difficult for the state to commit offences against an individual *qua* individual, but easier to commit crimes against society which mediates the relationships between individuals and the state.

DEMOCRACY, LAW AND ORDER AS ORGANISED VIOLENCE

'Executive lawlessness' is a limited recognition by Fawehinmi (1993) that state officials or 'executives' break the law and get away with it under authoritarian regimes, although limited to the 'executive' compared to a similar, though broader, concept of 'state lawlessness' offered by the South African human rights lawyer, Dullah Omar (1990). However, in spite of the differences in scope suggested by the different emphases on the executives compared to the more embracing one on the state, both concepts are synonymous in terms of their referents – the criminality of state officials and the need to try suspects and possibly punish them. Compared to the theory of 'authoritarian populism' as developed by Hall (1979, 1980, 1988), the application of lawlessness to the state itself is more advanced in practice and in theory. Authoritarian populism seems to be concerned with the excessive exercise of state power under the ideology of law and order and the excesses suggest illegalities such as discriminatory decisions that disadvantage the marginalised. However, the recognition that state practice could be oppressive and popular at the same time is still a far cry from the cryptic allegation that the authoritarian state is a criminal state.

This difference between the theoretically sophisticated concept of authoritarian populism and the politically threatening concepts of executive/state lawlessness could derive from their respective origins. The one was the product of contemplative labour in an authoritarian democracy that is also populist, whereas the latter emerged from insurrectional thought in the front line of the legal battles against state crimes. What the two strands together contribute to social thought is that even the most authoritarian state power will have its degrees of populism, while criminality can be committed for various reasons by even the most democratic state. If this is a theoretical possibility for some and a practical experience for others, why has criminological theory been slow to develop a penology for state crimes even by those thinkers who recognise the reality of such crimes?

The state can afford to play the self-righteousness game not only because the state is traditionally regarded as an infallible despot, but also because the modern state insists on exercising a monopoly over force or institutional violence. Through the enactment of law, the state prohibits certain acts, prescribes definite penalties and obligations, and censors certain expressions. This has led Nicos Poulantzas to argue that 'the split between law and violence is false ...'. He maintains that, in every state, law is the *code of organised public violence* which is essential to the exercise of power and the organisation of repression. He goes on to show that the repressive role of law does not lie exclusively in the negative act of prohibition but includes the positive act of imposing prescriptions (Poulantzas, 1978: 76–92). But this does not mean that every law in the society serves the repressive interest of the ruling class for the oppressed classes struggle continuously, winning some material and ideological concessions from a grudging ruling class or from the cunning state that wishes to defuse discontent by appearing neutral.

Apart from functioning aggressively as an instrument of repression, law also contributes to state crimes by making it possible for the state to act without reference to the law which may be modified to suit the whims and caprices of the state or merely ignored as the despotic state bluffs its way through. Thus Poulantzas (1978) maintains that 'every juridical system includes illegality in the additional sense that gaps, blanks or "loopholes" form an integral part of its discourse. It is not a question of ideological oversights, blind spots or concealment but of express devices that allow the law to be breached' at will by the powerful. This indicates that Poulantzas concentrated on the structure of the capitalist state but recognised only the coercive apparatuses of the state, without paying attention to the hegemonic processes of populism especially in democratic settings. Moreover, Poulantzas identified the violent nature of capitalist state power, but was silent about the possibility of juridical responses from the society that suffers such violence.

It is often claimed that the strength of sociology is that it does not focus narrowly on the criminal justice system but studies this institution in its social context (Garland, 1990). It seems that the more central punishment is to a criminological theory, the greater the tendency to lump together practices that are distinct from, though tied up with, punishment with its concept. This was the case with Durkheim (1973), who tried to understand the structure of society by looking at its penal policies and thereby arrived at a dead wrong, and to a great extent, oversimplified picture of both social and penal changes.

Foucault appears to avoid this reduction of the reality of criminal justice to mere penalty by focusing on power instead of on punishment. However, he fell into the same trap of reductionism because his study of the history of power relations zeroed almost exclusively on what is done to the individual without mentioning inter-group power relations, especially in the form of imperialism and anti-imperialist struggles, unlike Fanon's analysis of violence (Said, 1993: 335–6).

Foucault's theoretical sophistication made it possible for him to see that even this most penal of all criminal justice institutions – the prison – carries on activities, like surveillance and discipline, which are not exactly punishment. Although he studied power relations in different institutions, his basic assumption is that all the surveillance, discipline and punishment that go on in the prison are working 'to adapt punishment to the individual offenders' (Foucault, 1977: 7–8).

Foucault is misleading because he gives the false impression that he is abandoning a position when all he is doing is augmenting it, for example, when he says:

a general process has led judges to judge something other than crimes; they have been led in their sentences to do something other than judge; and the power of judging has been transferred, in part, to other authorities than the judges of the offence (Foucault, 1977: 22)

he means that this is not always the case or that this is not all there is to it. He could not mean that judges never judge crimes. What he is saying is that the existence of the 'non-juridical elements' which 'function within the penal operation' should be recognised, but he seems to go about it as if he is saying that 'criminal justice functions and justifies itself only by this perpetual reference to something other than itself' (Foucault, 1977: 22).

Foucault's approach to power is carried to an extreme by Cohen (1985: 10), who claims that what 'orthodox Marxists' regard as 'Foucault's greatest weakness – his conception of power as a "thing" not reducible to the workings of labour and capital' is what he sees as Foucault's greatest strength. He adopted this 'uncritically' even though he regarded himself as the type of humanist with belief in human agency whom Foucault allegedly attacked with his structuralism.

Foucault actually rejected structuralism and distanced himself from Cohen's conception of power as a 'thing'. In contradistinction to this, he proposed (1978: 94) that:

1. Power is not something that one holds on to or allows to slip away.
2. Relations of power are not in a position of externality with respect to other types of relationships (economic processes, knowledge relationships, sexual relations), but are immanent in the latter.
3. Power comes from below, etc.

What these propositions mean is that power cannot be understood as an abstract 'thing' that could be possessed or lacked or be divorced from its political, economic, knowledge and ideological relational contexts. Cohen was right; power cannot be reduced to these contexts, because they are constituted also by relationships other than power. However, as Foucault would insist, power is meaningless when it is removed from these varied contexts. Convinced that power is not reducible to the political economy, Cohen applied the concept of control to 'those organised responses to crime, delinquency and allied forms of deviant and/or socially problematic behaviour which are actually conceived as such' (1985: 3). Conceived by whom or applied by whom? As Cohen recognises, society does not operate as an individual and, in any case, it is not only people who are seen as exhibiting problematic behaviours that are targeted by control agencies.

There are people who are innocent 'victims' of social control who are dealt with, not as a result of mistaken conception of their behaviours, but for the purposes of controlling 'whole groups and categories – through planned manipulation (with good intentions of establishing "brakes on crime") of the everyday life conditions of these groups and categories' (Mathiesen, 1983: 139). This development of 'total control systems' of surveillance and special policing, which Cohen and Mathiesen described, is seen by Mathiesen as a departure from the tendency to individualise punishment in prisons – a tendency that Foucault identified. What is implicit in the system of total control is that the assumption of guilt is not necessary to the operation of control. Members of targeted groups and categories are liable to special policing without actually exhibiting troublesome behaviour. All these are seen as future possible developments. There is evidence for them now as the widespread use of racial profiling in racist societies shows, but Mathiesen and Cohen see these developments as things to come in the future.

This chapter tries to understand, with reference to black women, for example, whether this discovery is related in any way to the ancient plough of criminal justice administration – guilt by association. To what extent has the control of 'whole groups and categories' always been a basic approach of legal control? It seems that guilt by association never disappeared from the tool box of the criminal justice system. Contemporary practice does not seem to be a break with individualised treatment but a continuation of what Kennedy (1976) called the ethic of collective responsibility, which he believed has disappeared from modern criminal justice systems.

Furthermore, what this preoccupation with control and punishment overlooks is that the criminal justice system does not merely control but also protects; it does not only punish but also cares. This is the point Bottoms (1983) made with his theory of the 'bifurcation' of penal policy into a welfarist non-disciplinary penalty for less serious offences and disciplinary penalty for more serious ones. Bottoms correctly points out that, contrary to the Foucauldian idea of Cohen that modern society is turning into a 'carceral city' revolving around the prison, and contrary to the Durkheimian 'law' that 'the deprivation of liberty', i.e. imprisonment, would become increasingly the most frequent form of punishment in organic-type solidarity with restitutive rather than repressive penal forms (Durkheim, 1973), the most frequent sentence in England and Wales is the fine, not imprisonment. One might even follow Bottoms and Cohen at once and call modern society the 'fine city' visited by Young's (1987) hypothetical 'Martian', who found that the fine as a form of penalty is actually increasing, while imprisonment is declining. The problem is that Bottoms is talking of the bifurcation of penal policies whereas his analysis shows that all the policies are not penal in character.

Moreover, Young (1987) found that the fine is one of the few forms of penalty which can be borne by someone other than the offender. This is indirect evidence that one does not need to offend in order to attract punishment and that the imposition of punishment does not presuppose guilt. One objection is that the person who pays the fine is not the person being punished, but the Criminal Justice Act 1991 recommended that parents should be directly fined for the offences of minors, thus formalising an ancient tradition according to which both hands are washed when one is soiled. Furthermore, the former Home Secretary, Michael Howard, later proposed an amendment to the Act that would make parents responsible for the court attendance of juveniles on bail. This means that the traditional focus on 'the punishment of offenders' (the first four words in the seminal work by Garland, 1990) is, to say the least, misplaced. Efforts should be made to interpret criminal justice practices as a whole to show the internal anatomy of foreign variables that are colonised by the imperialist concept of punishment.

It appears to be the case that what is bifurcating is not penal policy in particular, but criminal justice policy in general (Agozino, 1997a). Indeed, the bifurcation thesis was used earlier to characterise the divergence of law into civil and criminal branches (Kennedy, 1976). Moreover, theorists of quantum chaos, according to Milovanovic (1992: 237), also use the concept of bifurcation to describe 'far-from-equilibrium states' in which bifurcation is encountered at every level, with each new focal point being the germinal bud for further bifurcation. What the 'chaologists' fail to explain is why there have to be only two points to every divergence. Even the word 'divergence' delimits the possible directions to two. Why must it always be a bifurcation rather than, say, a trifurcation or simply a multifurcation?

What is bifurcating into care and penalty (the 'penal-welfare strategy', as described by Garland, 1985) is criminal justice policy and not specifically the penal policy. What is more – and this is the point easily overlooked – what is going on is more than bifurcation; it is the 'trifurcation' of policy into welfare, punishment and victimisation.

Victimisation As Mere Punishment (see Agozino, 1995a, 1995b, 1997a) does not affect the issue of trifurcation because Punishment Of The Innocent is only an aspect or effect of this trifurcation. If we take the trident held by Britannia or the three-pronged fork of the devil to represent a model of the trifurcation of criminal justice (very suitable models, given the good intentions, penology and criminology symbolised by the two forks), we will find different forms of victimisation, including Victimisation Of The Innocent, Victimisation In Punishment and even Victimisation As Welfare, to mention but a few, under the much neglected third point. This is probably why Ngugi wa Thiong'o and Micere Mugo, in their anti-colonial classic play, *The Trial of Dedan Kimathi*, defined criminal justice figuratively as a system that commits crimes under a law that is criminal. (For an application of this definition to the criminal justice system of apartheid, see Agozino (1991) on the trial of Winnie Mandela.)

What difference does this observation make? The difference is that punishment in general, and imprisonment in particular, lose the primacy which earlier theorists accord them. Whereas Foucault assumed 'that it is the court that is external and subordinate to the prison' (1977: 308), a more comprehensive approach would avoid false hierarchies and situate the whole criminal justice system within the context of the state and society. In other words, there are certain types of (artificial) legal persons against whom imprisonment as a penal measure is not only inappropriate but impractical. For example, there is no prison for companies that commit offences and there is no way a state can be jailed. A state can be blockaded, boycotted, sanctioned, rebelled against, fought over, lost, divided, united, weakened, strengthened, punished, but never incarcerated.

Another difference is that the penal system and the criminal justice system are not interchangeable in the way Foucault applies them. Garland and Young (1983: 13) have tried to solve this conceptual problem by adopting the elastic phrase 'the penal realm', which covers 'criminal and quasi-criminal courts, Home Office departments, prisons, detention centres, psychiatric institutions, community homes, etc.'. However, their solution extends the territory of the penal empire instead of decolonising welfare and victimisation from the conception of punishment. If anything, the penal realm shows that all penal practices are not aimed at offenders, and all criminal justice practices are not within the penal realm. It appears more appropriate to talk of the criminal justice system as a whole when it is the focus of attention.

A third difference is the practical political point that the intrusive traits found within the penal system will not be seen as non-penal aspects of penalty but as different issues to be contested in different ways. The point here is that when trying to understand the criminal justice system, it is important not to see everything going on as an aspect of punishment. However, this point should not be pushed too far to the extent that everything happening in the criminal justice system has nothing to do with punishment either (Agozino, 1997a).

This does not mean that punishment is not worthy of study as an independent subject. It only cautions the student against piling everything into the penal basket. According to Poulantzas (1978: 185–7), the pluralist approach to power inevitably leads Foucault to underestimate at the very least the role of law in the exercise of power within modern societies; but he also underestimates the role of the state itself, and fails to understand the functions of the repressive apparatuses (army, police, judicial system, etc.) as a means of exercising physical violence that are located at the heart of the modern state. They are treated instead as mere parts of the disciplinary machine which patterns the internalisation of repression by means of normalisation.

This is a valid criticism in the sense that Foucault never raised a question about the social justice of the law and the legitimacy of the state in his analysis of discipline, punishment, surveillance, madness, sexuality, knowledge and power. Foucault should have distinguished between the exercise of power under a democratic setting and the exercise of power under an oppressive and authoritarian setting, if only to emphasise his persuasive argument that power must be contextualised to make it meaningful. In this direction, Garland (1990: 162) observes that 'Foucault refuses to accept that there are elements of the penal system which either malfunction and so are not effective as forms of control or else are simply not designed to function as control measures in the first place.' It is not enough to assert that power is not always bad as Foucault did. Those who fight for power and not simply against power know what Foucault means, but Foucault focused on what he called the 'micro-physics of power' and thereby ignored the macro-physics of people's power with all its implications for structural penology in practice and theory. In short, Foucault's silence on imperialist power and anti-imperialist struggles while living and theorising the plurality of power relations in the era of imperialism must, along with his other silences, serve as an embarrassment to those writers who see in his biography the key to understanding his theory of knowledge–power relations.

The problem with Poulantzas' critique of Foucault is that he replaces the disciplinary machine with organised physical violence and thereby obscures the fact that it is not every aspect of the law and criminal justice practices that is physically violent. In other words, non-violent victimisation of innocent people is as likely as non-violent struggles against victimisation. Poulantzas might reply to this by saying that all forms of victimisation are violent to some extent, but still it does not follow that all aspects of criminal justice practices are violent since victimisation is not the only possible feature of such practices.

It could be said that all capitalist states are by definition criminal states because they are defined as the dictatorship of the *bourgeois minority* (Madunagu, 1982). Capitalist states are criminal states and neocolonial states in the Third World are the most criminal of all states. This is because all neocolonial states pursue policies that subvert the independence of their societies and are therefore guilty of treasonable felony. On a more serious level, neocolonial states are more criminal than other states not only because they criminally neglect the people's aspirations to essential social services, but also because they encourage the criminal practice of primitive accumulation of capital. Just as the colonial powers encouraged their citizens to rob and commit piracy, neocolonial states encourage the members of the ruling class to defraud the society in order to acquire the initial capital with which to consolidate their power. Such encouragement is both overt in the form of mild punishment or lack of punishment for crimes of the ruling class as opposed to severe punishment for pickpockets. It is in this sense that Ngugi wa Thiong'o and Micere Mugo (1976) stated, through the historical character of Dedan Kimathi, that the criminal justice system is just that, criminal. (More on this in the next chapter.)

The crimes of the state are usually disguised in such a way that even the victims of the crime are punished for the crime while the criminal state goes scot free. One of the reasons is that people do not believe this little heresy of ours – that the state can and does commit crimes. The most they can believe is that there are political crimes committed by the agents of the state and that such agents should be held solely responsible. People who argue in this way forget that the state itself has relative autonomy and can reproduce itself and ensure the continuation of its policies irrespective of who is in office. If you kill corrupt politicians (as Nzeogu attempted in the abortive coup of 1966 in Nigeria, as Rawlins did in Ghana following a military-style trial, and as Doe did – and as was done to him – without trial in Liberia) for their alleged crimes and leave the criminal neocolonial state unaltered, the state will continue to commit crimes against society.

A relatively unknown example of the punishment of victims by the criminal state, apart from the better-known cases of the victimisation of anti-apartheid activists and runaway slaves, is the arrest of 120 children in Ikom, Cross River State, Nigeria, for hawking during school hours. According to the local government officials, the kids would be held in a reformatory for six months if they failed to pay a fine of 100 naira (*Nigerian Chronicle*, 7 July 1987, front page). But is it the fault of the children that they cannot go to school? Most people would answer that it is not; it is the fault of their parents. That was the reply that I got from an educational meeting of workers and peasants in Ikom under the auspices of an NGO, The Directorate for Literacy, the administration of which I directed voluntarily while studying and teaching sociology at the University of Calabar. Is it a crime not to send a child to school? Is it rich parents or poor parents that are likely to fail to send their children to school? Which sort of parents would be able to afford a 100 naira fine in order to save their child from going to the 'deformatory'? If education is not free, it cannot be compulsory. Until education is made free and compulsory, it is not a crime to fail to go to school. But it is a crime to refuse children education by charging fees when it can be made free and compulsory. The knowledge acquired by children will be used to serve their society and so the state is duty-bound to provide adequate opportunities for education. Otherwise, the state is guilty of the crime of criminal negligence, at the very least.

REALISM, AUTHORITARIANISM AND DECOLONISATION

The theory of the state as organised public violence which Poulantzas advanced, and the statement of Peter Tosh that he 'really' does not see the (real) criminals accused of criminality in calls for peace that ignore questions of justice and equality, could be said to be examples of what self-professed left realists call left idealism (Taylor, 1982; Lea and Young, 1984; Lea, Kinsey and Young, 1986; Young, 1986; Young and Matthews, 1992). This is because Poulantzas focused exclusively on the crimes of the state and ignored the crimes of the poor which, according to the left realists, affect mostly poor victims. The left realists join those that they call right realists (see Wilson and Herrnstein, 1985) in a 'competition' to take crime seriously at the working-class level, but follow convention by saying hardly anything about the crimes of the state. (For a full discussion of the ways that left realists exaggerate the differences between those they call left idealists and themselves, see Scraton (1990). See also, Sim et al. (1987) and Gilroy (1987) for a detailed critique of the ahistoricity of left realism, especially with reference to the oppressive racialised relationships between black people and the police.)

Victimology and criminology generally continue as if crimes of the state are not problematic enough to be taken seriously. This 'culture of silence' on the crimes of the state, as Cohen (1993) puts it, does not mean that there is complete silence on the matter among victimologists, many of whom are beginning to address these issues more critically. However, the almost exclusive focus on the crimes of the underclass and the working class by self-professed left realists may seem to have nothing to do with the victimisation of people by the criminal justice system. However, by repeatedly showing that the majority of crimes are unknown to the police, left realism indirectly applies the heat to the police for higher clearance rates which could result in the use of dirty tricks on poor 'victims' of criminal justice.

The theoretical approach of victimology is not unprecedented. Crime is conventionally defined in criminology as the action or omission of an individual against the state. The courts dramatise the conflict as *The Crown* v. *X*. But the crimes of the state against the society are merely misrepresented as human rights violations which are addressed more like civil wrongs than like criminal acts. Such violations are often not listed in official crime statistics and therefore tend not to be seen as crimes. The concept of victimisation as mere punishment suggests that the state commits crimes against the society just as individuals commit crimes against the state. However, while the individual may plead guilty to crimes against the state,

The state will never look for the causes of *social imperfection in the state and social institutions themselves* ... In so far as the state admits the existence of *social* evils it attributes them to natural laws against which no human power can prevail, or to private life which is independent of the state or to the inadequacies of the administration which is subordinate to it. (Marx, 1961: 221–2)

The state can afford to play this game of self-righteousness not only because it traditionally commands consent and allegiance by appearing to care for all as an authoritarian populist (see Hall, 1979, 1988), but also because the modern state insists on exercising a monopoly of coercion or institutional violence against dissenters, subversives, nonconformists and the relatively powerless.

This is accomplished not through force alone and not without force at all, but through what Gramsci (1971: 57) analyses as the mechanism of class hegemony – the 'intellectual and moral leadership' of a class or the 'entire complex of practical and theoretical activities with which the ruling class not only justifies and maintains its dominance, but manages to win the consent of those over whom it rules' (Gramsci, 1971: 244). The approach of the present chapter requires a trans-legal conceptualisation of crime to include the crimes of the state, of the criminal to include the criminal state, and of 'victims' to include the 'victims' of criminal justice much along the lines advocated by Schwendinger and Schwendinger (1970) and more powerfully by the contributions to Barak (1991) and by Cohen (1993).

Paul Tappan (1977: 266–7) implicitly rejected the approach of the Schwendingers and Cohen in his critique of the elasticity of the concept of white-collar crime. (More on Tappan in the next chapter.) If it is accepted that oppressive social systems such as slavery, Nazism and apartheid, though (un)well grounded in law, organise crimes against the oppressed, then criminologists would be blindfolding themselves if they studied only police records and criminal codes without also exploring how the people perceive crimes of the state and how they judge and punish these crimes through popular action. The contribution of Julia and Herman Schwendinger in this regard is that they argue convincingly that violations of human rights, though not listed as such under the criminal code, satisfy the legal, moral and scientific criteria for criminality and should therefore be treated as such. Similarly, the concept of victimisation as mere punishment suggests that even without going beyond the criminal code, criminologists should be able to go beyond the conventional picture of the offender and the victim to recognise the offences of the state and the 'victims' of punishment. Pitch (1995: 69) recognises 'the increasing spread of a political and social activism expressing itself through a language of "victimisation" (rather than that of "oppression")'. By talking about victimisation from positions of strength, the new social movements do not mean that their members are simply victims for, as West (1993) argues, it is possible to talk about victimisation without seeing people as passive victims. The victimisation that 'new social movements' agitate around, however, is still about the criminalisation of individuals who are, for example, domestic rapists, violent racists, child molesters, homophobics, etc. This is, perhaps, why many critical scholars see the reformism of new social movements to be diversionary because their activism does not directly confront crimes of the state (see Herman, 1993, for a defence of the empowering practice of gay activists). The point being made here is that victimisation is not always inter-personal or inter-group; it is sometimes structural and institutionalised (see Barak, 1991; Cohen, 1993 for structural analyses of victimisation).

The approach of this chapter is not new; it is implicit in classical Marxism and in most critical legal studies. Naffine (1990: 150), for example, specifically talks about the gender- and class-based '"victims" of the machineries of law', although she is silent on race while writing from a postcolonial location in Australia. Rodney (1975) lists 'the extension of political repression and victimisation' as one of the seven key elements that combine in various ways to reproduce petty bourgeois rule in the English-speaking Caribbean countries – an observation that could be said to have been generalised from his earlier work on Africa (Rodney, 1972) which suggests the need for decolonisation.

The decolonisation of victimisation from the expanding penal colony must come to terms with the fact of internal colonialism at the institutional level of punishment and also at the levels of political space. The former is like the internal colonialism of Habermas (1987) who used it to describe the juridification or colonisation of economic power in particular and the life world in general by juridical power that is in turn colonised by economic power through the monetisation of criminal justice administration. At the level of political space, we have gone beyond the internal colonialism of Hecter (1975, 1983) which emphasises intra-national exploitation of culturally distinct categories.

To decolonise victimisation, we need to go beyond the conceptual liberation of victimisation from the constructed clutches of care and punishment. Also, we need to go beyond the Hecterian intra-national dynamics of exploitation as Campbell (1991) has demonstrated with the theory of the 'globalisation of apartheid'. To decolonise victim- isation, we also need to follow Fanon (1963, 1965) and address the international, if not global, perpetuation and extension of socio- economic exploitation and domination in spite of the gaining of formal independence and how the victimised respond with spontaneity that is necessarily weak in organisation, with demands for cultural nationalism that is vulnerable to co-optation by the phantom bourgeois, with psychosis that mirrors the madness of the oppressors but which is increasingly subjected to medical power for the more effective control of the wretched of the earth, or with disciplined organisational struggle for the power to leave Europe and move on in search of genuine humanism.

Wilmot (1986) did exactly this when he analysed 'the universality of repressed self-consciousness' and linked this to 'the schizophrenic state ... of the being of the colonised', which Fanon identified. The limitation here is that Wilmot retains the masculinist language of Fanon whereas, following Freire (1972), who now regrets the androcentric language of this earlier work (hooks 1993: 147), he insists that an international perspective on decolonisation is essential,

> Because the colonising forces are so powerful in this white supremacist capitalist patriarchy it seems that black people are always having to renew a commitment to a decolonizing political process that should be fundamental to our lives and is not. And so Freire's work, in its global understanding of liberation struggles, always emphasizes that this is the important initial stage of transformation – that historical moment when one begins to think critically about the self and identity in relation to one's political circumstances.

However, when internationalised and even at its institutional and intra-national levels, the struggle for decolonisation is no longer simply the 'black struggle', if it has ever been so. The struggle involves, and has always involved, people who are black and people who are not. The important thing to note is the need to relate the struggle for decolonisation and against recolonisation to the concrete political and economic circumstances of the people engaged in the struggle as well as to the cultural politics of the people. This means that the decolonisation process cannot afford to turn a blind eye to a cultural, political and economic problem like Africa's debt burden and African's demand for reparations for the crimes of the slave trade, colonialism and imperialism (Agozino, 1997a).

DEMOCRACY AS REDRESS FOR VICTIMISED SOCIETY

We have shown that what is legal is not necessarily just and this is so not only because some cruel laws are deliberately made and enforced, but also because 'many a horrifying act of tyranny has been committed because it seemed good at the time' (Archer and Reay, 1966: 12). We do not need to bore anybody with the historical or statistical evidence of state crimes, especially as they relate to human rights violations; these are well documented elsewhere. Nor do we need to go into the controversy of whether only western capitalist countries built on individualism can observe human rights as Milne (1979: 34) put it; or whether the claim of exemplary human rights by the US is simply hypocritical as Bolshakov (1984) documents. We agree with McCamant that 'violations exist in every country of the world ... without some criteria, the arrest of a person for criticizing his government cannot be compared with the absence of schools for children or laws forbidding the organization of labour unions' (McCamant, 1981: 123–4). He suggested that the criteria of scope, arbitrariness and severity could be used to judge political repression.

The 'scope' of the offence of the state is small when the extent of the restrictions of the forces of opposition are small. In such a situation, the society whose discontent remains latent begins to manifest it by relying on even the laws of the state for protection and/or reparation against the crimes of the state. But as the issues at stake increase in scope, the restrictiveness of the state increases, rendering such instruments of defence as law courts, propaganda or peaceful demonstrations meaningless or dangerous. For example, members of society may be illegally sacked and may go to court to seek redress, but the state may enact a retroactive decree to legalise their dismissal. As a Ghana Court ruled on 28 August 1961, any law made by the state is valid within that state and will not easily be challenged in the courts of the state. According to the court, 'the people's remedy for any departure from the principles of the declaration [of fundamental human rights] is through the ballot box and not through the courts' (cited in Archer and Reay, 1966: 22). The hands of the courts are tied and the ballot boxes are toys in societies where control over state power is achieved more regularly through rigging or gunfire than through voting.

But if society is hopeless under the laws of the state, it is even more helpless under international law, which the powerful states flout with impunity. The society is therefore forced to adopt extra-legal means of struggle which might still be peaceful. When this also fails, and when the state responds with more arbitrary and severe violence, it dawns on the society that liberation could not 'come about as a result of magical practices, nor of a natural shock, nor of a friendly under-standing. If violence was the glue, the cement holding the edifice of oppression together, violence was also the flame and explosion which will bring it crumbling down' (Wilmot, 1986: 139). When a violent state forces society to adopt violent means of struggle, of course, the state does not blame itself for starting it; it rather descends on that society with even increased violence justified by the ideology of national security.

> Against violations of human rights, we must recognize a right of resistance and opposition ... when power is utilized in ways that deviate from the requirements of the human rights system, it also deviates from legitimate authority. There is then a basis for resistance against the use of power. But resistance is in itself an exercise of power and must therefore conform to limitations and requirements of the human rights system. (Eide, 1984: 35).

Such limits are set by the scope, arbitrariness and severity of state crimes.

The right to rebel must be recognised as one of the most fundamental of all rights in criminal states. This was what the American revolutionaries did when they declared independence from Britain in 1776 and was later enshrined in the spirit of the Second Amendment to the American constitution as the right to bear arms (a right that the new right misinterprets to support easy access to firearms). Without the recognition of the right to rebel, society will remain a slave to the state, and theory will remain inadequate to account for this realisation. Some people say that we do not need to recognise the right to revolt as a fundamental human right because with or without recognition, people are bound to revolt wherever there is oppression. The same escapist argument can be extended to the fundamental right to life and in fact to any right. If we do not recognise the right to life as a fundamental human right, people will continue living as they used to before the recognition. However, recognition of the right to rebel is important because it brings social theory more up to date with reality. Thus the oppressed will become bolder to oppose the criminal state whenever the right to rebel is universally recognised as a fundamental human right. And criminological theory will be better able to account for the nature of penalty as something that society sometimes inflicts on the criminal state rather than only the taken-for-granted view that it is always the other way round (see Barak, 1991, for a similar point). Sumner (1990) makes a similar argument with his theory of censures, but his claim is limited to the reversal of moral categories and their application against individuals (rather than the state itself) who occupy hegemonic positions in order to expose the arbitrariness, partiality and superficiality of moral categories. There is no clear indication from Sumner, unlike Barak, of the need for a criminology of state crimes even though the latter has not offered a clear penology for what he called 'crimes of the capitalist state'.

Such a theory of democracy and justice is being developed by Cohen (1994), who pays careful attention to the differences between Western European and other states where the left realist injunction that 'people should work within the system' to change things might be impossible in the case of a terrorist state. Cohen recognises the adoption of 'informal justice' by the people in an oppressive state as a form of 'defence' against the state. This chapter concludes that such defences could be theorised as forms of punishment against the state. The knowledge–power implications here are many. First, the bifurcated search for truth and reconciliation in addition to a search for democracy and justice in the new South Africa will have to look beyond individuals and demand justice from the state for the state crimes of apartheid. This means that, at least, the state must be 'tried' and an appropriate sentence passed on it to redress or address or compensate the people who were victimised under criminal policies.

Second, the application of the concept of punishment to the state will move the political focus beyond demands for the populist release of prisoners of conscience or the demand that those under detention without trial should be charged or released. The criminal state must be made aware of the possibility of having to pay for its wrongs through the trial of individual officers and through the trial of the state as a legal personality. International relations have examples of powerful countries 'punishing' less powerful ones, but such powerful states are also the ones that most frequently break international law through imperialism. 'Yes, imperialism is criminal and ruthless but we must not place the whole burden of blame on its broad back. For as African people are known to say: "Rice only cooks inside the pot"', said Amilcar Cabral (1982: 109) in a homage to Kwame Nkrumah. Hence the issue of how to penalise a criminal state is an issue that must be left to the victimised society rather than something to be imposed globally by imperialism. What the imperialist powers could do is to impose sanctions on the individuals who are suspected of aiding or participating in state crimes, but ironically it is such individuals who are most readily protected by imperialism due to the loot that they have personally accumulated and invested in imperialist economies.

Sad tales of the arrest, torture and killing of pro-democracy activists in various parts of Africa and elsewhere are too well known to be recounted in a theoretical chapter such as this. What the chapter suggests is that theoretical knowledge could be improved and social action better justified if the relations of crime and society were reversed in recognition of the collectivised victimisation that people have frequently experienced under different regimes. Whether we are looking at apartheid South Africa or at neocolonial Nigeria, Liberia or Sierra Leone, Algeria or Sudan, Rwanda or Burundi, Ethiopia or Eastern Europe, Western Europe or the Americas, we will not fail to find examples of state crimes and societal reactions to these crimes. Some of these reactions could be better understood as penal measures against the state, especially if the activists view their actions in those terms.

In some societies, such actions are facilitated by the availability of the franchise with which voters put politicians on trial and collectively punish or reward them according to perceptions of their performance and abilities. In other societies, the electoral process is either restricted or commodified to the extent that discontent breeds apathy rather than an attempt to judge political practice. In such situations, and in situations where the ballot has been replaced by the bullet, some attempt civil disobedience of various sorts. For example, some mount public demonstrations which might begin peacefully and then get out of hand, sometimes because of the authoritarian law-and-order response to legitimate protest. Where many of these forms of popular justice against the criminal state have failed, workers sometimes embark on protracted strikes with obvious political motives and often with the support of students, who might boycott classes or march.

Finally, when all peaceful means of checking the criminality of the state have failed, popular justice often responds in kind through the continuation of the search for justice by violent means. The final suggestion from this chapter is that democracy might be imperfect in many ways, but states that make democratic accountability and popular control over state power impossible expose themselves to opportunistic military groups that could seize power unlawfully or make themselves vulnerable to civil war. Linked to this final suggestion is the observation that many of the informal experiments at juridification still focus on the criminality of individual state officials when such vigilantism rarely goes beyond concern with the predatory lawlessness of ordinary individuals (Campbell, 1986) instead of also addressing the question of the legal personality called the state. The major lesson to be learnt from the peasant army or *Sungu Sungu* experiment that Campbell documents is that all such projects that are targeted at the 'individual offenders' of classical criminology are vulnerable to co-optation by the state, as in the case of Tanzania where the movement was hijacked by the state and turned into vigilantism against perceived economic sabotage. By judging the criminality of the state directly rather than indirectly through the trial of the agents of the state, some of the practical problems facing people in Nigeria, Rwanda, and South Africa, to mention but a few, who have suffered countless state crimes, would be overcome by theorising and attempting to punish the state directly.

9. Radical Criminology in African Literature

This chapter examines the reflection of criminological theory in the work of African creative writers. Here, I try to show how the writers' views of their society influence their representation of the crime problem. A criminological reading of the plays *The Trial of Dedan Kimathi* by wa Thiongo and Mugo and *Oga Na Tief Man* by Fatunde and of the novels *Devil on the Cross* by wa Thiongo and *The Contract* by Iyayi demonstrates that criminologists should take creative writing seriously and creative writers should take criminology seriously.

This theoretical and methodological chapter, addressed to both criminology and literature, aims to illustrate that it is futile to single out crime or any specific problem for exclusive interpretation without questioning the social structural conditions that engender such a problem. The objective of this chapter is to show that criminologists can rely on creative writers for analogy and theory construction. This does not mean that literature should be treated as raw material for theory building, but that social theory should be, and is already, in-built in literature.

Criminological research faces official control from many sources of data. Furthermore, the difficulties of gaining access to many empirical sources and the controversy surrounding official records force many scholars to engage in philosophical speculations that are little nearer reality than fiction. My conclusion is in line with Talbot (1988: 142) that we must 'ignore the false dichotomy between science and arts in the pursuit of criminological truths'. However, I believe that criminologists should attempt to understand complex social phenomena rather than seek to discover 'truths'. Criminology has nothing to lose by encouraging a social history of crime through the addition of literary sources to non-literary ones.

THE PROBLEM OF CRIME

The seriousness of the crime problem in Africa is such that no African literature is complete today without a direct or indirect reference to it. It is only natural that literature should reflect reality. However, crime in literature does not correspond to crime in real life or its extent, but it is coherent with the images of real crime (Talbot 1988: 143). This is what makes literature a source of insights for an intuitive understanding of the crime problem.

Talbot (1982) attempted to provide examples of how sophisticated the criminology of literature could be by computing correlations between crime frequencies in literature and officially recorded crime rates. Talbot (1987) also compared violence against police in literature with actual police records of such cases. These are interesting comparisons, but the craving for respectable sophistication should not tempt criminologists to mystify the potential of literature as a source of analogy.

In order to prove theoretical assumptions about the nature of crime, what encourages criminality or the nature of social control and power relations, it is not enough to show similarities between the social construction and representations of crime in literature and the cultural and political construction of deviance in society. Talbot's statistical comparisons appear far too literal. Literature, whether fiction or biography, seems more suitable as a source of illustrative analogies than as an alternative source of crime figures.

Moreover, the illustrative theoretical potential of literature is not enough ground for Talbot (1988: 142) to push for a subdiscipline entitled the criminology of literature. All criminologists should make use of literary illustrations when necessary. Otherwise, the theoretical value of literature to criminology would be minimised – as in sociology, where the sociology of literature is recognised primarily as a subdiscipline, while it flourishes in departments of literature more than in sociology itself. This means that the study of literature by criminologists should not be marginalised as something of interest only to literary theorists, but should be promoted as worthwhile by all those interested in the crime problem and in crime literature. Foucault (1961) did this effectively by citing creative works alongside scholarly ones in his study of 'insanity in the age of reason'.

However, some writers see African writers' preoccupation with crime as derogatory and writers are called upon to portray the positive aspects of society. For example, according to Ebun Clark (1990), 'In African literature, to my horror if black is murderous, if black is evil, if black is corrupt I think that African literature corpus in English expression has unwittingly, unknowingly given [reinforcement to this stock type].' Yet, there is hardly any example of African literature in which all black people are negatively portrayed. It is usually a minority of black people who are realistically shown to be oppressively preying on the majority of black people independently or in alliance with a few non-black people. Besides, it is not only African literature that reflects the seriousness of the crime problem in Africa. No major political speech is complete without at least a nodding acknowledgement that the problem is increasing alarmingly. Neither a conspiracy of silence by African writers nor pretentious declarations by corrupt politicians can help Africa to overcome the crime problem.

There is no general consensus on what constitutes crime or just punishment. This controversy is more pronounced in societies like Africa, where those who make and administer criminal law have ideological and material interests that conflict with the objective interests of the majority of the people. While many crimes may be condemned with some unanimity, the application of the law and the machinery of justice tend to impose stiff penalties on activities that are open to the poor for survival, while the exploitative and oppressive activities of the ruling classes remain legal, are less severely punished or are covered up.

In conventional criminology, crime is defined one-sidedly as the exclusive grief of the state (representing individual and collective interests) unleashed by the selfish individual or group. This is a long way from what is now known as 'personal justice', by which wronged individuals rely on self-help and kin or community assistance for the enforcement of retribution or reparation. With the emergence of the state and public policing, every ruling class promotes the dogma that the state is a benevolent patriarch protecting the good and punishing the delinquent (Spitzer and Scull, 1982).

The concern of conventional criminology in Africa is almost exclusively with the crimes for which only the poor are arrested and repressed (see Clinard and Abbott, 1973). The alternative concern of radical criminologists in Africa is to show that crime control has never been the focus of colonial and neocolonial policing in Africa.

Ahire (1991), for example, has shown that the exercise of law and order in Nigeria has always been geared to the maintenance of political, economic and ideological imperialist hegemony. This alternative picture to that of conventional criminology is also found in radical African literature in the form of the theoretical offer of a trans-legal conceptualisation of crime which includes crimes of the state and regards all oppressive states as criminal states.

Neocolonial states are depicted in such literature as the most criminal of all states. This is because all neocolonial states pursue policies that subvert the independence of their societies and could therefore be said to be guilty of treasonable felony. Neocolonial states are depicted as being peculiarly criminal not only because of their criminal negligence of the people's aspirations to essential social services, but also because of their encouragement and sponsorship of the organised crime-prone process of the primitive accumulation of capital. Just as the colonial powers encouraged their merchants to rob and pirate from other nations at the rise of capitalism, so the neocolonial states encourage members of the ruling class to defraud the society in order to acquire the initial capital with which to consolidate their political power. Such encouragement is both overt and covert, in the form of ghost contracts to overnight millionaires, mild punishment, pardon or non-prosecution of political and economic criminals, alongside severe punishment for pickpockets and victimisation-as-punishment for the innocent poor – thereby exposing the carelessly concealed partisanship of the legal order.

Marx developed the theory of primitive accumulation to solve the riddle of the origin of capitalist accumulation. He argued that individual producers of commodities accumulate a certain amount of capital, which becomes the preliminary stage for the capitalist mode of production. He assumed that this process takes place mainly (but not exclusively) in the period of transition from handicraft to capitalistic industry: 'It may be called primitive accumulation because it is the historic basis, instead of the historic result of specifically capitalistic production' (1954: 585).

It may be objected that an individual who accumulates private capital has not committed any offence. But Marx (1954: 668) emphasised that 'In actual history, it is notorious that conquest, enslavement, robbery, murder, briefly, force play the greater part', but not every part, in capitalistic accumulation.

This does not mean that primitive accumulation ended when capitalism became hegemonic, as Shivji (1982) and Caudwell (1975) imply. The idea that primitive accumulation occurred only at the infancy of capitalism derives from a mistaken reading of the analytical method of historical specificity as if it means that law and crime, for example, are peculiar to capitalism. The method simply means that phenomena assume historically-specific forms under definite epochs. Not even the generation of surplus value is peculiar to capitalism, although the process assumes a specific form under this mode of production.

The period of primitive accumulation is distinguished by being the key source of investment by emergent capitalists. But the process did not disappear with the period and it can still be identified in even the most advanced capitalist societies – as recent revelations (see Nelken, 1994) from Japan, the US, Britain and, especially, Italy demonstrate. New capitalists must keep emerging even in the most advanced capitalist economies. Old-established ones must keep struggling against the upstarts and against one another for monopolistic capitalist accumulation through the well-trodden path of primitive accumulation. However, not all methods of primitive accumulation are criminal (winning the lottery or inheritance could be legitimate sources), but crime is assumed by Marx to be the most frequent method.

Again, it does not follow from the theory of primitive accumulation that such crimes will disappear once the magic wand of socialism has been waved. In socialist societies, individuals who wish to restore capitalism or who wish to enjoy capitalistic privileges might resort to this criminal building block of capitalism. Nevertheless, primitive accumulation is likely to be relatively rare in a truly socialist economy; since social security would be guaranteed to all, there would be no opportunity for the private investment of the loot, its conspicuous consumption would facilitate detection, and punishment would be more certain and more severe as opposed to the selective leniency or even condonement of such crimes by capitalist states.

This may explain in part why the New Criminologists, who were dreaming of a crime-free and (by implication) a control-free society in the 1970s, abandoned their idealism and now claim that they are left realists who want to reduce the crime rate by taking working-class crimes seriously, since 'they are very divisive in their adverse impacts on working-class victims' (see Young, 1986: 27–8). The major limitation of this new realism is that it fails to take the crimes of the powerful and the crimes of the state against the poor as seriously as it claims to be taking those of the working class. The danger in this is that the exclusive left realist focus on working-class crime could reinforce a right realist ideology of repression which could affect poor people most adversely even when they are innocent. A detailed analysis of the relationship between capitalist accumulation and contradictions in the rule of law is given by Picciotto (1982).

It is within the framework of the Marxist theory of primitive accumulation that I propose to evaluate the contribution of wa Thiongo, Mugo, Iyayi and Fatunde to radical criminology in Africa. They do not necessarily share my interpretation of primitive acumulation, but they can be shown to reflect this framework with varying emphases and tendencies. These writers were chosen as a departure from the usual trend in African literary discourse by which Ngugi wa Thiongo is usually pitched against Wole Soyinka or Chinua Achebe. The choice of exemplars might differ, but the form often remains the same: one renowned radical writer is usually presented in polar opposition to another well-known liberal or conservative writer (see Gugelberger, 1985). Such an approach ignores the fact that radical aesthetics and politics have a plurality of forms and tendencies which permit fruitful comparisons within this broad category.

The decision not to compare Ngugi wa Thiongo with other radical gurus of African literature such as Sembene Ousmane, Alex La Guma or Nurudin Farah is deliberate to show to what extent the younger writers who claim to be following wa Thiongo's style of socialist realism (see Fatunde 1990, for instance) are close to him. I proceed by considering how Iyayi and Fatunde have addressed the major questions of the sociology of crime: What is crime? How is law related to society? How should the society respond to offending behaviour?

WHAT IS CRIME AND WHAT CAUSES CRIME?

Iyayi and Fatunde start from a common assumption that crime has a class character. They both demonstrate that what the state routinely represses as serious crime is less serious than the permitted predatory activities of members of the ruling class. Everything wa Thiongo has written boils down to explanations of the roots of crimes of imperialist domination and neocolonial exploitation. He consistently identifies the forces and processes of overcoming these crimes through popular struggles. In his prison diary, for example, he defines imperialism as 'the capitalistic robbery and theft of a country's wealth by foreigners aided, of course, by a few sell-out natives' (1981: 136). This theme runs through all his writings, but it is most dramatically captured in *Devil on the Cross* (1982), which he wrote secretly on toilet paper while in detention. It is not surprising, therefore, that in the opening pages of this book, he defines the role of the writer as that of the 'Prophet of Justice' (1982: 7).

Iyayi's three novels confront the reader with revolting pictures of institutionalised crime organised by a handful of rulers against a powerless people. *The Contract* (1982) is so far Iyayi's least reviewed but, in my opinion, his best effort to describe how this crime is organised and how ruthless the criminals are. Iyayi (1991) claims that were he to rewrite this book, he would focus it even more directly on the crime of corruption.

Likewise, every play Fatunde has written is a campaign against social injustice, but *Oga Na Tief Man* (literally, 'Master is a Thief' – a premier production I had the honour of producing and directing in 1986), written in Nigerian English for popular understanding, is his most frontal attack on the existing legal system. He shows how 'real' criminals are protected while the victims are punished. These assumptions are in line with *The New Criminology* (Taylor et al., 1973) without falling into the trap of glorifying all crimes of the poor as political struggles for liberation.

Given the consistent reflection of criminological theory by these African writers, Opolot is mistaken in thinking that African novelists were not 'aware of the tremendous contribution they were making to a fledgling discipline like African criminology' (1982: 208). Moreover, Opolot failed to identify any of the alleged unconscious theoretical contributions of African writers; he merely reviewed the contents of several African novels without linking them to criminological discourse. Of course, the writers under discussion did not set out to write criminological texts, but that is not to say that they were not aware of trying to enhance the understanding of the crime problem in Africa. It may be more appropriate to say that criminologists are the ones who are not aware of the contributions African literature is making to their field.

While these writers are in agreement over the nature of the crimes of the elite, they seem to disagree slightly on what to call breaches of the existing law by the underprivileged. On this issue, Fatunde is unequivocal in heaping responsibility for such acts on the exploiters of the people. In *Oga Na Tief Man*, in defence of the starving redundant worker, Akhere, who is refused credit at his former employer's supermarket and has to run away with the food items, Fatunde repeatedly argues that the real thief is the employer who misappropriated the foreign exchange allocated to him for the importation of raw materials and thereby caused job losses. Fatunde argues that if the capitalist had imported raw materials instead of 'holy white sand', Akhere would have kept his job and would not need to 'take' (not steal) from Alhaja Alao's supermarket. The writer has no problem here because he is dealing with a poor worker 'taking' from his exploiter's wife. But, given 'the fact that most working class crime is directed at working class people and that the "challenge to property relations" is more often the appropriation of working class property than any threat to capitalism' (Young 1986: 16), can we say that exploiters are the only real criminals and that poor thieves are not so real? Fatunde must have been aware of this, but his preoccupation appears to be the demonstration of the relative seriousness of the crimes of the elite compared with the survival tactics of the poor.

Wa Thiong̃o and Mugo differ from Fatunde in this respect. In their *The Trial of Dedan Kimathi* (1977), the streetwise boy tells the female Mau Mau leader that he used to 'steal' from his father even the little that he used to earn for both of them. This makes it easier to understand why he was bullying another city-groomed juvenile, a girl who cheated him of a few shillings that a white man had paid them for carrying his loads. The female guerrilla sums up the situation as being 'the same old story. Our people ... tearing one another ... and all because of the crumbs thrown at them by exploiting foreigners' (pp. 18–19).

Ngugi wa Thiong̃o depicts the internal contradiction among the ruling class in the ironical *Devil on the Cross* (1982), in which Mwireri wa Mukiraai is assassinated by the hired 'Devil's Angels'. His crime is that, after praising capitalism as the 'theft and robbery [which] are the measure of a country's progress', he makes the mistake of advocating self-reliance in theft and robbery by saying that Kenya should be robbed by Kenyans alone (1982: 79). Wa Thiong̃o explains his subsequent elimination with a Gikuyu saying that 'the thief in rags often becomes a sacrifice for the thief in finery' (1982: 158).

Iyayi pursues this theme further in *The Contract* when the taxi driver, representing a commonsensical understanding of the problem, condemns the whole society as irredeemably rotten. According to the taxi driver, 'Everybody wants money. People are bought and sold, the same way beer is bought and sold' (1982: 9). The young and the old alike are shown to steal from each other. A father cheats a son of millions of embezzled public funds, the son steals from the father and the father shoots him dead, mistaking him for an outsider. Contractors poison their rivals in the ruthless struggle for monopoly and wives and daughters are pawned and swapped for favours. In all, the poor are the prime victims because they produce the public funds being looted and also because they lack the means to protect themselves from the desperate poor robbers who rarely penetrate the fortresses of the rich.

What is common to these writers is that they follow the Marxist theory of primitive accumulation by demonstrating that economic crime is more a basis of capitalism than its consequence. These crimes form the easiest path to capitalist development and capitalists have little scruple regarding how wealth is accumulated. Furthermore, these authors do not share the preoccupation with what are conventionally called 'violent crimes'. The relative immunity of powerful people from prosecution for whatever crimes they commit has always been a central concern of radical criminology (see Pearce, 1976).

This concern is not exclusive to Marxists; Sutherland (1949) stimulated a great deal of research in this direction. However, what distinguishes the Marxist approach from that of Sutherland is that even though his research shows how corruption pervades social stratification, he talks of white-collar or elite crimes as if certain kinds of crime are committed exclusively by certain social strata. Apparently following Sutherland's conflict perspective, Odekunle (1986) argues that the '"real criminals" are the "haves" who engage in elite crimes like white-collar crime; corruption, and organised crime'. Odekunle claims that the 'have nots' are not real criminals and that the 'misperception' of the 'real perpetrators and real crimes' is deliberately instigated and deliberately propagated by the real criminals, who punish conventional crimes severely and treat elite ones mildly.

The Marxist approach talks of the crimes of the powerful and not of powerful crimes, with the full knowledge that there is nothing like real and unreal criminals (except that some innocent people or political activists are often criminalised or victimised). Nor are there exclusively elite or conventional crimes, because even murder could remain uninvestigated (the occasional prosecution of the powerful notwithstanding), as if it were a civil matter, when it is committed by state agents (see Usman, 1982, for example). What these writers show is that the conventional distinction between 'violent crimes' and 'white-collar crimes' is false because the latter are often violent in their consequence and the former are not the exclusive preserve of 'blue-collar workers'.

The attempt to go beyond the traditional focus of conventional criminology is also reflected in the concern of these writers with feminist issues in criminology. With the Mau Mau woman and the bullied girl in *The Trial of Dedan Kimathi*, Wariinga and Wangari in *Devil on the Cross*, Mama Ekaete and Alhaja Alao in *Oga Na Tief Man* and with the wives pawned for contract or the women Ogie Obala abused in *The Contract*, the writers intuitively illustrate how women encounter the formal and informal criminal justice systems as offenders or as victims. Women are relatively ignored in conventional criminology.

Such feminist criminological issues become even clearer when one attempts a criminological reading of African female writers such as Bessie Head, Ama Ata Aidoo, Nadine Gordimer, Buchi Emecheta, Mariama Ba, etc. It does not follow that any portrayal of women in African literature is necessarily feminist. In fact, the dominant image is patronisingly stereotypical (see Little, 1980). The works being considered here debunk the assertion of separatist feminists that no man should speak for or even on women (see Stanley and Wise, 1983). The works display gender awareness in the sense that women are represented in them as people who suffer oppression and exploitation with men, and who struggle with men to overcome the oppressive and exploitative conditions. These works show that it is not all men that oppress women; that some men are also oppressed on the basis of gender; and that some women (especially Fatunde's Alhaja Alao) oppress other women and men as well. Incidentally, Mugo, the co-author of *The Trial of Dedan Kimathi* (wa Thiongo and Mugo 1977), is a woman.

Furthermore, the works demonstrate that Chinweizu (1987) was wrong when he said that issues of race, gender and ethnicity are outside the scope of Marxism. He was misled into this conclusion by Ngara (1985), who believes that Marxism is concerned only with the political economy of class struggles. The works discussed show that Marxism is not distinguished by the peculiarity, exhaustiveness or exclusiveness of its subject matter, but by the effectiveness of its dialectical historical materialist methods. This means that gender and race can be better analysed in articulation with class relations, and not in the essentialist mechanical ways adopted by Chinweizu (1987), who asked all black sheep to unite against all non-black 'jackals', and later (Chinweizu, 1990) contradicted himself by inviting all men to unite against all women, as if their interests are necessarily coherent or polarised.

For example, Ngugi wa Thiongo took a radical decision to stop writing in English and start writing in Kikuyi, his native tongue. That was the first time that the Kenyan authorities detained him: they understood the potential of speaking directly to the people in their own language. The propaganda against wa Thiongo is that writing in Kikuyi, with characters whose names are meaningful only in Kikuyi, is tribalist in a multi-ethnic society. This seems to confirm wa Thiongo's claim that writing in English is an act of imperialism over the minds of the readers and the writers whose original languages are not English. Fatunde and Iyayi also seem to show an awareness of the politics of ethnicity by naming their characters from the different ethnic groups in Nigeria and, in the case of Fatunde, by writing in Nigerian broken English, which is spoken across ethnic boundaries with dialects across West Africa. What is missing from the accounts of these radical writers is any sense of the ethnic stereotypes and rivalries that are part of the social realities or any attempt to question such stereotypes through characters who do not conform to conventional expectations.

HOW IS LAW RELATED TO SOCIETY?

The writers under consideration seem to argue that the existing legal systems operate to legitimise the crimes of the ruling classes and to bludgeon the working classes into submission. However, Fatunde believes that legalist battles in bourgeois courts, led by radical lawyers, could win a victory for the oppressed. He argues that there are two types of lawyers: those who defend the looters of the economy and those who defend the suffering workers. Subscribing to the radical theory that sees law as the terrain of class struggles rather than as an exclusive instrument of the ruling class (Toyo, 1984), Fatunde believes that the courts and other institutions of society can still be used to bring about a workers' government (1986: 34).

Fatunde's faith in the legal system is reaffirmed at the end of the play, when Ismaila promises to appeal against the ten-year jail sentence given to the poor worker for 'theft'. For him, that is the way to continue the struggle for social justice. This strong faith in the legal system is understandable in that the protagonist of the play is a lawyer whose wealthy family background and professional optimism moderate his radicalism, even while he warns of the inevitability of revolutions in societies full of oppression and exploitation (1986: 53). What is not clear is why this lawyer did not lose faith in the courts after witnessing the passing of judgement on the worker, at the home of his wealthy father, even before the trial.

Fatunde's conviction that significant victories can be won by the working class in court is not shared by wa Thiongo and Iyayi. In *The Contract*, Iyayi (1982) believes that it is almost impossible, though desirable, to hang corrupt officials so that they can die slowly and, therefore, more painfully than the blindfolded armed robbers who are tied to a stake and given a 'quick' and 'merciful' execution. Iyayi believes that this is only wishful thinking 'because these same people are those who are now doing the sentencing and the shootings and the hanging. They are the law of the land' (1982: 29). The novel sceptically tries to show that everybody is trapped and that those who attempt to resist corruption will eventually be claimed as victims – like Ogie, whose father is manipulated to steal public funds and later shot dead. Surprisingly, Iyayi does not oppose the idea of capital punishment even though his narrative shows that it is applied almost exclusively to the poor. He would find it 'desirable' if the corrupt rich are hanged, but by calling for this he is indirectly legitimising this barbaric form of punishment, the majority of whose victims are poor. Yet his call is understandable in the context of the jurisprudence of former communist countries where corruption received such penalties.

Wa Thiongo and Mugo go beyond Fatunde's optimism and Iyayi's scepticism to reject the existing legal system in its entirety. This is captured in the dialogue between Kimathi and the colonial judge, who happens to have been his boyhood playmate:

> *Kimathi*: To a criminal judge, in a criminal court, set up by criminal law: the law of oppression. I have no words ...
> *Judge*: Law is law. The rule of law is the basis of every civilised community. Justice is justice.
> *Kimathi*: Whose law? Whose justice?
> *Judge*: There is only one law, one justice.
> *Kimathi*: Two laws. Two justices. One law and one justice protects the man of property, the man of wealth, the foreign exploiter. Another law, another justice silences the poor, the hungry, our people ...

Judge: ... No society can be without laws to protect property ... I mean protect our lives ... civilisation ... Investment ... Christianity ... order.

Kimathi: I despise your laws and your courts. What have they done for our people? What? Protected the oppressor. Licensed the murderers of the people ... I recognise only one law, one court: the court and the law of those who fight against exploitation, the toilers armed to say we demand our freedom. That's the eternal law of the oppressed, of the humiliated, of the injured, the insulted. Fight Struggle Change. (1997: 25–7)

The law might be literally criminal in the sense that Kimathi argues against the circular argument of the judge that the law is the law and justice is justice. However, Kimathi also believes that every law is not necessarily 'criminal law'. According to him, there is an alternative to the existing legal system even if it is a criminalised alternative. The question that remains is whether the people have any hope in the existing legal system. Can the oppressed, the injured, the humiliated and the insulted not explore all the chances in legalistic struggles? The attitudes of African writers to law have to be placed within their specific historical contexts. The Mau Mau leader Dedan Kimathi was addressing a court of occupation that protected a political economy against which he had led an armed struggle. He was not expected to share the optimism of Fatunde's Ismaila, the learned son of a millionaire, who was addressing a relatively legitimate court in a politically independent country.

However, wa Thiongó insists that political independence does not alter the law of theft and robbery, and so neocolonial law is as unjust as its colonial predecessor. In *Devil on the Cross* (1982) he exposes the bankruptcy of neocolonialism and at the same time shows how workers, students and peasants are organising to drive out the robbers. He criticises people like Wangari, the peasant woman, who believed that the law of thieves can be relied on to stop robbery. Against the advice of the students and the labour leaders to mobilise the people to drive away the feasting and boasting robbers from the cave, she reports the honourable thieves to the police, who promptly arrest her for spreading dangerous rumours about respectable people.

This position is very close to the instrumentalist theories of law which assume that only the ruling class benefit from the existing law. The ruling class receive better protection and less severe sanctions than do the working class, but the latter also benefit from the laws that protect individual rights. The curtailment of different aspects of these rights is what makes the law an area of continuing though unequal contests between opposed interest groups (see Toyo, 1984). African writers should highlight the possible gains (of politicisation, for instance) that workers can make through legalistic struggles, while showing the limitations of such struggles and pointing out the forms of struggle that could supplement them. The question should no longer be 'reform or revolution' but 'reform and revolution – how?'

HOW SHOULD SOCIETY RESPOND TO OFFENDING BEHAVIOUR?

Radical African writers distinguish between two kinds of offenders: the wealthy and the poor. The writers seem to agree that the offences of the poor are symptoms of the more dangerous offences of the rich. Fatunde is emphatic in demanding that the poor be set free and the rich jailed. However, it is not clear how the judiciary that is dominated by the rich can routinely punish its patrons.

Iyayi (1982) agrees that corrupt officials should be punished more severely than armed robbers, but he does not believe that this is possible. Nor does he believe that the people are prepared to change the situation. According to the taxi driver in *The Contract*, people 'worry all right. They complain at home. They talk about it in the taxis, as we are doing now. They talk about it in their offices. They complain and they talk, but they do nothing.' Iyayi (1991) is of the view that even this ability to talk about the problem is a healthy sign that things will not remain the same forever. The driver believes that the people cannot do much because 'The police are always watching, the army too. The police watch for what they call the trouble-makers, warn about them, imprison them, even without proof' (Iyayi, 1982: 29).

Thus the only forms of popular struggle that we find in *The Contract* are sporadic student demonstrations. The first is reported indirectly through the party which Chief Obala gives to celebrate his son's safe return after his university was closed following a police massacre of demonstrating students. The second time is only a nightmare: Chief Obala dreams that his undergraduate son has led a protest against him, publicly disowned him and pelted him with pebbles for stealing public funds.

Fatunde (1986) advocates that the people should express their resistance collectively. Comrade Umar, a labour leader, asks all workers to show solidarity by accompanying the lawyer and their arrested comrade to the police station to frighten the police. But the legalistic form of struggle which Fatunde adopts in this play is such that the people can participate only as spectators or, at best, as isolated witnesses. When they dare as much as grumble to show their dissatisfaction with the judicial procedure, the judge cows them into silence by threatening to eject them from the court or convict them for contempt. However, the lawyer warns that a workers' party will emerge one day to win victory for the masses.

For wa Thiongo, primacy should be given to the mobilisation of the people and their organisation into a formidable force against the system of oppression and exploitation. In *The Trial of Dedan Kimathi*, such a movement was the Mau Mau; in *Devil on the Cross* he agitates for the formation of a workers' and farmers' party to lead the struggle of all oppressed people. He shows how to organise the struggle effectively by dramatising a planned rousing of the people. The message here is that popular struggles would be more effective if they were less spontaneous. Both works end in neither victory nor defeat for the people, but in a reaffirmation that the struggle continues.

Thus, when the colonial judge condemns Kimathi to death, the two city youths stand up and shout 'No!' One of them pulls a gun, given to them by the female guerrilla fighter in an attempt to rescue Kimathi. Again, Wariinga (in *Devil on the Cross*) stands like a judge over her former 'sugar daddy' who has ruined her education and nearly driven her to suicide with an unwanted pregnancy. Mr Citahi kneels down, begging her not to marry his son in exchange for becoming the sugar baby of the rich old man once again. '"Look at me!" Wariinga commanded, with the voice of a judge' (p. 253). She shoots him and maims other 'thieves' who have gathered to receive her and her fiancé. She walks away with the conviction 'that the hardest struggles of her life's journey lay ahead ...'. The final actions in both works are taken by people with grievances against the system but who have been more or less spectators in the earlier struggles. This is to show that more people are joining the struggle and that the people will have the final word.

The above discussion shows that radical African writers have reversed the traditional emphasis of criminology by relatively ignoring the offending behaviours of the poor in their advocacy of how society should respond to offences. There is a need for African writers to extend the logic of their treatment of the offences of the rich to the offences of the poor in order to go beyond the biases of the conventional approach rather than duplicate them. Can the theory of primitive accumulation be applied to the predatory crimes of the poor? Probably not, but there are similarities between primitive accumulation and predatory acquisition. The process of primitive accumulation is characterised by its scope and goal, and only partly by its method and period. Predatory crimes may share the period and method of primitive accumulation, but they lack the scope that permits the investment goal of the acquisition.

DISCUSSION AND CONCLUSION

This chapter has shown that African literature reflects the African historical experiences of crises and is therefore valuable to the African social scientist, both as a heuristic device for the elaboration and illustration of social theory, and to demonstrate the efficacy of the practical implications of abstract theory. I have tried to do this by looking at the radical sociology of crime in radical African literature. Similar studies can be done more substantively by analysing the treatment of certain categories of offence, or by focusing on positivistic functionalist theories of crime and punishment, or on gender or racial issues in African literature of relevance to criminology.

Such efforts need not be restricted to creative writing but should rather be extended to non-fictional literature like the biographies of the Mandelas, the prison notes of George Jackson and to official records, in order to determine how much criminology can be found in fiction and how much fiction can be found in criminology. By this I mean that the so-called records of actual crime are also socially constructed and do not correspond one-to-one with 'real' crime. This is all the more reason why the division between fiction and non-fiction should be re-examined for the benefit of criminological theorising (Talbot 1988: 142). Literary representations of the crime problem can be used to illustrate theoretical analysis, just as theoretical constructions of crime can be represented creatively in literature.

I acknowledge that many literary critics would adopt different approaches to these texts. The closest literary theories to my approach are Eagleton (1976) and Jeyifo (1985), who insist that the international political economy of imperialism, mass poverty, repression, nuclear armament and Third World debts are inextricably intertwined with literary theory. They advocate the abolition of the 'fiction' of literary theory if by this is meant a community of knowledge autonomous from historical, political or sociological theory. By this they do not mean that literary theorists should adopt political and ideological approaches; they mean that even the most pretentious formalist or structuralist critics already harbour these inevitable 'biases'.

Without concealing my own bias, I have tried to show here that radical African writers are convinced that the crime problem is socio-structural and that this can be challenged effectively only through a revolutionary transformation of the entire society. This corresponds to the implicit assumption by these writers that the state can and does commit crimes against the people and that the crimes of the state can be best checked not merely by removing corrupt officials but by overhauling the criminal state as a whole.

Paul Tappan (1977: 266–7) rejects this approach in criminology. According to him, criminology is a science and therefore needs 'reasonably accurate descriptive information, it cannot tolerate a nomenclature of such loose and variable usage'. Crime must remain what the criminal law says it is. Tappan believes that

> The rebel may enjoy a veritable orgy of delight in damning as criminal most anyone he pleases ... The result may be fine indoc-trination or catharsis achieved through blustering broadsides against the 'existing system'. It is not criminology. It is not social science.

So it is not only what is crime that is determined by the limits of the existing law; social science must also not go beyond the criminal code.

If it is accepted that oppressive social systems like slavery, Nazism and apartheid, though well grounded in law, organise crimes against the oppressed, then criminologists will be misleading themselves if they study only police records and criminal codes without also exploring how the people perceive crimes of the state, and how they judge and punish these crimes through popular action. The 'rebel' label does not detract from the social scientific quality of the variable ways in which people understand this reality of crime.

10. Committed Objectivity in Race–Class–Gender Research

In this chapter I argue that objectivity and commitment are different but that they are articulated rather than being separate issues in social research. This chapter challenges those who believe that objectivity is impossible or undesirable as well as those who believe that commitment is undesirable in social science. This approach is close to the call by Sandra Harding (1991, 1993) that the methods of science should be applied to science itself by raising the women question in science and the science question in women's studies. Here, she develops her earlier analysis of feminist research agenda in science in terms of empiricism, standpoint epistemology and postmodern feminism. In this chapter, a slightly different formulation will be advanced to resolve what could be said to be a false dichotomy between objectivity and commitment. Committed objectivity or objective commitment could be used to capture the inextricability of the articulation of the processes of commitment and objectivity. The chapter concludes that both objectivity and commitment are necessary to good research irrespective (or even because) of race–class–gender differences.

Harding attempts to answer the reservations of postmodernist feminism regarding the desirability or practicality of applying the objectivism of a flawed Enlightenment epistemology to a liberatory scholarship. She argues that 'physics is a bad model for physics', but suggests that this is because the objectivism of physics is not strengthened by socially situated knowledge. In conclusion, she calls for a science that is not illiterate of race–class–gender standpoints. This is because such literacy would contribute to the strengthening of objectivity that scientists aim at. Harding refers to the black standpoint feminist Patricia Hill Collins (1986), who argues that

> as outsiders within, Black feminist scholars may be one of many distinct groups of marginal intellectuals whose standpoints promise to enrich sociological discourse. Bringing this group, as well as those who share an outsider within status vis-à-vis

sociology, into the center of analysis may reveal views of reality obscured by more orthodox approaches.

The call by Collins (1986) for the outsider within to be brought in in order to reveal what might remain concealed reminds us of Gouldner's (1970) response to Becker's (1967) call for sociologists to adopt the perspective of the underdog. According to Becker, underdog perspectives are more likely to be credible than the powerful perspectives of the topdogs who are wrongly rated higher on the hierarchy of credibility, according to conventional wisdom. According to Gouldner and Collins, the perspective of the outsider is essential to the strong objectivity advocated by Harding, not simply because it is more truthful but because it is a perspective that is not likely to be as well known as superordinate perspectives for the simple reason of being placed outside.

However, there are differences between Collins and Gouldner. The latter wrote as if all sociologists are white men while the former consciously admitted that black women are not the only ones whose perspectives are marginalised. Furthermore, Gouldner and Becker wrote as if it is up to the sociologist what perspective to adopt, while Collins clearly suggests that people from marginalised groups are discriminated against in the allocation of tenures, prestige and rewards. Collins calls for the outsiders to be brought in, a very careful choice of words that recognises that, in scholarship under the domination of white-supremacist-capitalist-patriarchy, it is not up to the 'outsiders within' to move into privileged positions of truth-claims that are fiercely guarded by gatekeepers at every turn.

hooks (1984, 1994) demonstrates the need to go beyond the demand to be brought in and focus instead on the ways that the epistemological advantages of occupying multiple marginal standpoints from which insurectionally to oppose and decentre the centre without wishing to be brought into the centre of the present system, which is patently unjust. The response to hooks could be that she is not very marginal now; she is a distinguished Professor of English with tenure and an incredible track record of publications despite continuing rejections of some of her works by publishers. However, hooks' call for the goal to be shifted from the demand for inclusion to the questioning of the centrality of the centre suggests that the emphasis of Harding on 'strong objectivity' needs to be re-examined in terms of why she did not place her emphasis on strong social-situatedness in research. In Harding's formulation, objectivity is still privileged over commitment because she suggests that commitment instrumentally makes for a stronger objectivity without also suggesting that a strong objectivity would contribute to a better commitment. In her formulation, 'strong objectivity' seems to be the primary end of epistemology, and standpointedness is only one of the means to that goal of strength.

The argument in this chapter is contrary to the 'purist' definition of the role of research by Hammersley (1993: 429) as the search for 'truth claims, not their practical implications or practical consequences'. Unlike Hammersley, Nagel (1986: 5) offers 'a defence and also a critique of objectivity'. He argues that a defence and a critique are both necessary in the intellectual climate of the 1980s because objectivity tended to be overrated and underrated even by the same persons. As he put it, objectivity

is underrated by those who don't regard it as a method of under-standing the world as it is in itself. It is overrated by those who believe it can provide a complete view of the world on its own, replacing subjective views from which it has developed.

This is similar to the view held in this chapter, except in the sense that Nagel (1986: 7) went on to suggest that 'The limit of objectivity ... is one that follows directly from the process of gradual detachment by which objectivity is achieved.' This chapter is sceptical about the necessity or even the practicality of any detachment as an element of objectivity. On the contrary, objectivity is being interpreted here as the process of taking a position and not the process of detachment.

This view of the articulation of detachment and involvement is captured by Deutscher (1983: 2), who argued that 'Every detachment is another kind of involvement – the idea of complete objectivity as complete detachment is a complete fraud.' However, Deutscher concedes that although 'the myth of detachment is a distortion, it is a distortion of real needs'. He explains what he means by analogy to an explorer who subjects himself to an arctic climate in order to study it and the fact that even when you are 'embarrassed, angry and astounded' you will need to have the objectivity to subject yourself to the force of an argument. In this regard, he quotes John Anderson as holding the view that 'objectivity was interested disinterest'. According to Deutscher, 'This aphorism reminds us that disinterest is not the opposite of interest and that objectivity requires interest as much as it does disinterest' (Deutscher, 1983: 54).

Where this chapter differs from Deutscher is on the view that, according to him, only liberals are capable of being objective because, 'To maintain our objectivity, we must maintain our liberality, though we must live in an acute consciousness of the tensions within it, and recognize that we must develop and defend many other different and competing values' (Deutscher, 1983: 72). This chapter argues that objectivity is not a monopoly of liberals but a process that even political radicals of whatever shape and shade cannot altogether escape. Moreover, when taking a principled stand against certain values like apartheid and Nazism (for example), and struggling against them instead of defending a liberal competition of values, the anti-fascists cannot simply be written off as lacking in objectivity.

Given so many different voices in defence of objectivity, it is somewhat surprising to hear from Rescher (1997: 1) that 'Objectivity has fallen on hard days.' (Oh dear, should we call an ambulance?) According to Rescher, the misfortune of objectivity lies in the fact that some people fail to understand that it is linked with rationality, while those who understand this link very well simply dismiss objectivity as repugnant. As he put it, feminists see objectivity 'as a male fetish, new-agers reject it as mere left-brain thinking, radicals dismiss it as a cover for bourgeois self interest ... We live in an era where the spirit of the times favors the siren call of subjectivism, relativism, skepticism' (Rescher, 1997: 1).

This is an extreme version of the only-liberals-are-objective-or-rational type of thesis, already critiqued under Deutscher above. The present chapter does not disagree with Rescher that the universality of rationality must be accepted, but the chapter argues that such an acceptance will have to extend universalism to feminists, new-agers and radicals, instead of assuming that only liberals are enlightened. For example, Rescher argues that only a rationalist can objectively provide the right answer to a question such as 'Was there a Nazi Holocaust that killed more than six million people in execution camps?' Perhaps he chose a bad example because I have taught Jewish students who argue in class that they cannot write about the Holocaust objectively, whereas I encourage them to write about it as passionately as they can without detracting from the objectivity of their claims. In other words, it was not rationality alone that defeated the Nazis. It was committed objectivity that united the world against Nazism, and thank goodness for that. Deutscher (1983) gives a similar example about the Australian involvement in the Vietnam war by arguing that those Australians who campaigned against the participation of their country in an unjust war could not be simply dismissed as radicals who lacked objectivity and rationality; most of them were rational liberals.

Even among feminists, there is no consensus that objectivity is repugnant. For example, in the volume edited by Lennon and Whitford (1994), objectivity is critiqued by some feminists and defended by others. Yet, according to the editors, it is not objectivity that is the focus of much of the criticism but a certain Enlightenment conception of knowledge as referential,

> it is about something (the object) situated outside the knower ... Putative knowledge reaches these goals by conforming to a set of criteria for testing and validation. These criteria are universal. These criteria can also in principle be applied by anyone, with the same results. Genuine knowledge does not reflect the subject who produced it. (Lennon and Whitford, 1994: 2)

This is the conception of objectivism that feminists joined radicals in questioning both its desirability and its possibility. In her contribution to the editorial, Lazreg (1994), however, argues against the privileging of women's experiences by standpoint epistemology. Lazreg is supported by Mangena (1994), and both of them were the only non-western feminist contributors. Both of them were opposed by Stanley (1994) and by Seller (1994), who defended the epistemological values of first-person accounts. This chapter contends that the dichotomy between these positions is a false one given that the two positions are not separable even though they are different. When a radical claims to lack objectivity, such a claim should be interrogated instead of being taken as sufficient indication that the speaker lacks objectivity. Similarly, when a liberal claims to be only rational and objective, no one should take his or her word for it without further interrogation.

RACE–CLASS–GENDER IDENTITY IN RESEARCH

Many feminists (hooks, 1984; Harding, 1987; Cain, 1990; Collins, 1990; Gelsthorpe, 1992; Daly, 1993) agree that men can study and understand the problems facing women, contrary to the separatist epistemology of people like Hartsock (1987), Mackinnon (1987); Stanley and Wise (1983); etc. The objection of the separatist feminists derives from the standpoint that 'who feels it knows it' and, since men do not experience certain things that women experience, they cannot understand them. Yet, experience is not always the best teacher given that we sometimes do not understand what is happening to us and that we still need to study what we experience – hence courses like women's studies and black studies, for example (Agozino, 1997a, 1997b).

Some feminists do concede that men can understand the problems facing women, but many still argue that men should not join the struggle because all men appear to be part of the problem. This is evident in the fact that some feminist journals still will not accept contributions from men as men; study groups on feminism (not necessarily feminist in membership) still refuse to allow men to participate in their discussions and urge them to start study groups on masculinism; and women who protest against nuclear power also protest against men joining the protest. This is an indication that even among marginalised groups, some categories might be even further marginalised in the sense of the multiple marginality that Collins and hooks talk about.

This chapter argues that research on women could be neither feminist nor anti-feminist (Agozino, 1995). Particular attention should always be paid to feminist literature for what can be learnt from it, but such attention would not necessarily make every research a feminist one (in the sense of identity), even though the research could be said to advocate feminism, among other issues, as hooks (1984) advised. This is not a chapter on or for women alone, but a chapter on the politics of researching underprivileged women by an underprivileged man. The focus on black women is necessary because they have been relatively ignored in the past, but this focus is also strategic in the sense that the comparative approach advocated shows how many of the problems of black women are shared by black men and by white women.

It is suggested in this chapter that the subjugation of black women, for example, can be best understood within the context of domination in general (including class, ethnic or racial, etc. domination). One does not have to be a black woman to understand that black women are subjugated on the basis of their race, class and gender. Being a black woman does not guarantee any researcher perfect understanding of the problems facing black women. Nor does black femininity command unflinching commitment by all black female researchers to black feminists; and nor does support for black women amount to black feminism.

Three problems that could confront a man who is doing research on women in the criminal justice system are problems of his middle-class relations that the women are less likely to share, his gender relations that differ from theirs, and his ethnic relations that the women may or may not share (Agozino, 1997a). Feminists like Stanley and Wise (1983) and Hartsock (1987) do not agree that a man can understand the problems facing women because they do not believe that the masculine world-view can allow a man to sympathise with women. Any researcher, male or female, black or white, rich or poor, could tackle the problems of race–class–gender relations in research with a conscious sense of social commitment to the research subjects and also a commitment to be as objective as possible, even though objectivity is unpopular with many researchers who share the sense of socially relevant scholarship. This chapter suggests that objectivity does not preclude, but actually presupposes, perspectivity.

OBJECTIVITY IS NOT POSITIONLESSNESS

The problem of whether social science can be objective is not the same thing as what Mackinnon (1987) calls 'point-of-viewlessness' or 'aperspectivity'. Objectivity is not positionlessness but is defined here as the procedure of taking a position without concealing or distorting oppositions to the position taken. Mackinnon (1989: xii–iii) seems to recognise this when she states: 'I do not defend "subjectivity" over "objectivity" or elevate "differences" over "sameness" but criticise the method that produces these symbiotic antinomies.' Mackinnon's paradoxes seem to have been derived from Nietzsche, who concluded by affirming the complex articulation of subjectivity with objectivity (Nietzsche, 1969: 119).

This reference is one of the instances where Nietzsche came close to those of Marx. The significant difference, however, between Marx and Nietzsche is that while Marx adopted the perspective of the oppressed while remaining objective, Nietzsche was 'a belligerent opponent of almost every enlightened liberal or democratic value ... a precursor of the Third Reich' (Eagleton, 1990: 244). This demonstrates that the epistemological assumption that subjectivity and objectivity are articulated rather than separate can be employed for either oppressive or emancipatory purposes. To be objective presupposes having a view or taking a position – an objective view or position – which could be for or against the oppressed. It follows from this that objectivity does not preclude but in fact rests on perspectivity.

What appears to be a false contradiction between objectivity and politicality in scholarship arose from the long-standing view of the nature of science reflected in Weber's lecture ([1918] 1989) on 'Science as a Vocation'. According to him, social research cannot help being 'value-relevant' in the sense that the choice of research topics is always value-laden, but sociology should be 'value-free' so that even political opponents can use its methods to compete fairly for academic status without undue appeal to political sentiment by rival scholars. In Weber's own words, 'it is one thing to state facts, to determine material or logical relations or the internal structure of cultural values, while it is another thing to answer questions of the *value* of culture and its individual contents' (Weber, 1989).

It is important to note that Weber was speaking with specific reference to the situation in the German lecture halls of his time. Lecturers were paid according to the number of students who subscribed to their lectures. Weber was saying that prophets and demagogues belong to the streets and the public arena 'where criticism is possible'. Politics did not belong to the lecture room, according to him, because

> In the lecture room, where one sits opposite one's audience, the audience must be silent and the teacher must speak. I consider it irresponsible for the lecturer to exploit the fact that students must attend a teacher's course for the sake of their careers and that nobody present can criticise him, in order to stamp them with his personal political opinions. (Weber, 1989: 20–1)

If that was the structure of power in German universities in Weber's day, it is amazing that such silenced students ever emerged to be such original thinkers! It is noteworthy that Weber never used the phrase 'value-free' to describe social science as a vocation. The closest he came to this was when he talked about a 'science free of preconceptions in the sense of religious lies' about miracles and revelations. However, he also emphasised that although personal sympathies could distort analyses, 'To let the facts speak for themselves is the most unfair method of all' (Weber, 1989: 20–1). This is a recognition on his part that facts do not have their own mouths and so, invariably, it is people that speak and they do not speak just to lend their voices disinterestedly to facts, that is, they do not speak for facts but with facts in the instrumental sense, rather than in the sense of camaraderie. Weber regretted that it might be impossible to exclude personal sympathies completely from scientific analyses, but advised that each researcher should be left to the mercy of the sharpest critic of them all – personal conscience.

Weber did not use the 'value-freedom' concept at all, but gave enough indication that it is a desirable aspiration for vocational social scientists. Consequently, his disciples use the concept very freely to describe the level of purity they want their analysis to attain (see Lassman et al., 1989, for example). This indicates that some social scientists are still striving for what Weber called 'pure science' in which truth and commitment are kept in separate compartments.

This fact/value separation is supported by many social scientists. Becker (1967: 244), for example, argues that 'our problem is to make sure that, whatever point of view we take, our research meets the standard of good scientific work, that our unavoidable sympathies do not render our results invalid'. However, Becker was defending the choice made by some sociologists to study social problems from the perspective of subordinates as distinct from an explicit choice by the researcher to oppose such subordination. A similar view was taken by Bankowski et al. (1991), who argue that two permissible commitments in scholarship should be first and foremost to 'truth and objectivity' and second, a necessary commitment to 'rationality' in theory and practice and to the ways that 'norms and values can inform material content of practical justifications'.

Similarly, Hammersley (1993) argued that Peter Foster has been unfairly criticised for concluding from a study of one school that teachers are not racist even though anti-racist education presumes that they are. According to Hammersley, the truth of Foster's finding cannot be debunked with reference to the political possibility that it could be used to undermine the anti-racist struggle. However, Hammersley presents an apolitical conception of truth which is questionable given that truth in social science is a matter of interpretation. For instance, the finding that teachers in one school are not racist could mean that anti-racist education has succeeded in eliminating racism among teachers in that particular school.

Furthermore, if teachers are not racist at one school, they could be at another and, even if all teachers are anti-racist, there might still be some racist students to justify an anti-racist education programme. Moreover, even if all teachers and all students are known to have become anti-racist (whether as a result of the success of anti-racist education and struggles or not) there is still racism in the wider community that demands anti-racist education. All these are political

considerations without which meaningful interpretation of
Hammersley's pure 'truth' would be impossible.

 This sharp separation of commitments from theoretical facts is
rejected by most radical scholars and almost all feminist writers as a
myth. Back and Solomos (1993) argue 'that it is impossible to see
research in this field as simply an information-gathering process'.
However, they are critical of Ben-Tovim et al. (1986) for carrying
commitment too far in claiming to be the advocates of the oppressed.
The present writer does not see any problem with any attempt by
researchers to advocate the interests of the oppressed. It is always
good for those who have a voice to speak up for the silenced rather
than hide behind the mask of scientific objectivity to speak only
about silences. It is commendable to hear white, middle-class, male
scholars, for example, state that they wish to advocate the interests
of poor black people in their scholarship. However, it will be even
more commendable for scholars to speak in solidarity *with* the
oppressed rather than simply speak *for* them as if their silence implies
voicelessness. What is more problematic is the claim by Ben-Tovim
et al. (1986: 5): 'Widespread condemnation of racism amongst
academics sits uncomfortably alongside a commitment to objectivity
in the production and use of research findings.' The present chapter
argues that objectivity and commitment could be and are often
comfortable neighbours. They are different principles but they are
rarely separate in any good research.

 Gouldner (1961: 204) argued that 'the value-free doctrine' failed
because it emphasised 'the separation and not the mutual connect-
edness of facts and values'. According to him, the doctrine was often
adopted as an excuse for political passivity whereas Weber deemed
the cautious expression of value judgement to be both permissible
and compulsory in certain situations, so long as such a value
judgement is cautiously separated from factual statements. As he put
it, 'If Weber insisted on the need to maintain scientific objectivity,
he also warned that this was altogether different from moral
indifference' (Gouldner, 1961: 200). The point here is that the
recognition that facts and values coexist is contradicted by efforts to
separate them. Facts are different from values, but they are articulated
rather than being separate.

 However, when Gouldner (1970: 112) wrote that he found himself
'in the uncomfortable position of drawing back' from some people
– Becker in particular – who found his above position persuasive, he
could be said to have recanted. But Gouldner was not drawing back

from his position; he was drawing back from a particular (mis)inter-
pretation of that position. Gouldner did not change his mind about
the inseparability of facts and values. He was afraid 'that the myth
of a value-free social science is about to be supplanted by still another
myth ... the myth of the *sentiment-free* social scientist' (Gouldner,
1970: 112 and 118). We will return to the dialogue between Becker
and Gouldner shortly.

The position of the present writer is that it is both undesirable and
impossible to separate social science from social action if for nothing
else, because the conduct of social research itself involves social
action. The major question behind all social science research
(implicitly or explicitly) is the problematic 'What is to be done?'
There is no social science research that has no direct or remote
practical implication. Those who pretend to be describing social facts
like discrimination from a value-free position cannot deny that such
descriptions could be used to support the continuation of discrimination. Value-freedom is therefore pretentious in concealing its own
value-ladenness, as is evident in its refusal to oppose oppressive
practices that directly utilise its findings and provide its funding.

While Weber saw the political lecturer in an uncritical lecture hall
to be irresponsible, it is similarly irresponsible for the apolitical social
scientist to try to understand the world of oppression without a
commitment to changing it. Whereas Weber saw what is now known
as value-freedom as a formula for making social science relevant, it
is seen by radicals as a prescription for what Soyinka (1973: 2) termed
the 'erudite irrelevances' with which sociologists are armed.

According to Rubin and Babbie (1989: 63): 'Nowhere have social
research and politics been more controversially intertwined than in
the area of race relations.' Social scientists may pretend that they are
studying race relations (and by implication, gender and class
relations) with point-of-viewlessness, but their findings eventually
inform political practices of different tendencies. For example, the US
Supreme Court established the apartheid principle of 'separate but
equal' in 1896 in order to deny black people who were victimised by
segregation the benefit of the Fourteenth Amendment's legislation
of racial equality. The judges pretended that they were not influenced
by social science research but their judgement has been linked to the
work of William Graham Sumner (1906) who maintained that
'stateways do not make folkways'.

W. G. Sumner may have presented the statement that 'stateways
do not make folkways' as a democratic critique of authoritarianism

but the converse implication that it is 'folkways that make stateways' could result in oppressive rule, especially in societies structured along race–class–gender dominance. The Supreme Court must have been influenced by Sumner to reject the belief that 'social prejudices may be overcome by legislation'. The court opposed 'laws which conflict with the general sentiment of the community' (Blaunstein and Zangrando, 1971: 308). This reasoning appears to be also an application of Durkheim's theory of collective conscience which critics have shown to be a mythical representation of hegemonic ideas (see Garland, 1990).

The link between social research and practical politics became clearer in 1954 when the same Supreme Court in *Brown* v. *Board of Education of Topeka* cited the findings of Myrdal (1944) regarding the adverse impacts of segregation on black children as part of the reasons for overturning the doctrine of 'separate but equal'. But when the US Commissioner of Education, as required by the 1964 Civil Rights Act, appointed James Coleman to direct a research into inequalities in education, Coleman et al. (1966) reported that black children in segregated schools did not perform better or worse than those in integrated ones. Coleman and his colleagues concluded that segregation had a neutral impact at a time when many social scientists were actively campaigning for black civil rights.

Although the conclusion of Coleman and others that good school facilities and effective teaching methods have less impact on performance than family and neighbourhood backgrounds could be interpreted to mean that desegregation was not enough, it more readily supported the widely criticised theory of Jensen (1967), who held that genetic inferiority accounted for black students' lower IQ scores. This chapter chose not to plunge into the outdated but still dangerous water of the debate about the genetics of intelligence or the intelligence of genes.

Michael Rutter (in Giddens, 1989: 424) has since shown that while Coleman was right about the influence of pre-school experiences and conditions outside schools on examination results, Coleman failed to consider the influence of teacher–pupil interaction. Rutter found, in a study of London schools, that a co-operative and caring atmosphere between teachers and students and well-organised course preparation influence students' motivation and that these principles were practised by better teachers who tended to be attracted to better schools. The unstated implication here is that, even in good schools, some good teachers could interact with students from different backgrounds differently. Thus Bourdieu (1986) has argued that schools are not simply institutions working for social equality, but also institutions that reproduce and amplify the existing culture with the existing inequality.

THE EXAMPLE OF THE INSTITUTE OF RACE RELATIONS

This can be illustrated by the case of the Institute of Race Relations (IRR), which claimed to be detached and to be surveying race relations in Britain with scientific objectivity and value-freedom. The Institute was challenged by one of its own staff, Robin Jenkins (1971), who forcefully demonstrated that the research of the Institute was value-laden and ideologically loaded against the black people who were being surveyed.

Jenkins' chapter was initially delivered to the British Sociological Association and it focused on the gigantic survey by the IRR on *Colour and Citizenship*. Jenkins charged that the perspective of the survey was not scientific, contrary to the claims of the researchers and their supporters, but ideologically exploitative of the black communities studied. According to Jenkins, the knowledge produced by the Institute tended to empower the 'power elite' at the expense of black communities. The controversy raised by Jenkins resulted in self-criticism by the Institute and gradually transformed it 'from an institute *of race relations* to an institute *against racism*', according to Sim et al. (1987: 30).

Other IRR researchers, notably Mullard (1985) and Sivanandan (1974), have pointed out that the controversy over objectivity and commitment had gone beyond the initial critique by Jenkins to embrace the fundamental roots of racism and the strategies for fighting racism. Jenkins was all for 'strong objectivity' and he recommended that black people should tell social researchers to get lost until they stopped being biased. Jenkins' views were obviously shared by many researchers at the IRR and his bold intervention encouraged many other researchers at the Institute to make their research even more critical of the state and its agencies.

The now defunct journal of the Institute, *Race Today*, became more accessible to black perspectives for the articulation of black realities. Notably, collections of the works of radical black poets like Linton Kwesi Johnson were published by *Race Today*, even though they were openly critical of the state. For example, Johnson's poem 'Sonny's Lettah', in the form of a dramatic narrative from an imprisoned son to a disturbed mother, exposes the injustice of the use of the Criminal Justice Act 1982 by the police against black youth whom they suspected of being involved in crime or of planning to engage in crime. Hall (1979: 13) points out that 'the pervasive application of "arrest on suspicion"' which is popularly known as 'sus' operated 'under the ancient statutes of the Vagrancy Act of 1824'. The poem was also published with the sub-title 'anti-sus poem', by Island Records as a track in Johnson's 1979 classic album *Forces of Victory* and in the 1985 selection of his best for Island's 'Reggae Greats' series (Johnson 1981: 11–13).

'Sonny's Lettah' illustrates a number of points that are relevant to the present chapter but readers can check out the record for themselves. The fact that the letter was a work of creative writing means that certain readers dismiss it as lacking in objectivity whereas this chapter argues that even poems can be passionate representations of objective reality. The fact that the poem is addressed to a mother to cheer her up illustrates that even when black men are the focus of repressive policing, the women close to them are also affected (Agozino, 1997a). But since the poem is concerned with a single incident, can it be taken to be representative of more widespread encounters, or should it be treated as an isolated event?

It is significant to note that the IRR published this poem. It could be said that the poem is not a documentary but a one-sided, fictitious account of an imaginary encounter, which has little or nothing to do with real events. However, the poem very closely predicted the case of the 'Tottenham Three', who were jailed for killing a policeman following protests that greeted the death of a black woman during a police raid on her flat. Just as the 'Tottenham Three' have had their convictions quashed because the police fabricated evidence to convict them, Sonny could be said to have been innocent of the murder with which he was charged because it appears that he acted in self-defence and had no intention to kill.

The poem must not be trivialised as fiction because it seems to illustrate what is probable if not predictable in situations of oppressive policing. Johnson may have used irony to exaggerate in order to capture attention and also to emphasise that black youths are not underdogs on their backs but militant underdogs fighting back, as Gouldner (1970) would say. That the policeman died from Sonny's kick just as a policeman died during the Broadwater Farm Estate protests should not conceal the fact that most of the kicks and the killings that occur in such encounters are directed against poor people by the police and yet hardly any police officer has ever been convicted as a consequence (Scraton and Chadwick, 1987). The present chapter argues that researchers should make use of similar literary allusions to provide illustrations when appropriate. It will be seen that such literary texts, like 'Sonny's Lettah', will tend to focus on single events and so care will be taken not to present them as generalisations but as specific illustrations or analogies to clarify certain lines of argument.

WHAT IS COMMITTED OBJECTIVITY?

Theories of inequality have forced many radical scholars to conclude that objectivity is either undesirable or impossible or both. For example, Hall (1987) was unnecessarily apologetic about his commitments in the analysis of race relations. He pleaded that he found 'it impossible to muster the scholarly detachment and academic calm which is often felt to be appropriate in discussions of this kind, and if I transgress in any way this frontier I hope that you will forgive me'. Maximum respect is due to Hall for confessing his commitments; he should go in peace for, as Bob Marley sang in 'Jah Live', 'Truth is an offence but not a sin.'

Marx was aware that he was developing an objective method for studying and (with commitment) for changing the world. So the belief that it is possible to be objective and still be politically committed is not new; that is what most radicals have been doing (see Hall, et al. 1978, for example). But it is not only radicals that do it; non-radicals claim that they are not committed and that they are simply objective (Tappan, 1977, for example). Radicals have easily shown how much the so-called objective methods are also committed. They in turn deny being objective and clearly demand the spelling out of commitment (Becker, 1967, for instance).

Those who doubt that objectivity is possible in the social sciences do so because they define objectivity in natural science terms of complete detachment. In the present chapter, objectivity is operationalised not to mean pretentious value-neutrality in social research, but the ability to take a position and argue it logically without concealing or distorting opposing positions. Thus operationalised, objectivity does not guarantee truth. The finding could be objectively shown to be false or true, empirically tenable or otherwise, politically viable or inefficacious, etc. There are different possible truths relating to the logical adequacy, empirical tenability and policy efficacy of the claims and interpretations of individual analysts. Since the empirical terrain of social science is political and dynamic, there is no guarantee that objectivity could deliver an absolute truth, but there is no doubt that, as operationalised here, objectivity that presupposes rather than denies commitments could increase our understanding of social phenomena. However, some studies could be more objective than ideological, and vice versa.

It should already be clear from the beginning that the present writer calls for identification with oppressed research subjects not because they are research subjects, but because researchers should identify strongly with all oppressed people everywhere, even when they are not research subjects and even when they are not researchers. Social research should be partially stimulated by a desire to contribute to the amelioration of all sufferings through a better understanding of avoidable problems.

It is known that black women, for example, are not the only people who suffer discrimination and so the problems they face can be best understood only in solidarity with the problems faced by other relatively powerless people in society. This approach, which values the freedom of all human beings, irrespective of class, race and sex, will help the researcher to remain objective and honest while showing commitment to the overcoming of the problems facing those more marginalised than others.

11. How Scientific is Criminal Justice? A Methodological Critique of Research on *McCleskey* v. *Kemp* and Other Capital Cases

Where the issue of the death penalty is concerned, law follows politics, and conservatives won the socio-political battles of the 1980s on the basis of an agenda that included a ringing endorsement of capital punishment. The venerated principle of *stare decisis* – following rulings of previous judicial decisions – meant little in the politically charged judicial arena. Statistical methodology and scientific and sociological studies, once valued tools for challenging state practice, now serve as meaningless academic exercise. (Abu-Jamal, 1995)

McCleskey v. *Kemp* (481 U.S. 279, 1987) was chosen as the focus of this chapter because of the role that social science methodology played in the case. In that case, McCleskey's appeal was largely based on a sophisticated statistical analysis demonstrating evidence of racial bias in the application of death penalty statutes (Baldus et al., 1989). The Supreme Court also offered a legal and factual critique of the social science methodology produced for the appeal in the case. Finally, David Baldus and his colleagues wrote extensive method-ological critiques of the Supreme Court's decision (hereinafter the Baldus study).

In this chapter, I will not go into detail about the Supreme Court critique of the social science methodology or the counter-criticism offered in the Baldus study. However, the goal of the chapter is to examine the possibility that criminal justice is a science, as in 'scientific criminal justice', that approximates principles of scientific rationality and not simply an administrative field where the criminal justice sciences (such as forensic science, criminology and psychiatry) are employed. If criminal justice practitioners and actors can be seen as consciously or unconsciously employing scientific methodology in the performance of their duties, then the standards of scientific validity tests could be extended to the outcomes of capital cases, for instance. This possibility will be examined by exploring the assumptions that underlie criminal investigations, prosecutorial decisions, jury selection, presentation of evidence, jury verdicts, acquittals or convictions, sentencing, appeals and criminological research.

This chapter is divided into five broad sections: (1) a background summary of the McCleskey case; (2) an examination of investigative, judicial, appellate and correctional processes in capital cases; (3) a critique of criminological research on capital cases; (4) a comparative review of the cases of Mumia Abu-Jamal and Ken Saro-Wiwa; and (5) a concluding section on the role that a scientific view of criminal justice could play in the capital punishment debate.

THE CASE OF MCCLESKEY

In the case of *Furman* v. *Georgia* (1972), the US Supreme Court declared by a 5–4 majority that every death penalty statute in America had a potentially discriminatory and arbitrary racial impact. Thus, such statutes violated the Eighth Amendment. As a result, the federal government and all 50 states declared a moratorium on death sentences until satisfactory safeguards against arbitrary and discriminatory decisions were put in place (*Furman* v. *Georgia*, 408 U.S. 238, 1972). Concurring with the leading opinion in this decision, Justice Thurgood Marshall stated that 'The question with which we must deal is not whether a substantial proportion of American citizens would today, if polled, opine that capital punishment is barbarously cruel, but whether they would find it to be so in light of all information presently available.' Hopefully, this chapter will contribute to the task of informing the public better.

The response to *Furman* came in the form of three promised reforms (Baldus et al., 1989: 1):

1. The reduction of prosecutorial discretion by limiting the number of cases that qualified for the death sentence and by calling the attention of the jury to mitigating and aggravating circumstances in each case;
2. The promise that state supreme courts should exercise stricter oversight through 'comparative proportional review' to prevent excessive and arbitrary use of death sentences; and

3. The Supreme Court promise to provide stricter oversight of state capital case decisions to ensure that death sentences are passed even-handedly.

In 1987, in *McCleskey*, and again by a 5–4 majority decision, the Supreme Court rejected an appeal on the ground that the appellant failed to show that the death sentence imposed on him was administered arbitrarily or in a discriminatory manner. This narrow decision was reached even though a comparative quantitative analysis by social scientists suggested that there were racial disparities in the imposition of death sentences and that promised reforms had failed.

In *Furman*, Justice Thurgood Marshall was probably optimistic about the power of the 'light of all information available' to influence the American public into opposing the death penalty given that legislators and his fellow justices at the Supreme Court obviously knew the facts but continued with the centuries-old bias against the poor and minority men who were more likely to be sentenced to death. In *McCleskey*, the fact that support for the death penalty is not based on lack of information about discrimination is brought out by the revelation that Justice Antonin Scalia voted with the 5–4 majority to deny McCleskey's appeal. However, Justice Scalia sent a memo to his colleagues which he did not want published, in which he stated that 'The unconscious operation of irrational sympathies and antipathies, including racial, upon jury decisions and [hence] prosecutorial decisions is real, acknowledged in the decisions of this court, and ineradicable, I cannot honestly say that all I need is more proof.' This awareness should have made him cast his vote on the side of McCleskey and perhaps pave the way for the abolition of the death penalty in America, but he failed to do so, apparently because he believed that there would always be racism in the justice system. However, he must have been uncomfortable with the logic of his memo, hence he asked for it not to be published and it became known only after Justice Thurgood Marshall donated his own papers to the Library of Congress (quoted in Kennedy, 1997: 339).

In the case, McCleskey confessed that he participated in a robbery but insisted that he did not fire the shot that killed a white police officer. However, the prosecution matched one of the bullets that hit the officer to the type of gun McCleskey was carrying during the robbery. The prosecution also presented two witnesses who stated that McCleskey confessed to them that he shot the police officer.

INVESTIGATION AND ADJUDICATION AS RESEARCH

It is often assumed that criminal justice researchers and criminal justice practitioners are completely separate professionals. Practitioners are expected to be concerned with pragmatism while researchers are supposedly concerned only with abstractions. Barbara Boland (1996: 213) has challenged this assumption by arguing that community police officers and prosecutors should apply the research methodology of 'grounded theory' in their practical work. Grounded theory is contrasted with grand theory as a method that requires social scientists to approach their fieldwork without grand deductive theoretical preconceptions. Grand theory requires such 'hypotheses' right from the beginning and then goes on to test such assumptions empirically, but grounded theory requires that researchers begin their qualitative analysis in the field inductively through the coding and recoding of information as it becomes available. Barney Glasser and Anselm Strauss (1967: 124–5) stated that grounded theory requires:

> The development of a systematic understanding which is clearly recognizable and understandable to the members of the setting and which is done as much as possible in their own terms; yet it is more systematic, and necessarily more verbal, than they would generally be capable of expressing. It uses their words, ideas and methods of expression wherever possible, but cautiously goes beyond these.

This is how most detectives work, or how they should work if prejudice and racial profiling did not exist. Prosecutors, jurors and judges should also start without the presumption of guilt in an ideal court, but this requirement is not always present in actual cases where racial/class/gender profiling is a reality. The following is an example of grounded theory in practice. Members of the jury are supposed to approach the case with a presumption of innocence. They are expected to hear all the evidence before deliberating and deciding on the guilt of the defendant that they were required to presume innocent. But in reality, jurors do not wait for all the evidence to be presented before they start forming an opinion. They start coding the evidence and go on recoding it in the light of new information rather than waiting until the end of summations before commencing what social scientists would call the 'analysis' of the evidence (Champion, 2000).

A common-sense assumption in investigative fieldwork is that police officers and prosecutors focus on one case at a time because of the uniqueness surrounding each case. However, according to Boland, officers tend to 'look for patterns' when they are investigating crimes. She gives the example of community prosecution officers in Oregon who started their investigation with the hypothesis that serious crime by repeat offenders was the major problem in the area. However, when an officer tested this hypothesis by talking to residents, it became clear that people were more concerned with social order offences and the danger posed by campers. The residents believed that disorderly conduct could result in complex crime problems if it was not tackled quickly. In other words, the officers started their investigation with assumptions and coding schemes, but their findings quickly forced them to recode and theorise the evidence (Boland, 1996: 213). Since the officers in the Boland study started out with a hypothesis, it could be argued that they started with the deductive logic of grand theory before switching to the inductive logic of grounded theory which Boland found more suitable for the nature of their work.

The observations of Boland support the suggestion by Barbara Hart, Legal Director of the Pennsylvania Coalition against Domestic Violence, that the grounded theory approach could offer an opportunity for criminal justice professionals to improve criminal justice research (Maxfield and Babbie, 1998: 33–5). According to Hart, practitioners utilise the methodology of grounded theory without realising it. She argued that 'probation officers, judges, case managers, victim service counselors and others tend to formulate general explanations to fit the patterns they observe in individual cases' (Maxfield and Babbie, 1998: 33). The suggestion is that such theory guides the actions and decisions of criminal justice practitioners as if they were engaged in grounded theory research. The coding by officials supposedly continues until they find cases that do not fit the existing theorisation that is always in the making, forcing them to re-examine or recode their original theorisation, modify it, reject it or defend it, and dismiss the new evidence as an isolated exception to the emerging grand theory that is always a possible by-product of grounded theory.

Further support for the view that criminal justice practitioners adopt the scientific approach in their work comes from Robert Emerson (1995), who argues that social control agents do not focus on isolated cases when making decisions. He argues that they consider the holistic effects of their total workloads in deciding which cases are to be treated as serious and which are to be treated as minor. Emerson also argues that even among such practical scientists as medical doctors, it has been found that if their caseload involves very serious cases, other serious cases would be coded as minor cases whereas another doctor with a lower range of serious cases would code 'minor' cases as serious. Emerson concludes that social control agents take into consideration the amount of resources available to them in deciding which cases to prioritise. Officials also pay attention to precedent and the sequence of cases at any particular time that they are making a specific decision as the guideline for deciding whether a case is serious or not.

The above authors suggest that the scientific method influences the practice of criminal justice officials and other actors in official positions. Taken together, what can be inferred from the work of these authors is that a scientific view of criminal justice should be approached with caution. This is because the scientific method is error-prone and should not be confused with a guarantee of infalli-bility, hence grounded theory prescribes the trial-and-error procedure of coding and recoding instead of starting out with preconceived foundational assumptions. The awareness that science is applicable to criminal justice practice should warn us that scientific truth is always, by definition, a falsifiable truth. What is scientifically proven beyond all reasonable doubts today should remain as a thesis until an antithesis successfully challenges it and advances knowledge towards a synthesis. When applied to capital punishment – the 'final solution' – we find an unscientific dogmatic faith in the judgement of facts and law that could quite easily be mistaken. If members of the jury know that the proper scientific attitude to adopt when considering the case for the prosecution is that of scepticism, then there will be no room for such irreversible punishments as the death penalty, given the ever-present chance of error.

SCIENCE HAS NO ROOM FOR FINALITY

Kate Malleson (1994) reviewed the principle of finality in legal reasoning in a special issue of the *Journal of Law and Society* which focused on The Royal Commission on Criminal Justice in the United Kingdom. The Commission was set up to examine why so many Irish descendants were wrongly jailed for terrorist offences in the 1970s. Needless to say that if the UK had not abolished the death penalty, many of the cases of miscarriages of justice that gave rise to the Royal Commission could have resulted in wrongful executions of the innocent.

According to Malleson, many submissions to the Commission identified the reluctance of judges to review cases that resulted in a conviction as the principal reason for the delay in releasing convicts even when there was evidence of a wrongful conviction. She argues that the judges' reluctance to review convictions stems from their inability to tamper with the principle of finality in judicial decisions. She also argues that criminal justice researchers have rarely focused on this principle. This chapter suggests that if judges were trained in criminal justice research methodology and if criminal justice officials were familiar with the scientific principle of falsifiability, perhaps both parties would not hold to this principle.

The suggestion that judges would be more flexible if they were trained in the scepticism of research methodology is obviously optimistic. Criminal justice scientific experts are themselves stubborn in the defence of their theory even when there are more persuasive interpretations or theories available. However, the scientific methods allow room for all the contested theories to be evaluated for as long as necessary without imposing an arbitrary limit in the form of finality. Also commenting on the cases that gave rise to the Royal Commission, Paddy Hillyard (1994) reviewed the case of an Irishman who was condemned as a terrorist in the press even before his trial. When he was eventually acquitted, the Home Secretary used the powers granted him by the Prevention of Terrorism Act to deport him and exclude him from entering the UK again. This indicates that even when marginalised suspects have been acquitted, certain legislators refuse to accept the finality of their innocence and continue to profile them as offenders. It is only when the marginalised challenge their conviction that lawmakers seek to set limits to the appeal process in the form of the Effective Death Penalty Act which President Bill Clinton signed in the US, setting a limit to the appeals against the death penalty. There are civil rights justifications for the principle of finality when defendants have been acquitted (double jeopardy), but no similar justification for the finality that is imposed to prevent an innocent person from presenting new evidence that could have led to an acquittal.

Peter Alldridge (1994) notes that the wrongful convictions that led to the setting up of the Royal Commission were based on forensic evidence. According to Alldridge, the police did not begin questioning and coercing false confessions from the six Irishmen later convicted of bombing a pub in Birmingham until forensic scientists assured them that those men were the culprits. Yet, those forensic scientists did not come forward later to admit that they were mistaken in their analysis even after serious doubts about the convictions were raised. Moreover, none of the 300 recommendations by the Royal Commission questioned how scientific forensic evidence was utilised in the convictions. This serves as a reminder that scientific evidence deserves to be treated with scepticism. Once again, this evidence supports the argument that finality in the law, when applied to the convicted, is wrong because even forensic science (like any science) can be wrong in identifying the innocent as the guilty party.

DNA evidence provides a clear example of the need for scepticism towards scientific evidence. Many American politicians believe that DNA tests should be used to prove that a person condemned to death is guilty. Some death row inmates and lifers believe that DNA tests will clear their names. However, this faith in scientific evidence should be tempered with caution since DNA evidence is relevant only in a small number of capital cases. Also, since DNA evidence is scientific, it should be subjected to the scepticism afforded to all types of scientific evidence. In general, we should err on the side of caution in order to avoid executing an innocent person. The only way to guarantee that there will be no miscarriage of justice is to eliminate the death penalty.

A SCIENTIFIC ARGUMENT AGAINST THE DEATH PENALTY

There is startling evidence in support of the above scientific argument against the death penalty. However, no scientific argument exists in support of the death penalty. In 1991 the Chair of the US Senate Committee on the Judiciary asked Professor James Liebman of the Columbia University School of Law to calculate the frequency of relief in habeas corpus cases. The following summarises the disturbing results from the unprecedented research (Liebman et al., 2000):

1. Nationally, during the 23-year study period, the overall rate of prejudicial error in the American capital punishment system was 68 per cent. In other words, courts found serious, reversible error in nearly seven of every ten of the thousands of capital sentences that were fully reviewed during the period.

2. Capital trials produce so many mistakes that it takes three judicial inspections to catch them – leaving grave doubt as to whether we *do* catch them all. After state courts threw out 47 per cent of death sentences due to serious flaws, a federal review found 'serious error' – error undermining the reliability of the outcome – in 40 per cent of the remaining sentences.

3. Because state courts come first and see *all* the cases, they do most of the work of correcting erroneous death sentences. Of the 2,370 death sentences thrown out due to serious error, 90 per cent were overturned by state judges, many of whom were the very judges who imposed the death sentence in the first place; nearly all of whom were directly beholden to the electorate; and none of whom, consequently, was disposed to overturn death sentences except for very good reasons. This does not mean that federal review is unnecessary. Precisely *because* of the huge amounts of serious capital error that state appellate judges are called upon to catch, it is not surprising that a substantial number of the capital judgments they let through to the federal stage are still seriously flawed.

4. To lead to reversal, error must be serious indeed. The most common errors – prompting a majority of reversals at the state post-conviction stage – are (1) egregiously incompetent defence lawyers who didn't even look for – *and demonstrably missed* – important evidence that the defendant was innocent or did not deserve to die; and (2) police or prosecutors who *did* discover that kind of evidence but *suppressed* it, again keeping it from the jury. (Hundreds of examples of these and other serious errors are presented in Appendices C and D to this Report.)

5. High error rates put many individuals at risk of wrongful execution: 82 per cent of the people whose capital judgments were overturned by state post-conviction courts due to serious error were found to deserve a sentence less than death when the errors were cured on retrial; *7 per cent were found to be innocent of the capital crime.*

6. High error rates persist over time. More than 50 per cent of all cases reviewed were found seriously flawed in 20 of the 23 study years, including 17 of the last 19. In half the years, including the most recent one, the error rate was over 60 per cent.

7. High error rates exist across the country. Over 90 per cent of American death-sentencing states have overall error rates of 52

per cent or higher; 85 per cent have error rates of 60 per cent or higher; three-fifths have error rates of 70 per cent or higher.

8. Illinois (whose governor recently declared a moratorium on executions after a spate of death row exonerations) does not produce atypically faulty death sentences. The overall rate of serious error found in Illinois capital sentences (66 per cent) is very close to – and slightly *lower* than – the national average (68 per cent).

9. Identifying so much error takes time – a national average of nine years from death sentence to the last inspection and execution. By the end of the study period, that average had risen to 10.6 years. In *most cases*, death row inmates wait for years for the lengthy review procedures needed to uncover all this error. Then, their death sentences are *reversed*.

10. This much error, and the time needed to redress it, imposes terrible costs on taxpayers, victims' families, the judicial system and the wrongly condemned. And it renders unattainable the finality, retribution and deterrence that are the reasons usually given for having a death penalty.

I have quoted extensively from the executive summary of *A Broken System: Error Rates in Capital Cases, 1973–1995* as evidence of unreliability in the imposition of the death penalty with finality. Some criminal justice scientists try to reform the system by calling for a moratorium until an error-proof method of identifying guilt has been devised. Some supporters of the death penalty see the ability of the legal system to identify errors as proof that the system is working accurately and does not need any more reforms. However, the view that criminal justice practitioners intentionally or unintentionally apply the scientific method in the process of investigation and adjudication suggests that it is naïve for criminal justice scientists and criminological researchers to seek ways of reforming an error-prone system on the basis of error-prone science. The following section will challenge criminology researchers who ignore the possibility of innocence in their death penalty research.

A CRITIQUE OF CRIMINOLOGICAL RESEARCH ON THE DEATH PENALTY

During his appeal, McCleskey argued that the imposition of the death sentence on him was due to the fact that his alleged victim was white.

To support this theory, David Baldus and his colleagues presented statistical evidence from a Procedural Reform Study, which showed that the accused was more likely to be sentenced to death in cases involving white victims than in cases involving black victims. The state's expert social scientists challenged the validity of the samples and the statistical procedures used in the Baldus study. According to the state scientific experts, the apparent racial disparity in capital cases could be explained by the fact that cases involving white victims tend to be more aggravated than cases involving black victims. They also stated that this was true in cases where life sentences were imposed. The state experts concluded that if racial bias existed, then the life sentence cases involving white victims would be less aggravated than life sentence cases involving black victims. However, this did not appear to be the case, according to the expert social scientists for the state. The implication is that the reason why defendants in cases involving white victims were more likely to be sentenced to death or to life is because their cases had more aggravating than mitigating circumstances and not because of racism (Baldus et al., 1989: 311–12).

Criminal justice scientists should easily recognise that the issues raised by *Furman* and *McCleskey* in the administration of death penalties are issues of validity and reliability. How do we know that the people sentenced to death deserve to die (validity) and if an impartial jury-prosecutor-judge retries the case with a competent defence attorney, how can we be sure that the verdict would not be different (reliability)? In answering these questions, every criminology undergraduate student would expect academic criminal justice researchers to be more sceptical than Supreme Court Justices; however, the reverse appears to be the case.

For example, in *McGautha* v. *California*, Justice Harlan argued that the promised reforms were 'beyond present human ability' to deliver. Moreover, Justice Renquist, in *Woodson* v. *North Carolina,* argued that it was impossible for state supreme courts to carry out the proposed comparative proportionality review (*Woodson* v. *North Carolina*, 428 U.S. 280, 316, 1976). James Tyrone Woodson was the lookout who did not participate in a first-degree murder but was sentenced to die because the death penalty was mandatory for such offences in North Carolina. The Supreme Court allowed his petition and found that mandatory death sentences were unconstitutional. Justice Renquist dissented.

To Justice Renquist, the reviews would have been particularistic, involving individual cases with unique individual facts which would lead state supreme courts to decide arbitrarily which condemned prisoner should live and which should die. Surprisingly, the Baldus study (Baldus et al., 1989: 2–3) which formed the basis of the appeal by Warren McCleskey, disagreed with the two justices who found the promised reforms impossible. Instead of supporting the methodologically sensitive critique of promised reforms offered by the judges and pushing the logic in scientific directions unanticipated by the pro-death penalty judges, the social scientists felt that they would have more credibility if they offered a scientific argument for validating the death penalty. The justices seem to be saying that there is no need for reform because the death penalty would always be arbitrary and the social scientists are saying that they could remove arbitrariness by applying systematic scientific methods. Yet, systematic methods of science are by nature error-prone, suggesting that the arbitrary application of death penalty statutes can be checked only through abolition rather than through reform.

Throwing methodological caution to the winds, the social scientists in the Baldus study asserted that 'we are not yet convinced that arbitrariness and discrimination in death sentencing are inevitable'. They claim to have demonstrated that 'the system has improved since *Furman*' and suggested that not all death sentences are arbitrary and discriminatory. 'Indeed,' they asserted, 'many death sentences are imposed each year in highly aggravated cases in which racial features play no role whatever' (Baldus et al., 1989: 3). They conclude that the problem is that a large proportion of death penalties are imposed on defendants who are not the most blameworthy. In their view, what should be done is to strengthen the first promised reform by further restricting the application of death sentences to the worst cases. If this was their view, it is hardly surprising that Warren McCleskey lost his appeal based on the ideologically loaded argumentation that they tried to present as being value-free regarding the death penalty itself.

Given the established fact that every research has a margin of error, a scientific model of the criminal justice system would maintain that there is no such thing as perfect justice. Social scientists who think that the death penalty can be reformed to eliminate bias and arbitrariness are mistaken, given that even the best examples of social science research contain some errors. The question is how to correct errors in death penalty cases after the execution. As many commentators have said, that is simply impossible. This impossibility of correcting the inevitable errors that are made in research, investigation or judgment after someone is already dead is the strongest argument against the death penalty.

In another study, Hugo Badau and Michael Radelet (1992) found 400 cases involving erroneous convictions, yet Baldus et al. (1989: p. 2) did not identify one person who was convicted but innocent out of the nearly 2,000 cases analysed. They indicate that they studied 153 pre-*Furman* cases and 594 post-*Furman* cases which resulted in a Georgia jury conviction for murder between 1973 and 1978. In addition, they also analysed data from the Procedural Reform Study involving 1,066 defendants indicted for murder or voluntary manslaughter between 1973 and 1979. Incredibly, none of these cases raised the issue of innocence on death row or the need to abolish the death penalty for the Baldus study. If the Baldus study started with the assumption that the death penalty should be abolished, rather than reformed, perhaps they would have been more sensitive to the protestations of innocence that many death row inmates maintain. In the state of New York, eight people who were executed were later found to be innocent (cited in Albanese, 2000). Moreover, 92 people on death row in 21 states had their sentences either overturned or reduced on further appeal, leading to increased scepticism about the validity and the reliability of the death penalty statutes (Rovella, 1997: 7).

The Baldus study did correctly highlight the racism in the administration of the death penalty in America. However, it mistakenly assumed that the racist aspects of the death penalty only involved excessive punishment for black men convicted of killing white victims. Warren McCleskey's proclaimed innocence was not examined in their research because the study was not interested in the possibility that people on death row could actually be innocent. It is not enough to indicate, as Tracy Snell (1996) did, that black people disproportionately made up 42 per cent of the 3,000 Americans on death row or that they disproportionately made up 38 per cent of the people executed since 1976. Researchers should not assume that all of those black men were guilty and were simply being punished disproportionately due to racism. Rather, researchers should also explore the probability that many of them were simply innocent.

The US Controller-General (1990) conducted a systematic review of 28 studies on the death penalty for Congress and issued a finding that the majority of the studies concluded that racism was inherent in the charging, trial and sentencing of death penalty cases. The Controller-General could have further explored whether the punishment of the innocent was also racialised in such a way that more innocent black people were likely to be sentenced to death than innocent white people were. However, since the Controller-General was simply reviewing existing research, silence on possible innocence of death row inmates can only be blamed on criminal justice scientists who assumed that all the convicted were guilty. Scientists wrongly assume that they cannot call for the abolition of a flawed policy without being accused of bias whereas their qualified support for a racist penal policy lacks any scientific basis and is every bit biased.

Since 1976, the state of Illinois has executed twelve inmates. However, due to the research of undergraduate journalism students and law students, 13 people on death row were found to have been wrongly convicted and released. Their findings forced the Governor to declare a moratorium on the death penalty in the year 2000. Death penalty opponents say that a moratorium is not enough and call for outright abolition. If the death penalty was a drug and the chances are that 13 healthy people out of 25 who took the drug would die, no one would license such a drug for public consumption. The Death Penalty Information Center[*] reported in 2003 that, 'Since 1973, 197 people in 25 states have been released from death row with evidence of their innocencd.' The racial distribution of the innocent who were exonerated is as follows: 48 of them were black, 45 were white, 12 were Latino and one each were Native American or Other. The Death Penalty Information Center also lists a number of people who remain on death row while protesting their innocence.

In *Black Women and the Criminal Justice System*, I argued that criminologists are preoccupied with the punishment of offenders. Consequently, theories of the punishment of the innocent are lacking in criminology (Agozino, 1997: 11–16). That forced me to develop the concept of victimisation as mere punishment to theorise the treatment of innocent black women in the criminal justice system as if they were guilty in different historical epochs. That study demonstrated that those who are marginalised in race–class–gender relations are more likely to suffer victimisation as mere punishment. Although that study did not cover cases of the death penalty as such, the argument can be extended to capital cases by challenging criminologists to be more scientific and sceptical about the criminality of

* Point to http://www.deathpenaltyinfo.org/innoc.html#race

everyone who faces punishment. This is not the place to review that theoretical debate. Instead, this chapter will end by reviewing two disturbing cases of innocent people sentenced to death. One of them is now dead, but researchers can still add their voices to the calls to save the life of another innocent man. This can be done by opposing the death penalty on scientific principles instead of trying to reform the flawed system with the aid of empiricist logic.

MUMIA ABU-JAMAL: ANOTHER KEN SARO-WIWA?

Mumia Abu-Jamal and Ken Saro-Wiwa, both with double-barrelled surnames, won awards for their writing with which they campaigned for a better world. Both of them were accused and convicted of the murder of prominent citizens. For Ken Saro-Wiwa it was the murder of Ogoni chiefs and in the case of Mumia Abu-Jamal it was a white police officer. Ken was leading the struggle for his people, the Ogoni, who are marginalised and endangered by the hyper-ethnicist neocolonial politics of Nigeria. Mumia is still campaigning for his people, poor African Americans, who are marginalised and endangered by the hyper-racist internal colonial politics in America.

Ken was judicially murdered in November 1995 by the Sani Abacha dictatorship which denied him the right of appeal and confirmed the death sentence without even seeing the trial transcripts from the kangaroo military tribunal that convicted him. Ken was hastily hanged with eight other Ogoni campaigners in spite of protests and pleas from the international community.

Mumia was to be executed in November 1998 by the Republican government of the Commonwealth of Pennsylvania, but due to protests and pleas from the international community, Governor Tom Ridge granted him a stay of execution pending the determination of his latest series of appeals. His 29-point writ of habeas corpus details evidence of abuse of his constitutional rights in a prejudicial trial. The appellate court ruled that Mumia should be granted a new sentencing hearing while upholding his conviction for a murder that he did not commit. Needless to add that a new sentencing hearing instead of the new trial that he was seeking could still return a sentence of the death penalty or impose a life sentence which means no chance of parole in Pennsylvania. Mumia could still be judicially murdered.

However, unlike Ken, who was a member of the Nigerian elite – a former government commissioner who went on to develop a profitable business in the media as writer, publisher and television producer/director, with enough resources to send his children to elite private schools in England – Mumia was under police surveillance from the age of 17 when he became an official of the Black Panther Party. However, after compiling a 650-page dossier on his activities, the FBI found no evidence of a criminal record. Unlike McCleskey, who admitted that he was part of the gang that killed a police officer but denied firing the shot, Mumia was never linked to any criminal activity before the shooting.

Mumia went on to win awards as a radio journalist, especially for his live coverage of the police bombardment of an African American communal organisation known as Move Afrika. For his politically sensitive journalism, the award-winner lost his job and no other radio station would hire him or use his freelance materials. As a result, he became a taxi driver in order to support his family. By contrast, Ken was flown to the presidential villa in an Air Force jet to have breakfast with his friend, General Abacha, who reassured him of his support for the Ogoni shortly before he was arrested. General Abacha would eventually sign Ken's death warrant.

Ken Saro-Wiwa and Mumia Abu-Jamal have very different stories. What they have in common is that they have had the death penalty imposed on them without due process and with no regard to their protestation of innocence. These two brothers serve as examples of how cruel and unusual the death penalty is and why its imposition should not be available in a world structured along race/ethnic/gender/class articulation of dominance and prejudice.

The Abacha dictatorship later admitted that the Ogoni nine were hanged without due process. Under the criminal justice system, there is a reasonable expectation that if they had been given prison terms they might have had a better chance of proving their innocence through the appellate process. Yet the case of Mumia illustrates that even where appeals are provided, if the appellant is denied the resources along with a prejudiced judiciary, Abacha could have given Ken a million appeals and still murdered him judicially. Wole Soyinka (1996: 150–1) suggested that the multiple murders for which Saro-Wiwa was convicted were probably committed by Abacha's soldiers who were in the habit of impersonating Ogoni youth when launching attacks against neighbouring communities in order to divide and weaken the opposition. Without coming out clearly against the death penalty in principle (especially when it is used against the poor masses), Soyinka questioned why the Abacha dictatorship hurriedly rushed Saro-Wiwa and the other eight Ogoni activists to the gallows when:

There are hundreds of convicts on the death rows of our prisons, some of them held over ten years, maybe twenty, awaiting their date with destiny. Some are violent armed robbers, cold-blooded murderers. Several are functional sadists, mindless butchers who took advantage of religious or ethnic riots to practise their stock-in-trade. Years after they slaughtered their victims and turned the streets, markets and especially places of worship into slaughter slabs, years after they were sentenced, they are still kept alive in our prison cells, awaiting rescue by executive clemency. (Soyinka, 1996: 150)

President Olusegun Obasanjo of Nigeria's Fourth Republic and 50 others came close to being executed by the same regime for a fictitious treasonable felony. Perhaps because of this near-death experience, Obasanjo proclaimed his commitment to abolish the death penalty. In January 2000, he announced an amnesty for some death row inmates and in an interview with Jonathan Power stated that he was not going to announce a moratorium because 'The trouble with moratoriums is that they come to an end. And it's a wasted opportunity if one has to go back. I want to abolish the death penalty. I'm working towards it but I have a lot of educating to do' (Power, 2000: 5). Amnesty International (1997) reports that 'On 2 August 1994, 38 people were executed by firing-squad in Enugu, southeastern Nigeria. One of them, Simeon Agbo, apparently survived, stood up an hour later, bleeding profusely, to protest his innocence and plead for water. Police reportedly threw him onto a lorry load of corpses and his subsequent fate was unknown.' This mass execution of convicted armed robbers was under the Abacha dictatorship that framed and convicted General Olusegun Obasanjo and 50 others of the capital offence of treasonable felony. Thirty-nine people were executed in Nigeria in 1976 for treasonable felony under the previous rule of General Obasanjo, ten were executed in 1986 and 69 in 1990 under the dictatorship of General Ibrahim Babangida for similar offences (Amnesty International, 1997). Hopefully, this chapter will contribute to President Obasanjo's education, although it is doubtful that the supporters of the death penalty among judges and legislators are simply uneducated.

The key judicial argument against the death penalty is that the standard of impartiality required in capital cases was beyond human ability due to the emotional impact of the crimes for which the death penalty was imposed. How about the family of the victims who suffer the loss of their loved ones? That is the question that every member of the jury or the bench will ask themselves and they will probably decide that an eye for an eye is better, even if the world eventually goes blind. Yet examples of bereaved families like that of Bill Cosby, saying that they do not wish to have the death penalty as an option in their case, is exemplary and principled in opposition to the death penalty.

The answer to the question of the fate of the victim in the cases of Ken and Mumia is that killing an innocent suspect does no justice to the victim. However, the argument in this chapter is that the death penalty should also be abolished because it is administered wrongly and innocent people are suffering as a result. This is supported by recent evidence from the state of Illinois. Mumia Abu-Jamal (1995) also makes the point in his book *Live From Death Row*. According to him, we should not think that he is the only one wrongly convicted and placed on death row, and we should be asking every country in the world to abolish capital punishment because it is cruel, unusual and open to abuse without remedy.

CONCLUSION: HOW SCIENTIFIC ARE CRIMINAL JUSTICE SCIENCES?

This chapter serves as a wake-up call to criminologists and criminal justice scientists urging them to be more scientific in their general research, especially when the subject is the death penalty. Most of the arguments for and against the death penalty are moral, but the argument being presented here is a scientific one against the death penalty. The Baldus study used its research to offer a scientific argument in support of the reform of the death penalty instead of its abolition. This chapter is using the logic of the philosophy of science to call for the total abolition of the death penalty throughout the world. Criminal justice practitioners and researchers alike have a choice between two equally error-prone methods – the inductive logic of grounded theory or the deductive logic of grand theory. Both methods demand a healthy dose of scepticism which will inevitably lead to the conclusion that the death penalty should be abolished.

Grounded theory assumes that researchers approach their fieldwork without theoretical preconceptions. As I have pointed out, some social scientists argue that this is how criminal justice practitioners actually investigate, prosecute and try cases. Even when criminal justice officials are not following grounded theory, they could still be said to be following the deductive method of grand theory – starting with a presumption and testing that presumption against available data. The deductive scientific method of grand theory proceeds by stating a hypothesis or guiding assumption and then testing the assumption against empirical evidence. By analogy, the original hypothesis of the prosecution is that the defendant is guilty of a capital offence. As is expected, this is not the hypothesis tested by the jury. Rather, the jury tests the alternative hypothesis that the defendant is innocent. In the end, proof is accepted at the level beyond all reasonable doubt that the alternative hypothesis should be rejected and the original hypothesis of guilt affirmed. However, reasonableness is a problematic category in scientific research, it remains a fiction in law given that what is reasonable to a white, middle-class jury might not be reasonable to a black, working-class jury, and vice versa. Hence, science does not look favourably at finality in the search for truth – there is always room for more research whether you prefer grand theory or grounded theory.

Given the argument presented above, there is reasonable doubt on scientific grounds that the death penalty is valid, fair and reliable as a just means of punishing any offence. Orlando Patterson (1998) likens the death penalty to the religious rites of human sacrifice involving scapegoats. He traces such human sacrifice in America from the public lynching and hangings of mainly Afro-Americans by Euro-Americans to the death penalty today. He argued that it would be wrong to say that all the people lynched were innocent of the accusations against them given that a large number of the accusations were those of murder. This suggests that many of those lynched may have killed, perhaps in self-defence, given the antagonism against the new freedom of the former enslaved people of African descent, especially in the South.

By the same logic, it is true that not everyone (African American or European American) on death row today is innocent. However, due to the political nature of the death penalty, its impossible correction once given in error, and the persistence of racism in the criminal justice system, the death penalty should no longer be an option in a scientifically informed criminal justice system. This logic can be extended to all those in prison and all those who are being punished. We must not rush to the conclusion that they are all criminals since they may have been convicted in error or forced to plea bargain in a criminal justice system that tries only 10 per cent of the cases while 90 per cent are settled through plea-bargaining (Alschuler, 1995). At the very least, prisoners stand a slight chance of being released if they were later found to be innocent. It is also true that being released from death row is no proof of innocence either, but the criminal justice system should make it difficult to punish innocent people even if it means some guilty people are free.

In a comparative review of Jürgen Habermas (1996) and Jean Baudrillard (1996), in chapter 7 of this book, I argued that criminologists follow the modernist orientation of Habermas too closely by claiming that they pursue truth, the whole truth and nothing but the truth. Baudrillard, on the other hand, offers a postmodernist caution that we should be more sceptical of such claims because virtual reality all too often masquerades as reality (Agozino, 1999). The cases in which innocent people are condemned to death illustrate why we should strive to be more scientific by being much more sceptical. Habermas has been consistently defending the Enlightenment faith in rationality as the guide to the completion of the project of modernity. He suggests that what we need is more rationality rather than less in our search for justice. Baudrillard and the postmodernist critics of the Enlightenment project of modernisation insist that rationality is frequently used as an alibi to conceal the desire to dominate and oppress the marginalized sections of society.

Most criminologists would side with Habermas against Baudrillard, but I pointed out in my review that both the modernists and the postmodernists are right. Reason is important in the search for justice but pure fiction also plays a role in the use of analogies, metaphors, creative thinking and force in the struggle for domination within the law. The reason why many innocent people are on death row or why a flawed policy such as the death penalty remains is not simply because it is rational or because its advocates are right and the opponents are wrong or illogical. Fictions of deterrence and retribution remain the emotional basis for the support of the death penalty even when these have been faulted with scientific, rational, economic and moral arguments.

In scientific research, truth is never absolute, but tentative and falsifiable. Hence, truth beyond reasonable doubt of the guilt of a defendant should be taken with a grain of salt. The most scientific argument against the death penalty is that it lacks validity and reliability and it is impossible to correct once the error is noticed after the execution. Of course, these arguments are also ethical, but they should not be seen only in ethical terms because ethical issues are also broad methodological questions. In research methods, ethical questions about how to avoid harm to human subjects are part of the research design. This practice came about in an attempt to prevent some of the ethical nightmares such as the Tuskegee syphilis study in which African American men who were infected with syphilis were deliberately denied treatment between 1932 and 1972 by researchers who claimed that they wanted to know how the disease developed in human beings (Brandt, 1978: 15–21). If the death penalty were a criminal justice research experiment, no Institutional Review Board would approve it because the margin of error and the chances of doing harm would be too high. The criminal justice system should do the same, or follow the same logic, by outlawing faulty policies that are capable of doing harm – especially to innocent citizens.

12. What is Institutionalised? The Race–Class–Gender Articulation of Stephen Lawrence

The consistent denial of allegations of institutionalised racism by the majority of police officers in spite of the contradictory confessions of a few top-ranking officers suggests that the meaning of the term is not yet clear to all those involved in the debate. Institutionalisation means something unambiguous in sociology, however, and this meaning should be shared with the wider public in order to differentiate stark ignorance from ideological hoo-hah. The chapter will conclude by carrying the debate beyond institutionalised racism and including a discussion of the institutionalisation of race–class–gender articulation. Note that this chapter will use the term institutionalised racism in preference to the preferred one of institutional racism.

According to the *Chambers English Dictionary*, to institutionalise is to turn something into an institution; to confine someone to an institution; and as a result of such institutionalisation or confinement, to cause to become apathetic and dependent on routine. Sociology borrowed this idea long ago and set out to elaborate it as a way of carving a niche for its discipline compared to biology or psychology. In other words, the problem of racism in the police force is not simply a problem of racist attitudes held by some individual bad eggs in an otherwise normal force (although that is a serious problem in itself), but also a deeper problem of the reliance on routine in an apathetic way.

In London, Stephen Lawrence, a black teenager studying for his A-levels, according to a unanimous verdict returned by the inquest jury in 1997, 'was unlawfully killed in a completely unprovoked racist attack by five white youths' (Macpherson, 1999: 3) on 22 April 1993. His best friend, Dwayne Brooks, managed to escape their racist attackers and called the police and the ambulance. When the police arrived, he told them that the five white youths shouted 'What, what, nigger!' before attacking them. Although the police arrived much earlier than the ambulance, they did not give any first aid to the 18-year-old as he lay dying in what they saw as a large pool of blood, claiming that they thought that he was in a recovering position and denying suggestions from lawyers that they refused to help in order not to dirty their hands with black blood. Although the police were given positive information that could have led to arrests, they refused to make any arrest. Even when one of the attackers was picked out in an identity parade, the police suggested that the survivor who positively identified him was probably guessing. The police confessed that one of their officers was carrying a clipboard at the scene of the crime and was asking people for information, but later he could not remember anything he was told and had no record of any notes he may have taken.

Later, the police mounted video surveillance on the suspected attackers and caught them on tape boasting about how they were going to cut up black people but, at the same time, one of the officers was seen socialising with the gangster father of one of the suspects under the pretence that he wanted to 'cultivate' the gangster as a witness (against his own son?) but without any instruction from the officer in charge to do so. That same cultivating officer was the person assigned to protect the surviving witness during the trial even though a photograph of him and the father of one of the suspects sitting in a car was already known to the police. The case against the suspects was dropped after the police claimed that the eye-witness account of the survivor was unreliable. Subsequently, they arrested him while he was on a public protest and promptly charged him, only for the judge to throw out the case. In pursuit of justice, the parents of Stephen Lawrence attempted a private prosecution of the suspects, but when that collapsed, they launched an unprecedented campaign for a public inquiry into the way that the police had handled the investigation. It was only then that the above facts became widely known.

During the public inquiry chaired by Sir William Macpherson of Cluny, this heated exchange took place between Michael Mansfield, QC, representing the family of Stephen Lawrence, and Inspector Steven Groves, who was in charge of the scene of crime operations that fateful night:

Groves: I thought that what we were dealing with here was probably a fight.
Mansfield: I am going to put to you Mr Groves, that I suggest to you very clearly, this is one of your assumptions because it is a black victim, was it not?

Groves: No, sir. You are accusing me of being a racist now, and that is not true. I would like it noted that I do not think that is fair, either. You have no evidence that I am a racist.
Mansfield: If I ask you if you are a racist what will you say?
Groves: Of course I am not. I could not do my job if I was a racist. It would not be possible, it is not compatible. (Norton-Taylor, 1999)

Although the police officers investigating the murder of Stephen Lawrence (like most police officers) denied that they were racist, they confessed that they saw it as just another case of gang fights among inner-city youths. Following severe criticism of the conduct of the investigation in the Macpherson Report, the officers involved all took early retirement except one senior officer who announced his early retirement only when the disciplinary hearings against him were approaching and who was only convicted on one count out of eleven and was simply cautioned by the disciplinary hearing in 1999. As the Inquiry reported,

There is no doubt whatsoever but that the first MPS investigation was palpably flawed and deserves severe criticism ... Nobody listening to the evidence could reach any other conclusion. This is now plainly accepted by the MPS. Otherwise the abject apologies offered to Mr and Mrs Lawrence would be meaningless. (Macpherson, 1999: 4)

Is the claim by the police that racism, sexism and class prejudice are incompatible with police work convincing? Is it not possible for a police officer to remain on duty long before enough evidence can be found to prove that he or she was racist on the job before being disciplined? But even if the officer is not racist, is it not possible for the same officer to implement institutionalised racism by, for example, disbelieving the information from an eye witness, associating with the suspects, arresting the witness and charging him, and denying that the murder was racially motivated? Should the police not have started investigating it as a racist crime, made prompt arrests, kept records of their investigation, and been more sensitive to the eye-witness? If the police deny being individually racist, why do they also deny the existence of institutionalised racism? Is it because they do not understand what the term means? Moreover, was it simply a racist crime or was the murder also gendered and class-specific, very much like the police investigation?

The *Daily Mail* took the unprecedented step of naming the five white youths as racist murderers and challenged them to sue for libel if they were sure of their innocence, but their mothers went on radio to deny the accusation and claim that if they had the money and if they could be guaranteed a fair hearing, they would sue. The newspaper repeated the allegation and the challenge to be sued, but we must not forget that the racist reports of the same newspaper in the past may have helped to fuel the racist violence that claimed the life of Stephen Lawrence. According to the *Daily Mail* editorial of 8 October 1985, following the protests of black people against police brutality:

> Either they obey the laws of this land where they have taken up residence and accepted both full rights and responsibilities of citizenship, or they must expect the fascist street agitators to call ever more boldly and with ever louder approval for them to 'go back whence they came'.

This editorial wrongly assumed that all black people had taken up residence in England as migrants, whereas many like Stephen Lawrence were born here, and that only black people who do not obey the laws of the land have anything to fear from fascist street agitators. Stephen Lawrence has proved (if anyone needed proof) that black people do not need to do anything wrong before facing institutionalised racist violence either in the form of slavery, colonialism, fascism or oppressive law-and-order politics. Such symbolic violence was institutionalised in the Enlightenment movement that denied the humanity of Africans even while calling for universal brotherhood of man. It was perfected under colonialism and has been sustained by neo-colonialism, re-colonialism and internal colonialism (Gilroy, 1993; Hall et al., 1978).

THE SOCIOLOGY OF INSTITUTIONALISATION

Different sociological perspectives offer competing approaches to the understanding of institutionalisation. This section will not attempt a comprehensive review of the competing perspectives but will simply give enough indications of what is known theoretically about institutionalisation. This brief treatment is arbitrary and not exhaustive since some adherents of some perspectives could be classified differently by other writers. The synthetic classification adopted here has been tabulated as follows:

Table 1: Key perspectives, adherents and definitions of institution-alisation applicable to the articulation of Stephen Lawrence

Perspective	Adherents	Definition	Application
Marxism	Marx, Engels, Lenin, Gramsci, Luxemburg, Sivanandan, Cabral, hooks, Hall, Davis, Rodney	Emphasises that social institutional-isation is structured unequally with dominant class–race–gender being privileged, while others who are oppressed tend to resist and struggle for justice.	Stephen Lawrence suffered from the fascist violence that is part of imperialist social institutions that encourage ideas of rich white male supremacy among poor white men whose false consciousness tell them that poor black people are their enemies.
Functionalism	Durkheim, Radcliffe-Brown, Parsons, Luhmann	Stresses the consensual nature of social institution-alisation under a collective conscience that is strengthened through the systems of expected reward and punishment.	Wrongly suggests that there is a consensus that those who killed Stephen Lawrence were fascists and that they should be punished but the killers remain free and appear to be rewarded with false senses of heroism despite the fight to bring them to justice.
Rationalism	Weber, Giddens, Habermas, Beck, Mills	Sees institutionalisa-tion as the establishment of repetitive social action that is meaningful to all concerned and is supported by social norms under a system of rational domination that is legitimate as opposed to irrational forms of domination.	Suggests that a rational bureaucratic administration of justice would have arrested the suspected killers of Stephen Lawrence sooner without any personal considerations. In other words, Weber saw English law as historically denying justice to the poor because it is based on empirical justice rather than the rational bureaucracy.
Poststructuralism	Foucault, Fanon, Baudrillard, Lyotard, Frugg, Smart, Bhabha, Irigaray	Sees social institutions as socially constructed systems of discourse of power and knowledge designed to subjugate, control and discipline.	Suggests that the fascist violence of white youth and the legitimate force of officials derive from the same source of the will to dominate and so they must be deconstructed together.

It could be said that the Metropolitan Police Commissioner, Sir Paul Condon, was following the structural-functionalist conception of institutionalisation when he denied that racism is institutionalised within his force, although he was led by the Inquiry to admit in a letter that racism 'can occur through a lack of care and lack of under- standing ... almost unknowingly, as a matter of neglect, in an institution' (Macpherson, 1999: 24). The Inquiry responded indirectly by pointing out the difference between admitting that something could happen and acknowledging that it is happening. The Inquiry called for the debate to move beyond the problem of definition to the problem of what is to be done 'about the racism within the service' (Macpherson, 1999: 30–1).

The structural functionalist view regards institutionalisation as something that contributes to the survival of the social system. Therefore, only those things that contribute to the system's need for survival can be said to have been institutionalised. Whatever is dys- functional to the system is seen as an intrusion from the environment and such traits are supposedly identified and weeded out of the system in a cybernetic process eternally geared to stasis and equilibrium. That is the view that led Inspector Groves to assert that racism is incompatible with police work. Since police work is good work, it follows that anything that is not good, such as racism, cannot be seen as part of the institution of policing.

When Condon publicly warned 'leaders of the black community' to watch their backs because he was about to launch an operation specifically targeting young black males, he was exhibiting institu- tionalised racism–sexism–classism of the rational bureaucratic Weberian ideal type. First of all, he has never warned 'leaders of the white community' to control their kids even if neo-fascist murderers (who kill more people than muggers) in Britain happen to be white nor that there will be an operation targeting young white males as a result of white crime (Agozino, 1997a). In other words, even an officer who has admitted that he wants to eliminate racism from the police force can still carry on with institutionalised racism whether or not he acknowledges it. Some writers would argue that the policy statements of anti-racist racists like Condon represent a betrayal of the Weberian ideal bureaucracy but, as Zygmunt Bauman (1989) clearly illustrated, the rational bureaucratic logic is consistent with genocidal practices.

The bizarre investigation of the murder of Stephen Lawrence comes closest to the poststructuralist perspective in the sense that police officers are supposed to follow the truth and the rules and the seriousness of the crime, and so on, according to the rational bureaucratic ideal type of the administration of justice. Instead, Baudrillard would argue that they treated it as a *Perfect Crime*, or in other words no crime. Baudrillard uses this idea to expose the naivety of the faith that modernism places on the role of truth in the criminal justice system when it can be seen that virtual reality plays as much role as socially constructed ideas of reality in the investigation of crime (Agozino, 1999, see chapter 7 of this book).

The best example of the application of the Marxist perspective to the institutionalisation of racism–sexism–classism remains *Policing the Crisis* (Hall, et al., 1978). The authors of that book analysed the politics of mugging and demonstrated how the moral panic was imported into Britain from America at a historically specific time and why deep social structural forces condensed the themes of race, crime and youth into the images of mugging and blackness. The moral panic was triggered by the stabbing to death of an old man by three youths, one from a black Caribbean background, one of mixed race origin and one of Maltese origin. Although the victim was white, the motive for the killing was robbery and no newspaper reported it as a racist crime. However, most of the news reports presented 'mugging' as a black crime, a view that was backed by some politicians such as Enoch Powell and some senior police officers. The analysis shows that long before the public were made to panic about mugging due to police and media campaigns around sensational court cases, the police had institutionally defined the crime, linked it predominantly to black youths and mobilised before declaring that there was a mugging epidemic. The result of all this was that 'the police in the black communities have come, progressively, to perceive the black population as a potential threat to 'law and order', potentially hostile, potential troublemakers, potential 'disturbers of the peace', and potential criminals' (Hall et al., 1978: 45–6).

This explains the institutionalised racist assumptions by the investigating officers that they were dealing with a fight even after it was clearly reported that Stephen Lawrence had been attacked by five white youths. The zeal with which the police and the media 'amplified' the crime of mugging in their campaign against it differs markedly from the frequent denials and attempts to suggest that racist thugs are isolated individuals or groups whom the police presume innocent until proven guilty. In other words, racist violence is not amplified; on the contrary, the police do not take the investigation into such crimes as seriously as they take the crime of mugging. Hence there is no moral panic around racist violence. Instead, there is a moral crusade by the victims and their supporters while the police maintain a stance of incredulity and pretend that they do not have the evidence with which to mount a successful prosecution.

Hall and his colleagues went on to argue that the institutionalised racism evident in the policing of the crisis of hegemony derives ultimately from the role of the authoritarian state as a partisan in the class struggle. They suggest that the working-class movement is fragmented with sections of the black working class forced to fight over crumbs with sections of the white working class, especially when the postwar boom ended in a cataclysmic crash that divided the nation and undermined the consensus constructed by the welfare state. The scapegoating of black immigrants became fashionable populist rhetoric used by politicans to seek votes as if it was black immigrants who had caused the economic recession. Although the views of the politicians were populist because they were widely shared in society, Hall and his colleagues concluded that the political power of the state, including criminal justice agencies, makes the institutionalisation of prejudice and discrimination exceptional compared to the everyday racism that is shared widely in the society.

Compared to the above analysis of how conflict is tearing British society apart, the conflict functionalists theorise conflict as part and parcel of normal institutional practices. This approach to the analysis of racism proposes that the whole of society, not just the police, still survives on the fruits of the historical wrongs done to ethnic minority people and that the dominant ethnic groups seek to maintain the marginalised in positions of inferiority by perpetuating 'sets of advantages or privileges for the majority group and exclusions or deprivations for minority groups' (Rodriguez, 1987). According to adherents of the normal institutional practices approach, institutional racism 'is so embracing an operating principle that it no longer requires conscious or overtly racist acts to sustain it' (Rodriguez, 1987).

The opinion of the Chief Constable of Greater Manchester Police, David Wilmot, was close to a conflict functionalist view when he admitted on day 2 of part two of the Inquiry that the problem of institutionalised racism existed in his force, that he had had racist prejudice as a young officer and that he was tackling the problem especially in the 'canteen culture' of lower ranking officers. As he put it, 'there was still institutional racism, both in an internalised way (just as in society) and an overt way' (Macpherson, 1999: 31).

Institutionalised racism simply means that, in Manchester, if street crime occurs in the Moss Side area, for example, the police will mobilise a stereotypical image of the suspect as a black person until proven otherwise. This working assumption will be held by all police officers irrespective of their attitudes to black people and in spite of the fact that, statistically, the assumption has only a 30 per cent probability of being true, given that the majority of Moss Side residents happen to be white.

INSTITUTIONALISED RACISM–SEXISM–CLASSISM

What is it that differentiates racist attitudes from institutionalised racism? The difference is that one is conscious and the other is unconscious. However, it does not follow that they are separate; on the contrary, they are articulated. Racist attitudes are tolerated in institutionally racist organisations and institutionally racist organisations encourage the development of racist attitudes. This chapter focuses on a discussion of institutionalised racism instead of the Macpherson-favoured term of institutional racism which Stokely Carmichael and Charles V. Hamilton introduced in their pioneering definition of the term (Carmichael and Hamilton, 1967: 21–7).

The difference between the two terms is evident in the fact that institutional racism has been used by the Inquiry and the academics that submitted evidence to it as a reference to unwitting racism, a term that Lord Scarman preferred to allegations that the police was institutionally racist. Institutionalised racism suggests that the officers who implement it are not necessarily overtly racist but questions the assumption that they are not aware of the inherent racism of institutionalised practices. The difference here is an emphasis on the social construction of social institutions, hence institutionalised racism–sexism–classism as implemented by conscious social actors and not as something simply and exclusively left to the inhuman machinations of institutions.

Robert Miles argues that racism is institutionalised in state policies of immigration when the political discourse is overtly and covertly racist even without politicians arguing openly that immigrants are racially inferior. Apart from a correlation between phenotypic differences and official policies of exclusion from entry, people who had previous right of entry without visas, immigration was institutionally 'racialised' whenever reference was made to immigrants being 'the cause of economic and social problems for our own people' (Miles, 1993: 74).

Miles illustrated this with a detailed analysis of how the Aliens Act 1905 institutionalised anti-Semitism by seeking to exclude Jewish immigrants who had no means of supporting themselves in Britain. Although the Act did not mention Jews by name, the use of economic criteria to exclude poor Jews effectively excluded most of the refugees who could not demonstrate independent means of livelihood while allowing rich Jews (Jewesses were simply reduced to the status of dependants in this articulation of race–gender–class relations) to come with their money. Of course, it can be said that the immigration law today openly targets black immigrants for exclusion and even rich people of African descent have had their application for citizenship refused, in spite of their incredible personal wealth.

Stuart Hall (1979, 1980) warns that we should look beyond individuals and focus on institutionalised ways of doing things. According to Hall, in every society structured in dominance, race–class–gender are articulated or joined together in such a way that you will not understand any of these power relations in isolation from the others. For example, if Stephen Lawrence was a rich black boy, he could have been presented with a personal car on his seventeenth birthday, and hence there would have been no need for him to wait at a lonely bus stop, nor would his parents have been forced to bring him up in the Isle of Dogs. Moreover, if Stephen had been a millionaire white, black or Asian kid, there is no way the police could have started investigating his murder with the routine assumption that he might have been involved in drug gangs.

Secondly, if Stephen had been a young black woman, perhaps the racist thugs would have gang-raped her instead of butchering her on the spot (although being gang-raped is not necessarily better than being murdered – some would say that it is worse than death, perhaps because it could also end in actual murder). What this suggests is that racist-sexist violence is exercised against black men in a way different from how it is practised against black women in some situations. Similarly, if Stephen had been a girl, the police would probably have started looking at the way she was dressed to see if she had precipitated the crime. This is present in attempts to demonise Lawrence's grieving mother by accusing her of cop-bashing when, as a woman, she should stay at home and mourn, while her husband is left to speak to the press in the reasonable way that men are supposed to understand things.

Enough has been said about what the police would have done if
Stephen Lawrence had been a white, middle-class male like his
namesake, the headmaster whose murderers were immediately
apprehended even though they wore masks, perhaps because he was
white and his killer was Chinese. However, the point being made
here is that it is not only racism that is institutionalised in the police
force. What we have is the articulation, disarticulation and rearticulation of racism, sexism and class oppression within institutional
settings. Tony Jefferson (1992) is critical of academics who design
increasingly sophisticated techniques that increasingly fail to detect
'pure' racism. According to Jefferson, this is a case of using an
increasingly fine mesh for sieving flour until the mesh is so fine that
not enough flour comes through to bake anything.

A LETTER FROM HARLEM

In his essay 'Fifth Avenue, Uptown: A Letter from Harlem', James
Baldwin (1961) analysed what institutionalised police racism means
to poor black people in America. Although he did not use the phrase
institutionalised racism, he describes a condition in which black
people are forced to live in housing projects where a minority of the
young are fanatical churchgoers, and many more are 'muslems' who
organise 'buy black' street corner public meetings without admitting
that the big corporations that manufacture most things are owned
by whites. Some stay home and watch television all day except when
they go to the bar or the dole office, others are on drugs or selling it
on their way to jail. Those who avoided 'all these deaths' (of course,
Stephen Lawrence was not the only casualty), according to Baldwin,
are those who get up in the morning and go downtown to meet 'The
Man', the white man. In spite of the insults, cruelty and indifference
that they suffer at work, they keep going to work ritualistically as a
way of instilling some sense of honour in their own children. Baldwin
could have been describing the 'internal colonies' in the cities of
Britain today where black people are dying all these deaths.

Baldwin admits that there are other slums, besides Harlem, where
poor white people are 'fighting for their lives and mainly losing'.
However, he argues that the wretchedness of white people must not
be used to console him for the wretchedness of blacks. Nor is it
satisfactory simply to point out so-and-so exceptional white or black
poor who made it by working hard – Frank Sinatra and Sammy Davis
Junior. He points out that the rise of the few is not proof of equal

opportunities because a few have always risen, even under authoritarian regimes, and some of the few rose simply to join in the
perpetration of violence against the poor masses rather than to help
make the world a better place. Baldwin concludes that:

> The Projects [council estates] in Harlem are hated. They are hated
> almost as much as policemen, and this is saying a great deal. And
> they are hated for the same reason: both reveal, unbearably, the
> attitude of the white world, no matter how many liberal speeches
> are made, no matter how many lofty editorials are written, no
> matter how many civil-rights commissions are set up. (Baldwin,
> 1961: 63)

He adds: 'The people in Harlem know they are living there because
white people do not think that they are good enough to live
anywhere else.' He illustrates this by stating:

> the only way to police a ghetto is to be oppressive. None of the
> Police Commissioner's men, with the best will in the world, have
> any means of understanding the lives led by those they swagger
> about in twos and threes controlling. Their very presence is an
> insult, and it would be, even if they spent their entire day feeding
> gumdrops to children. They represent the force of the white world,
> and that world's real intentions are, simply, for that world's
> criminal profit and ease, to keep the black man controlled up here,
> in his place. The badge, the gun in the holster, and the swinging
> club make vivid what will happen should his rebellion become
> overt. Rare, indeed, is the Harlem citizen, from the most
> circumspect church member to the most shiftless adolescent, who
> does not have a long tale to tell of police incompetence, injustice,
> or brutality. (Baldwin, 1961: 63)

Baldwin concludes that it is difficult to blame the fact that the
police represent institutionalised white power on the individual
police officer who could be 'blank, good-natured, thoughtless, and
insuperably innocent'. The individual officer could also believe in
good intentions and might be surprised and offended at any
suggestions that he is individually racist. He may never have done
anything for which he deserves to be hated, 'and yet he is facing
daily and nightly, people who would gladly see him dead, and he

knows it' (1961: 63). Baldwin predicts the course of institutional racism by observing that the police officer

> can retreat from his uneasiness in only one direction: into a callousness which very shortly becomes second nature. He becomes more callous, the population becomes more hostile, the situation grows more tense, and the police force is increased. One day, to everyone's astonishment, someone drops a match in the powder keg and everything blows up. Before the dust has settled or the blood congealed, editorials, speeches, and civil-rights commissions are loud in the land, demanding to know what happened. (Baldwin, 1961: 64)

Compare this with the assertion by David Smith (1994) that cases like that of Rodney King reveal a vicious cycle in which the police over-react to black offending behaviour, leading to black anger and riots against the impunity of the officers in the face of the law, leading to more police response and the arrest of more black offenders. As I have argued elsewhere (Agozino, 1997a), Rodney King did not commit any offence and he was not charged with any, just as neither the West African immigrant fatally shot 40 times in New York by white police officers nor Stephen Lawrence committed any offence. The police officers claimed that Rodney resisted arrest for suspected speeding under the influence of drugs. Baldwin is pointing out above that it is not black offending that initiates institutionalised racism but that the latter calls for black resistance that is frequently criminalised.

However, as in the case of Rodney King, the commentary on Lawrence focused exclusively on institutionalised racism without acknowledging the role that gender played in the institutionalised racism that he suffered and how such racism was equally disarticulated and re-articulated by his subordinate class relations. Also as in the case of Rodney, most of the people who protested against institutionalised racism in Stephen's case did so peacefully, especially when they were middle class in appearance, clad in smart suits like the militant black Muslims who protested at the public inquiry against what seemed like the turning of the case into a media event, even for the suspected killers. We need to go beyond the police and see how institutionalised racism–sexism–classism affected the administration of other criminal justice agencies and other institutional services in the general society over the past 50 years.

WINDRUSH: A LAW AND SOCIAL JUSTICE WORKSHOP

As part of the commemoration of the 50th anniversary of the historic voyage of Caribbean workers to Britain on the *Empire Windrush*, a conference on the black experience in Britain was organised in Liverpool in 1998. The conference was structured into five sub-workshops on different themes following a plenary. The workshop on 'Law and Social Justice' was led by a leader of the Black Probation Officers Association, who made a very impressive presentation that anticipated almost all the issues raised by the workshop participants. A reading of the workshop proceedings will show that they are relevant to the issue of race–class–gender institutionalisation.

We started the workshop by going round the table to introduce ourselves. The workshop leader was a member of the Black Probation Officers Association; I came to facilitate the workshop from a criminal justice lecturing background; there were two police officers, two community education activists, one retired community activist and two victim support workers in the workshop.

The leader started with a presentation of statistics on the representation of black (meaning all non-white) people among criminal justice personnel between 1992 and 1998. For example, the proportion of black staff in the judiciary rose from 0.9 per cent in 1992 to 1.3 per cent in 1998. Magistrates' courts had 3.9 per cent black people among their staff and 1.92 per cent black magistrates in 1992. Black workers in the Crown Prosecution Service rose from 5.9 per cent in 1991 to 7.5 per cent. Black police officers made up 1.06 per cent of all officers and this rose to 1.75 per cent out of a total of 125,000 officers in 1998. The Prison Service increased the proportion of black staff from 1.9 per cent to 2.6 per cent but the highest increase of black workers was among probation staff who rose from 2.6 per cent to 7.6 per cent. Solicitors rose from 1.3 per cent to 4 per cent and barristers from 5.3 per cent to 6 per cent.

The speaker, who was of Asian descent, was obviously using 'Black' as a political category meaning all non-whites. The 1991 Census of the UK reported that the 49,890,277 population of England and Wales was made up of 94.1 per cent White, 1.0 per cent Black Caribbean, 0.4 per cent Black African and 0.4 per cent Black Other (Agozino, 1997a: 149), suggesting that there are more people of Asian descent in England than people of African descent.

After the presentation of these figures, we asked the leader to pause while the participants reflected on the figures. Two important comments emerged at this stage. Is there any relationship between unionisation or the formation of an association and the increase in black representation among the workforce? It seemed that black workers were better represented in the Probation Service, Crown Prosecution Service, solicitors and barristers where there are active black organisations campaigning against marginalisation, exclusion and discrimination within the professions. The relevant organisations here are the Society of Black Lawyers and the Association of Black Probation Officers. If this is the case, then the formation of a Black Police Officers Association can be expected to lead to increasing recruitment of black officers and an Association of Black Magistrates or Association of Black Criminologists could be expected to do the same. However, such a strategy might be ineffective in those areas where the number of black officers is too small to sustain a black association, among judges for instance.

In answer to this, the probation officer clarified that the Association of Black Probation Officers started just like that. It was two or three probation officers meeting up in Birmingham in the 1980s for a drink who found that they had similar problems and needs in their profession and decided to set up an association to address such issues and provide mutual support for one another. In other words, even two people can start an association and go on to mobilise or recruit new members like any other organisation. This is probably why many of the black associations adopt a political definition of blackness that is more inclusive of most minority ethnic groups instead of focusing only on people of African descent.

The more serious question was whether the increase in the numbers of black people has had any impact on the number of black people who are processed through the criminal justice system. If discriminatory practices contribute to the over-representation of black defendants and prisoners in the criminal justice system, is it not proper to expect that increasing the number of black officers would lead to decreasing discrimination and thereby decreasing over-representation? Are we suggesting that even black officers are racist because the more they are hired, the more black people end up in jail, or is it a case of setting a thief to catch a thief? This question is important given the suggestion that the Metropolitan Police are planning to use black officers as undercover agents to expose racist colleagues. When Tom clicked his magic button, the statistics stared us in the face. There seemed to be a positive correlation between the increase in black officers and the increase in black prisoners! The more black officers you have, the more black prisoners, or vice versa! At this stage, due to limited time, we asked the participants to respond in turn to the presentation.

The retired community activist saw the figures in terms of a personal challenge. She wondered if she should come out of retirement to try to do something about the increasing proportion of black people being sent to prison. In a way, she saw it as a personal failure that her years of campaigning for social justice in the community had done nothing to reduce the over-representation of black people in prison service establishments.

The victim support activists suggested that the increasing over-representation of black people in prisons indicates increasing racism among criminal justice officials. When asked to be more specific, they revealed that children as young as eight already know that the police are very racist, especially in Granby Toxteth, where they are always stopping black drivers and threatening to arrest them if children in their car are not wearing seat belts.

At this point, the police officers present said that they were in a no-win situation. According to them, when they stop white drivers in other areas and ask them to put seat belts on their children, they are told that they could never do the same in Granby. In other words, some sections of the white population suspect that the police favour black residents, while sections of the black population are sure that the police favour the whites. The police themselves seem convinced that they were just doing their jobs as fairly as they could.

The black youth education activists pointed out that the debates should not be made too narrow in terms of law-and-order issues only. They suggested that the issue of racism is a broad social justice one and not a narrow issue of law and order. For example, black children are still more likely to be excluded from school for various reasons and so more provisions and more efforts should be geared towards educating those black children who are being marginalised even before they are criminalised. Indirectly, this is suggesting that the children should be educated about road safety, personal responsibility and professional orientation whether or not this is what the police want.

In the end, the workshop pointed out that it is not the fault of black officials that black people are over-represented in prisons. It was argued that it would be wrong to say that it is the responsibility of black officials to prevent discrimination in the system and so if discrimination persists, then black officials are to blame. On the contrary, the black staff organisations were more concerned about discrimination against their own members within the professions and if they had not succeeded in preventing this completely, it was inappropriate to expect that their still limited presence would end all discrimination in the criminal justice system.

This point clearly suggests that the institutionalisation of discrimination is not always direct in terms of prejudice, but is also indirect in terms of institutionalised practices that routinely marginalise the relatively powerless. In other words, efforts to increase the numbers of black professionals in the criminal justice system must continue in spite of the increasing number of black prisoners simply because a decrease in the number of black professionals in the system cannot make the matter better but worse. It is not the increased number of black officials that leads to increased numbers of black prisoners but the increased number of black prisoners is what makes increased numbers of black officials necessary. Given the over-representation of black people in the penal system, a decrease or the elimination of black staff from the system is clearly not an option and so the struggle to increase the black presence among the staff must be seen as part of the struggle against direct and indirect discrimination in the system. The implicit recommendation from the workshop is that all black professionals should consider forming associations to address the problem of the under-representation of black people in their fields.

These observations by some of the workshop participants warn that police officers should stop complaining that they are not individually racist whenever the problem of institutionalised racism is mentioned. Even an officer who is not racist could be implementing institutionalised racism. For example, many black officers in the different criminal justice agencies would swear that they are not racist and that they themselves suffer from racism within their own establishments. However, such black officers are less likely to deny the existence of institutionalised racism, sexism and poverty as part of the problems facing black people in the criminal justice system. This was probably why the Chairman of the Stephen Lawrence public inquiry called on the police to stop denying the existence of institutionalised racism and start looking for ways of tackling it.

However, as Sivanandan (1990) points out, it is possible for some opportunistic black officials, consultants and researchers of the criminal justice system to see themselves as privileged and they might try to prove that they attained their positions on merit alone by denying that there is any racism in the criminal justice system. Such 'respected' black professionals are often used to oppose any demands for anti-racism awareness training in the criminal justice system given that the top officials prefer training in multiculturalism and diversity as ways to escape having to confront racism, sexism and class exploitation in the existing institutions of criminal justice.

In his speech to a conference evaluating progress in anti-racism since the Macpherson Report, Sivanandan argued that it is wrong to look at the report for the solution to the problem. What the report does is simply acknowledge that black struggles have taught the British state a lesson by making the state admit for the first time the institutionalisation of racism. Sivanandan points out that when it comes to the implementation of the recommendations in the report, it can be expected that the state will water them down by, for example, promising to extend the Race Relations Act to the police who were previously exempt, but the extension will not include instances of institutionalised racism; only direct racism by individual police officers will be prevented by the extended powers, as outlined in the Queens Speech of January 2000. Sivanandan concludes that it is up to black people and their supporters, especially in non-governmental organisations, to continue the struggle to teach the British state lessons in democracy and common decency because the struggle against institutionalised racism goes beyond the police. As he put it:

> The fight against institutional racism is a fight against state racism – against asylum laws, against deportations, against stop and search, against deaths in custody, against school exclusions, against miscarriages of justice. Which, in turn, calls into question the larger issues of accountability, freedom of information and judicial impartiality that constitute the fundaments of democracy. In the final analysis, institutional racism is the litmus test of a society's democracy. (Sivanandan, 2000)

CONCLUSION

> Racism, the word nobody likes. Whites who don't want to confront racism and who don't name themselves white recoil in horror from it, shun it like the plague. To mention the word in their company disrupts their comfortable complacency. To call a text or methodology under discussion in a classroom ... 'racist',

or to call a white person [to order] on her or his racism, is to let loose a stink bomb. Like a tenacious weed, racism [creeps] up everywhere – it has a stranglehold on everyone. It is cultivated and produced in families, churches, temples and state institutions. (quoted in Pfohl, 1994)

This chapter ends by echoing the call by Stephen Pfhol for scholars who are critical of racism to develop an analysis of the theoretical and 'methodological significance of race as a social construct'. He proposes that this could be done through the twin strategies of opposing 'the continuing violence of racism' and opening the ears of scholars to cultural traditions that have been silenced for a long time by Eurocentric perspectives on world history.

Given the fact that white supremacist views have been well established in religious, scientific knowledge and political practice, the question is no longer whether institutionalised racism exists but what forms it takes and how to combat it. In spite of the severe criticism in sociology regarding racist eugenic theories of race and crime, established criminologists still come up with mythical evidence of the inherent blackness of certain kinds of criminality (Gilroy, 1987b). Other social scientists minimise the significance of race by over-emphasising the significance of class and completely ignoring gender. Pfhol suggests that we should try to understand that (1) racial formations are socially constructed for the purpose of social control, (2) theory can play a role against racist violence, (3) the racialised standpoint of white culture should be studied, and (4) non-racialised cultural difference must be affirmed given the reality of multiculturalism.

This chapter has demonstrated that the debate around institutionalised racism should not proceed without realising how racism is articulated, disarticulated and rearticulated with sexism and classism. Furthermore, the chapter has argued that any debate on institutionalisation should be made sensitive to the rich sociological literature on the meaning of institutionalisation. Once this sociological meaning is grasped, scholars, activists and policy-makers would avoid the antiquated debate as to whether racism–sexism–classism is an institutionalised practice. Rather, we would all be searching for every manifestation of such institutionalisation and searching for feasible solutions through the increased democratisation of civil society.

The chapter has demonstrated that no single theoretical perspective offers all the answers to the question of form and the solution to institutionalised injustice. Rather, some of the manifestations are better understood through some theoretical perspectives while other perspectives offer better explanations of other manifestations or what could be considered the most efficacious solutions. I have not dwelt on what those solutions are except by indicating that social theory should be used to assist the search for solutions by analysing the practical struggles of the people in their effort to live in a more just and democratic society. Others may disagree with my characterisation of certain perspectives but no one can question my guiding assumption that theory should be taken seriously in the practical struggle to end racism–sexism–classism.

13. Criminal Records: The Toughest, the Police and the Thieves: The Policing of Peter Tosh and Popular Culture

This chapter attempts a critical reading of *Stepping Razor/Red X*, the biopic of Peter Tosh, and emerges with a broad view of policing as a process that goes beyond the police force to encompass other hegemonic processes of gatekeeping which result in the increasing marginalisation of oppositional thought and transgressive cultural practice. However, policing is also emphatically analysed in this chapter as more than a metaphor for exclusion, as a unique institutional arrangement that focuses on law and order though not necessarily on the 'equal rights and justice' that Peter Tosh tirelessly demanded in his songs. The chapter will show that the tragic-heroic cultural politics of Peter Tosh was typical of the daily experiences of the 'suffarahs' who ended up fearing and fighting the police sometimes more than they feared or fought known thieves in an authoritarian, neocolonial, white supremacist, imperialist political economy. This chapter is therefore not about the metaphysics of who killed Peter Tosh, given that the killers allegedly told the man that they had come to kill him, they left the house without stealing anything, the convict – whose death sentence has been upheld by the Privy Council – had an allibi and was dependent on Tosh for his livelihood (thereby raising doubts about a motive for the killing) and given that he gave himself up to a human rights organisation when he learnt that he was implicated in the killing. The chapter is not about the logic of the trial court which acquitted the company driver who admitted that a colleague asked him to drive the alleged 'thieves' to the scene of the crime in a company car and later drove them to safety without identifying the three killers (White, 1991). The policing of Tosh and the policing of Rasta culture generally offer a deep and challenging meaning to the term 'criminal records' especially because much of the oppressive policing Tosh and others experienced arose from their insurrectional lyrics. This conclusion will serve to clarify a neglected theoretical issue of what lies on the opposite side of the so-called 'dark figures' of crime. The chapter suggests that on the other side of the coin lie 'dazzling figures' that could be used to interrogate many of the truth-claims that animate the oppressive-repressive policing of popular cultures and counter-hegemonic cultural activism. Finally, the chapter distinguishes between policing against and policing for popular culture or between protective and repressive policing of popular culture, in order to show that policing is more than a simple threat to popular culture. Policing or self-policing is also a resource or service that is taken seriously by popular culture and the experience of Peter Tosh makes this very clear to sceptical cultural activists.

'EVERYONE IS TALKING ABOUT CRIME, CRIME, TELL ME WHO ARE THE CRIMINALS' – TOSH

The critique of criminal records or official crime figures is too well known to receive another take in this chapter. Those who are still interested in the old realism of the labelling perspective on how little the police know, how big the dark figures are and how to study the real impacts of deviant labels should read Pfohl (1994) for a sympathetic account and Sumner (1994) for an obituary of the perspectives on deviance.

The goal of this chapter is to chart the uncharted by doubting the relatively undoubted. The very meaning of criminal records seems to be unproblematically taken for granted, especially when applied to individuals who could then be said to have criminal careers, as Carlen (1992) does with a claim to realism. If someone stole a packet of biscuits at the age of 14 and is involved in a drunken fight at the age of 25, longitudinal studies will have no hesitation in identifying that individual as someone with a criminal career. I am sure that you have heard the one about the farmer who claims to have saved a man but was not called a life-saver, who told many jokes but was not called a joker and who was, to his surprise, branded a sheep-shagger for shagging one sheep. The farmer could even argue that he never shagged any sheep, that he was simply shearing the sheep when the informer saw him and wrongly concluded that he was shagging. Perhaps he would not object if people called him sheep-shearer because that is something he has been doing on a regular basis since he started farming sheep.

This indicates that doubts about the meaning of 'criminal records' are very old. Such doubts suggest that the error in criminal records is the error of omission or the error of the tip of the iceberg (as if the tip of the iceberg is made up of only ice and not also of sand, grass and debris). Who knows how many sheep the sheep-shagger shagged in secret before being caught? Who knows how many more packets of sweets were nicked on the day that the unlucky little girl was nicked? Who knows the danger concealed by the dark figures of the unknown? All shades of realism have tried to bring enlightenment to the incomprehensible Other through victim surveys, self-reported criminality and local crime surveys. The conclusion of the realists is not hard to guess: lo and behold, crime is real and not merely a moral panic invented by the gutter press for quick profits (see Matthews and Young, 1992). Smart (1990) has questioned the anti-positivism positivism and empiricism of the left realists and opted for a post-structuralist scepticism about the disguise of knowledge – power relations as the search for purer and purer truth. Cain (1995) defends what she calls the realist epistemology (note that she omitted the left realist adjective from her notion of realism) and maintains that realism does not commit anyone to the universalism of positivistic claims to objectivity.

This chapter contends that what is relatively neglected in the realist debates is the other side of the coin of dark figures (Agozino, 2002). The chapter is not asking whether dark figures (like dark holes) exist, but seeks to show that darkness follows enlightenment, and vice versa. The suggestion here is that the errors in criminal records are not only those of exclusion and incompleteness but of inclusion and superfluity. It is no longer a problem of darkness but of excessive enlightenment also. Wherever there are dark figures, we must expect to find dazzling figures in accordance with the amplification of deviance thesis of Cohen (1972) and Hall et al. (1978) and the hyperrealism thesis of the simulacrum by Baudrillard (1996). The reason why prisons are full of poor people is not simply because poverty causes crime; who knows how many more poor desperadoes are out there trying to survive as best as they can? Another reason that cannot be dismissed as loony left idealism is that the poor lack the resources to defend themselves effectively even when falsely charged with a crime that they did not commit. Plea bargaining means that many poor defendants may be coerced into a guilty plea on the vague promise of mitigation. Such cases and the more spectacular cases of the miscarriage of justice constitute what this chapter refers to as dazzling crime figures, or what has been called elsewhere victimisation as mere punishment (Agozino, 1991, 1995, 1996, 1997a, 2002).

'I AM WANTED DRED AND ALIVE, NO PLACE TO HIDE' – TOSH

The metaphor of dazzling criminal records can be explored in greater detail by applying it to the autobiographical tape-recordings that formed the basis of the feature film, *Red X* (a mark that Tosh saw regularly on his name in police files). His criminal records went beyond being busted and nearly being beaten to death by the police for possession of just one spliff and include his anti-imperialist, anti-racist and anti-'downpressor' (though not always anti-sexist) lyrics. His records were often banned from the public radio, only to be selling like hot cakes on the streets. Maureen Cain (1995) warns against both an instrumentalist reading of the policing of popular culture and the postmodernist preoccupation with discourse analysis. According to her, only a realist approach will show that there is power in the drums of the carnival and there is knowledge in the 'wining' of the waist by calypso dancers. It is this inherent knowledge-power content of culture that makes it a target of repression by a political authority that sees it as something out of the unknown dark frontier, as the Other. She did not extend her examples to reggae music, perhaps because she focused on Trinidad and Tobago, where calypso is hegemonic, rather than on Jamaica, the birthplace of reggae. However, she notes in her preliminary survey of the literature that there are richer examples from Jamaica but her focus is Trinidad and Tobago.

If Cain had extended her focus to Rastafari, as Campbell (1985) authoritatively did, she would have had no doubt that this form of political culture is directly instrumentalist in the sense of being insurrectional. This is not a case of 'coolies' smoking the kali weed and dancing themselves into a frenzy that frightened the police into opening fire, or the case of shame-faced black bourgeoisie clamouring for a ban on the 'wining' of the waist by provocatively dressed young black women.

This is the type of music that wails 'I'm not gonna give it up', 'Fight Apartheid', 'I am Wanted Dred and Alive', 'Equal Rights and Justice' or 'Legalize It'. In an interview with Roberto (quoted by White, 1987), Tosh defined reggae music as reflecting the articulation of race and class consciousness which Campbell (1985) identified as a feature of black political awareness. According to Tosh, reggae is a king of kings music played by the kings inspired to play this music. It is a music for the poor. It's an educational musical entertainment where people can learn and dance at the same time. It's the only music that has that potential. It's the music of the Rastaman's inspiration, and it's origination is Africa and in this time Jamaica. (quoted in White, 1987)

Of course, there is 'Word Sound and Power' (The name of Tosh's band) in the music, but to imply that the knowledge-power constitution of this popular culture is the reason for its repression, as Cain seems to suggest, would appear to be a case of blaming the victim. A realist epistemology cannot escape admitting that it is the repression of this popular culture that helped to shape its militancy and to necessitate its insurrectional orientation. This chapter is not offering an instrumentalist perspective as being more real than a realist perspective, but simply pointing out that Peter Tosh was not just a singer; he saw himself as an instrumentalist in three senses that he considered to be non-criminal:

1. As an instrument of Jah for the fight against vampires.
2. As an internationalist activist against ignorance, injustice and disease.
3. As an instrumentalist who saw his music as a weapon for fighting the above battles in the interest of truth and justice.

This is why Tosh titled the first tune that he ever recorded 'I'm the Toughest' – 'I can do what you can do, you never try to do what I do, I'm the toughest.' This defiant chant was directed not only against those who are visibly bearing the mark of the beast (police officers, according to Tosh), but also against the exploitative music industry bosses whom he tirelessly fought in court for control over his own talents.

Regarding one of his many experiences of police brutality, Tosh narrated to Timothy White (1987) what happened while he was composing 'The Mark of the Beast' – a song that was released as a single in Jamaica but has been tactically excluded from all of Tosh's albums for the global market ever since:

I was not only arrested! I was *to-tal-ly brutalized!* I was taken to Kingston Public Hospital on North Street under police guard two or three years or so ago for smoking herb. And I was totally brutalized! ... I was at me 'ouse on Solitaire Road, I was there, smokin' a spliff while a dance was 'appening outside, and I was writing, making a tune called 'The Mark of the Beast'. There was a party outside in the same yard. I was singing the words when in comes the police – the Beast – to manifest itself. See, the words took on a phy-si-cal self /So they jus' used the party as an alibi to enter my 'ouse, and dey beat me up. I got seven stitches 'ere [Pointing to his forehead], and they get my ribs dislocated. And dey mash up my abdomen with the butt of a riffle. I was taken to de hospital hand-cuffed as a fuckin' criminal. And I had to lie down on the floor and beg a nurse to come attend to me! Just for smoking herb. That is why Iman have to stand up predominantly and say, 'Legalize it!' /I'm not a criminal! And the world know dat! I sing music to my people, yet I suffer many police brutalities and harassments. I don't do nothing, subversion to no government. The only thing I do is smoke 'erb and I will smoke 'erb in Buckingham Palace or the White House!'

Believers in the validity of the term criminal records will say that the above statement supports their claim. They will point out that Tosh was not brutalised for playing criminal records (musically) but for breaking the law against the use of narcotic drugs, even though Tosh alleged that the party was the 'alibi' for the police to enter his house and beat him to the point of death, suggesting that the music at the party was Rasta music for Rasta people in an upper-middle-class area of Kingston, where the neighbours even complained about the red-gold-and-green painting of his house.

Criminal records believers could grant that the police used excessive force which they probably use on a daily basis when dealing with the poor generally. However, if Tosh had committed class suicide by joining the middle class rather than retaining his friends and associates from the ghetto in spite of his success, it is very unlikely that the police would have brutalised him in the way that they did even if he had smoked a million spliffs in his own house. If his music is of the rock and roll variety, that is apolitical love songs, it would have been even more unlikely that the police would have targeted him as a suspect in the first place.

The point Tosh was making was that even though he smoked herbs, he should not be considered a criminal because he believes that marijuana should be legalised, if only for its many proven medicinal uses. In other words, the musician refused to accept some of the categories of crime officially defined by the state and also advocated for greater consistency in the handling of the education of the youth who are taught that the cow jumped over the moon and that pirates were very brave men. He made this point very poignantly at the Peace Concert (One Love Concert) where he lectured the audience of leading politicians and the youth gangs that organised the event about the deadly implications of peace without justice in an 'imperialistic shituation'. Two days after the event, Tosh was nearly beaten to death again by the police, allegedly for smoking herb.

'GET UP STAND UP, STAND UP FOR YOUR RIGHTS' – TOSH AND MARLEY

Iyorchia Ayu (1986) has argued that the dehumanising conditions of capitalist production relations are antagonistic to oppositional art which, according to him, should be regarded as an essential element in any society experiencing capitalist dehumanisation. This type of reading could be said to be an example of what Cain (1995) rejected as a simple 'instrumental' reading of the policing of popular culture. Ayu (1986: 6) argues that

> when art runs counter to the interest of the dominant class in society, the attitude of that class to art changes. In capitalist society, the bourgeois state becomes hostile to art that seeks to humanize its alienating conditions of existence. In advanced capitalist states, however, subtle devices are employed to incorporate oppositional art. But in dependent capitalist states direct repression seems to prevail.

This was the case in Chile, as it was in Nigeria, South Africa and the Caribbean. The point Cain makes by rejecting an instrumentalist reading in preference for a realist alternative is that it would be misleading to say that any art is being repressed simply because it is oppositional, or even that it is simply oppositional in an instrumentalist sense. This does not mean that an instrumentalist reading is wrong but that a realist reading would show how the repression of oppositional art is only a part of the total repression of 'the Other'. It could even be argued that the instrumentalist reading presumes a possible ending of oppositional art when the goal of that instrument has been achieved. However, this interpretation could be replied to by the instrumentalist who could insist that liberation should not lead to an ending of open criticism, self-criticism and oppositional arts. This was the view of many South African cultural activists who argued that peace and reconciliation should not be seen as a gag on oppositional art. The instrumentalist could go further and charge that any attempt to deradicalise art in dehumanised societies in the name of realist epistemology is suspicious. This is because the realist assumes that instrumentalism is any less realistic than realism. Whose reality is it anyway? The reality of scholars or the reality of the subjects of scholarship who cannot be accused of lacking in realism and who only regret that they are not instrumentalist enough in their cultural practice?

The instrumentalist reading insists that there is no non-instrumentalist reading or that all realistic epistemologies are instrumentalist in themselves. The instrumentalist does not claim that all art is oppositional nor that only oppositional art is instrumentalist. In other words, the 'deodorised dog shit' of Chinua Achebe – art for art's sake – would be seen as a nonentity by the instrumentalist. The realist claims to have discovered that there is power and knowledge in the drum beats but Peter Tosh goes beyond to ask 'Mama, what we gonna do?' with the power and knowledge that we have. That is an instrumentalist question and it is also far from being unrealistic in the 'shituation' brought about by the 'shitstem' of imperialism.

Peter Tosh was not alone in bringing out what a Rasta elder in *Red X* described as the double standards in society. Victor Jara faced similar brutalisation for his oppositional lyrics, which he saw as his 'weapon'. Jara's *El soldado* (The Soldier) is authoritative morally rather than being angrily confrontational:

> Soldier don't shoot me, don't shoot me soldier:
> Who pinned those medals on your chest?
> How many lives did they cost?
> I know that your hand is trembling, don't kill me,
> I am your brother.
>
> (Quoted in Ayu, 1986: 40)

Jara was butchered 'live' in a national stadium full of adoring fans who probably wondered as Bob Marley did, 'How long shall they kill our prophets while we stand aside and look?' Peter Tosh reasons that if the pirates are the ones given medals, and if education is for domestication rather than liberation, then you can't blame the youths of today for acting like gangsters:

> You teach the youth about Christopher Columbus
> and you said he was a very great man
> you teach the youth about Marco Polo
> and you said he was a very great man
> you teach the youth about the Pirate Hawkins
> and you said he was a very great man
> you teach the youth about Pirate Morgan
> and you said he was a very great man ...
> All these great men were doing
> robbing, raping kidnapping and killing
> so-called great men were doing
> robbing, raping, kidnapping and killing.
>
> (Tosh 1977)

According to Ayu, the conditions under which these popular artists were working were similar to those of Fela Anikolapo Kuti in Nigeria. He analysed the aesthetic and the political in Fela's music and came to the conclusion that it remains a powerful instrument for advancing the resistance of Nigerians against neocolonial fascism. Fela was repeatedly brutalised like many ordinary Nigerians, but maintained his reputation as a social critic. However, Ayu is critical of Fela for his sexist earlier songs which projected a patriarchal authority as traditionally African (hear his 'Lady' and his statement in 'Shakara' that when a woman says no to a man she actually means yes (see Nzegwu, 2000)). The irony is that ten years after 'yabbing' (Fela's term for critique) Fela for his 'Lady', Ayu blindly served the most brutal dictatorship (under General Abacha) in Nigerian history as a minister of education who collaborated in the repression of freedom of expression by the organised unions of university students and staff (Agozino and Idem, 2001).

Peter Tosh also sang in his early Wailer days that 'anywhere you go, woman is the source of all evil' – probably reflecting the Eve syndrome that was part of his strict Christian upbringing. He later sang songs that are no less abusive of a (certain) woman whom he repeatedly reminded that she was only 'a brand new second hand' no one wanted. Much later in his career, Tosh saw the light and embraced feminism as the most potent charm against the forces of evil. He claimed that he was conscious of being too paralysed to move in his bed due to a spiritual attack. He cast off the spell only at the point of death because he uttered a word that is almost completely censored by decent Jamaicans.

That word is 'bumboclaat' and as soon as he uttered it, according to him, every spell was released. He concluded that this was probably why the modern-day vampires rule out the use of the spell-breaking word from everyday usage. Bumboclaat, rassclaat, bloodclaat, pussyclaat are all patois words for the sanitary towel (bum cloth, arse cloth, blood cloth, pussy cloth). They are dreaded curses, more dreaded than the 'F' word in the West. Tosh went out of his way to sing a song praising bumboclaat for helping him to chase away the vampires. He also asked an interviewer jokingly, 'what about women's liberation? Women are running everything anyway' (Sheridan, 1987). He went on to sing his acclaimed praise of 'Mama Africa'. He was said to be dominated by his common law wife, Marlene Brown, whom his friends suspected of being a practising witch, or Obeah. Peter trusted her, but it is reported that those who shot him dead claimed that she (Eve) was the cause of all the troubles.

This remarkable transformation mirrors what Teresa Turner (1994) identified as the 'new Rastafari' that shuns the chauvinist treatment of Rasta women by old Rastafari which Campbell (1987) criticised, but which Turner missed when she accused Campbell of being silent on this issue. Turner argued in line with C.L.R. James that the new Rastafari reflects the new society which is emergent and that the black feminist movement has matured to help shape a new Rasta movement that will be anti-sexist and anti-class exploitation.

CONCLUSION: GROUNDINGS

A million men have marched on Washington to bring home the message that perhaps Peter Tosh was not realistic enough when he said that 'you can't blame the youth'. When he wondered why everyone is talking about crime, crime, he should not have said that he really could not see the (real) criminals – even if he meant the powerful criminals. Perhaps his ganja activism was a bit over the top given that many Jamaicans smoke it without making a big fuss. Many others campaigned through reggae music for the legalisation of the herb, but it was not a key issue in their politics.

Bob Marley, for instance, would defiantly state that he 'wanna have kaya now' with complete disregard of the criminalisation, and when a sheriff calls round fictitiously to tell him to kill his seeds before they grow, he shoots him down in self-defence and confesses to the crime. This is a brave act which Eric Clapton copied without facing the hostility that Marley and the Wailers had to endure from the police. However, Marley was never arrested by the police for ganja or beaten up for it, even though he survived an assassin's bullet. Tosh made it clear that he was politicising the personal when he called for the legalisation of marijuana and his call has resonated among other artists and even among top government officials from around the world.

Oppositional artists should not oppose only the causes of 'raping, robbing, kidnapping, and killing'. Such acts should be condemned and prevented through political education of the sort that Rodney (1969) tried in his *Groundings with my Brothers*. Linton Kwesi Johnson makes a similar pedagogical distinction between a just war when the people fight the oppressors and a war of madness in which the people fight one another. Similarly, bell hooks (1994) contends that white supremacists and sexist imperialism should take the rap for sexist gangsta rap (and by extension, misogynist strands of ragga and jungle music) because imperialism glorifies hegemonic violence against marginalised people. The point made by left realists that we should take crime seriously at the working-class level is valid because it is always the poor and their prophets who are raped, killed, kidnapped and robbed the most (Matthews and Young, 1992). However, taking crime seriously at this level does not imply the left realist silence on crimes of the powerful that Peter Tosh, Bob Marley, Walter Rodney, bell hooks and many others have opposed even more fiercely than they have condemned the 'phoney' gangsterism of certain forms of black popular culture expression while pushing for an end to imperialism, sexism, racism and other forms of oppression.

The popular oppositional Jamaican poet, Michael Smith, for instance, was stoned to death at a place called Stonehill. As Mickey himself would say, 'Me cyaant believe it' that anyone would suggest that only the imperialist powers or the politicians are to blame for these savage killings by their hired mobs. The mobs should also be blamed, even when they are in uniform as in Jara's *The Soldier*. Such a deep understanding can come about only if we learn the humility of Walter Rodney, who took the risk of sitting on the bare ground (grounding) with the Rasta brethren of Jamaica to learn/teach with them about the shituation of African people everywhere in the world.

The lesson that we black intellectuals and all intellectuals can learn from Rodney and Rastafari intellectuals like Bob Marley and Peter

Tosh is the extent to which they struggled to control their own work; *Groundings with my Brothers* was published by a collective press (Bogle L'Ouverture) which was set up by Rodney (1969) and his comrades for this purpose. Everything Marley published in his later years was published by Bob Marley Music Ltd and Peter Tosh published his work through his own label, Intel Diplo (or Intelligent Diplomat of Jah).

When Peter Tosh died, it was rumoured that he was about to set up a Rasta Radio station for broadcasting black consciousness music and teachings. The radio DJ who was shot along with him, 'Free I', was said to have been a joint applicant for the licence. The lesson here is that we should try to publish our own work, especially if commercial publishers are unwilling to do so. It is painful to read tales of rejection by such established black intellectuals as bell hooks (1994). Taking the initiative would not necessarily be self-publication if it is not an individual effort and if it is conceived as a project that should go beyond the owners to seek and publish the work of other struggling writers or artists. This is being done today by many organisations that are media-marginalised. Perhaps such efforts should become more co-ordinated and resources should be pooled for a wider reach.

The final lesson is that policing must not be left to the police alone, especially when the security of someone like Tosh is at stake. He had over a dozen guard dogs but not a single security guard. Anything could still happen to a self-proclaimed 'rebel' even if he engaged a dozen security guards, but Tosh had none even though he gave money regularly to 'friends' and hangers-on who owed him no obligation as employees would. Andrew Tosh, Peter's son, understands this when he claims that he too is watching his back and that his friends are also looking out for him (Snowden, 1988).

The policing of popular culture goes beyond oppositional policing to incorporational policing. This is most evident at major concerts where private and public policing could work together to ensure a peaceful event. In their private lives, top performers in the West are protected by professional body guards. Peter Tosh had nothing to fear from poor robbers, but he frequently expressed his fear that the police were out to get him. This is confirmed by a friend of his who claimed in *Stepping Razor* that he had heard many officers state openly that they would like to 'take him out'. The money that Tosh spent on feeding 15 huge dogs (all but two of which were attack-trained; ICA, 1988) could have been added to the handouts to a few friends who should have been 'promoted' to be in charge of his security arrangements.

However, artists in the Third World rarely earn enough to enable them to afford the elaborate security of western pop stars who have little to fear from the police and who seem more scared of their fans, quite unlike Rasta artists who preach 'one love and unity' to the 'brethren' and 'sistren'. According to the ICA report compiled by Joe Borzeki, a business associate of Tosh, the day before Tosh was assassinated, his neighbours complained to the police that his dogs were tearing up their flowerbed and the authorities asked him to secure the animals. Tosh complied, tying up the 13 attack-trained dogs and leaving only the two tame ones to guard him the next day, 11 September 1987, the Maskaram, or the Ethiopian Orthodox New Year, when he was wasted.

The view that oppositional thinkers and activists should take security and surveillance seriously has been strongly advocated by Gill (1996: 189–90). According to him,

> it is important not to succumb to 'postmodern paranoia' regarding the malign aspects of surveillance, whether the chosen metaphor is Orwell's *1984* or Huxley's *Brave New World*. It is clear that the growth of surveillance cannot be reversed, not least because so many are convinced of its benign impact, for example, in providing safer opportunities for consumption and leisure. Rather, the case must be made for some greater 'specificity' of the knowledges sought by otherwise excessive surveillance schemes, more robust regulatory and inspections systems, and, as here, appropriate organisational changes aimed at minimising the 'gaze' of those surveillance apparatuses seen as most malign to the democratic political process.

This powerful argument was directed mainly at the policy-makers for the new Labour government in Britain as a warning that they should not contemplate sacking the 'spooks' just because the Cold War was over. Gill recommends that a better alternative would be to take away the power of state surveillance to repressively police peaceful democratic protests (such as the rebel music of Rastafari – my example) and concentrate such surveillance on manifestly violent protests. Gill did not extend the logic of this argument beyond the state security services, even though his analysis of 'domestic security' is very suggestive of privatised policing of personal space by groups and individuals within civil society. However, the logic of his rec-ommendation for the Labour Party could be extended to oppositional popular musicians by urging them to recruit their own 'spooks' and 'watch their own backs', if only to encourage the provision of 'safer opportunities' for consumption and (the production of) leisure. This view was acceptable to Peter Tosh in theory because he sang that he was 'recruiting soldiers for Jah army'.

Conclusion: Beyond Criminological Orientalism

From 1492 to the present the western theoretical imagination has been haunted by a shadowy history or racism and imperial conquest. For the most part, a lack of reflexive engagement with the methodological significance of race as a social construct has limited the critical power of even the most well-meaning of theoretical perspectives. Today, in a world where hierarchical differences between 'racialized' cultures are manifest almost everywhere – from Miami and the South Bronx to south central Los Angeles and from South Africa and Bosnia to the Israeli-occupied territories of Palestine, critical theory can no longer afford the hegemonic white standpoint that has long characterized its most dominant strands. Critical theory must both help to counter the continuing violence of racism and open its ears to the voices of cultural traditions long silenced by Eurocentric approaches to world history. These two objectives constitute the core of radical multicultural forms of critical theory. (Pfohl, 1994: 453–4)

Criminology was developed primarily as a tool for imperialist domination and it continues to operate largely as a repressive technology. Other technologies of domination crafted by imperialism, such as the army, the police and the prison, have been generally appropriated by neocolonial regimes around the world. Why has the transfer of criminological technology proved more elusive in the Third World while the discipline is enjoying an unprecedented boom in Europe and North America? Chinua Achebe (1983) is critical of politicians who shamelessly boast that they would steal, borrow or transfer technology from wherever it exists without realising that technology is a worldview and not an artefact waiting to be stolen. Achebe was reluctant to accept the usual explanation that under-development is entirely due to the legacies of colonialism for, according to him, the neocolonial regimes have had enough time to reverse the colonial legacies but have chosen to entrench imperialism instead. In a similar vein, Wole Soyinka (1994) argues that the thinkers who are normally expected to challenge dictatorial imperialist reason in the Third World are equally to blame for abdicating their duties through convenient silence. As he put it, 'the man dies in all who keeps silent in the face of tyranny'. Soyinka was wondering why many more Nigerian radicals failed to join him in opposing the military dictatorship that unleashed a bloody civil war on the citizens. For his patriotic act of opposition to the ethnic war, he was thrown into solitary confinement. In a preface to the 1994 edition of his prison notes, *The Man Died*, he responded to criticism that his memoir was not a manual for revolution by challenging his critics to speak out against the continuing civilian use of killer squads openly as part of the police force to commit atrocities worse than those committed by the military dictatorship in the country. In response to his critics, Soyinka (1994: xiii–xiv) speaks for this book too when he states:

> When power is placed in the service of vicious reaction, a language must be called into being which does its best to appropriate such obscenity of power and fling its excesses back in its face. Criticism of such language is simply squeamish or Christianly – language being expected to turn the other cheek, not stick out its tongue; offer a handshake of reconciliation, not stick up a finger in an obscene, defiant gesture. Such criticism must begin by assailing the seething compost of inhuman abuses from which such language took its being, then its conclusions would be worthy of notice. When it fails to do so, all we are left with is, yet again, the collaborative face of intellectualism with power – that is, the taking of power and its excesses as the natural condition, in relation to which even language must be accountable. But suppose we start accounting all arbitrary power – that is, all forms of dictatorship – as innately and potentially obscene. Then, of course, language must communicate its illegitimacy in a forceful, uncompromising language of rejection, seeking always to make it ridiculous and contemptible, deflating its pretensions at the core. Such language does not pretend to dismantle that structure of power, which can only be a collective endeavour in any case; it does, however, contribute to the psychological reconstitution of public attitudes to forms of oppression.

This must be part of the reason why African creative writers are the ones at the forefront of attempts to develop a relevant criminology for Africa while African social scientists, especially those trained in criminology, have been silenced by the imperialist reason that is dumbed down.

Samir Amin (1977) has argued that the transfer of technology is not all that difficult given the experience of Japan and Germany in the importation of machinery for reproduction by engineers in their country. According to him, Third World countries have also tried to transfer the technology of capitalist 'modernisation' farming from the West but with tragic consequences. Amin explains that such uncritical importation of techniques failed because:

> The new techniques are developed in isolation, in the laboratories and experimental farms of the monopolies and governments. Then, when these techniques prove useful, i.e., likely to extract surplus value from the peasants' labor, they are transmitted to the peasants, i.e., imposed by the government authorities. Dispossessed of the world, alienated, the peasants resist. They are accused of being 'reactionary traditionalists.' They are sent teams of sociologists and more often, policemen. They finally give in and allow themselves to be exploited, until such time as when they rebel – unless they simply flee the towns. (Amin, 1977: 175)

This warning is important to criminologists who wish to transfer their imperialist technology to the Third World where criminology remains underdeveloped. As Amin suggests, it will be very easy to import western textbooks and theories and assemble a factory line of scholars to translate them by inserting local news items, local cases and local places into the existing texts. It is likely that such an uncritical borrowing of criminological know-how would prioritise research methods, theories and policies that maximise the exploitation and repression of the masses. The main thrust of this book is to suggest that criminology in the Third World would flourish better if it did not uncritically adopt the imperialist reason of western criminology. For example, emphasis should be placed in the curriculum of criminology in Africa on reparations for the crimes of the slave trade, the crimes of colonialism, the crimes of apartheid and of neocolonialism instead of following the imperialist obsession with the crimes of the poor. At the same time, the crimes of the poor would be addressed with more emphasis on how to avoid victimisation as mere punishment and how to develop the technologies of peace and love instead of being fixated on the gunboat criminology of imperialism.

Criminologists in the Third World would make a greater impact by being sceptical of western theories of punishment instead of agreeing with western scholars who, according to Cohen (1988), arrogantly boast that there is nothing to learn from the Third World and that all that needs to be done is to apply the woefully failed theories of imperialist criminology to the rest of the world. In an essay published in *Theoretical Criminology* (Agozino, 2000), I posed two related questions: what would Fanon (1963) say about the dramatic increases in prison populations in the US and the UK? And what would Foucault (1977) say? My answer is that Fanon would argue that the disproportionate number of black men and black women incarcerated in the prison industrial complexes of the US and the UK is an indication that the wretched of the earth are still being victimised by white supremacist systems of power. Foucault, with his deliberate silence on colonialism in his analysis of micro-physics of power relations, would probably ignore the politics of imperialism altogether in favour of documenting the changing history of penal discipline imposed on the minds of individual offenders as opposed to corporal punishment imposed on their body in the past.

The lesson here for criminologists is clearly that of Fanon, who warned the Third World (and by extension, counter-colonial criminologists) that they should not follow the modernist example of the West where there is a lot of talk about humanism while human beings are subjected to abominable conditions everywhere. The Third World, in particular, could not afford the billions of dollars that the US spends on the scandalous number of prisons and prisoners it is warehousing. For example, America, with about 250 million residents, has about two million people in jail and half of them are minority individuals, mainly African Americans. In contrast, a country like Nigeria which is demonised in the West as being full of criminals, has a population of nearly half that of America but only a fraction of its jail population – fewer than 50,000 in total. While America spends over $20 billion a year to run the profitable prison industrial complex, Nigeria spends $5 billion to run the whole country. And so my fellow criminologists, get real and stop assuming that all those in prison are criminals.

The review of theories above demonstrates how modernist accounts of criminality appear unilineal in the construction of imperialist power as the polar opposite of decolonisation. Masculinity comes across as heterosexuality, as domineering force, as rational, as violent attack or defence, as muscular force in contrast to femininity and emasculation. This lineal equation of white supremacist, imperialist patriarchy with its mythology has been maintained by modernist discourse that promises a universal classification of all living things into male and female, black and white, rich and poor, good and bad species.

This book has examined whether this modernist obsession with the delineation of the contours of hierarchy is a symptom of an identity crisis or the symptom of a crisis in modernist paradigms of science. If we accept the premise of positivistic social science – that social relations are measurable, quantifiable, classifiable, predictable and generalisable – then we should adopt any of the numerous modernist perspectives on deviance and social control as the guide for this research. If, on the other hand, our guiding assumption is that deviance and social control are socially constructed, that they are observable but not easily quantifiable or measurable, largely unpredictable and historically specific rather than universal, then we should seek alternatives to the lineal geometry of modernist correlations.

An example of this alternative to the modernist geometry of social relations is offered by chaos theory. This was suggested by Goethe at the height of modernist philosophy of science as an alternative to the linear geometry of Newton, but it was largely ignored, perhaps because Goethe was more of an artist than a scientist. Newton experimented with a prism which broke a beam of white light into a rainbow of colours that could be observed throughout the spectrum. Newton concluded that the colours must be the pure colours that combine to produce the colour white. There was hardly any evidence to justify Newtonian optics except that the experiment can be repeated a thousand times with reliable results. Today, if you were to ask a physicist what the colour red is, he or she would state that 'it is light radiating in waves between 620 to 800 billionth of a meter long' (Gleick, 1987: 164).

An example of what Newton proposed can be illustrated with the following analogy: if a black boy is like a glass prism and masculinity is like a ray of white light, then if the light shines normally on one surface of the glass, we can calculate the angle of deviation of the ray after being refracted through the glass prism. Since the ray of light (masculinity) strikes the face of the prism (boy) normally, it will proceed through the glass (boy) until it strikes the opposite face at the point P (read politics). On emerging from the prism the ray of masculinity will be refracted away from the normal as shown. Now the angle the ray of masculinity makes with the normal in the glass boy is clearly 30°, and if the angle of emergence is e, we have, by Snell's law:

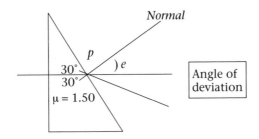

sin e divided by sin 30 = 1.50,
or sin e = 1.50 x sin 30,
= 0.75, giving e
= 48° 36′.
But the angle through which the ray of masculinity is deviated
= e – 30,
= 48° 36′ – 30°,
= 18° 36′ (Tyler, 1959: 106–7).

Although this is known as Snell's law because it is presumably invariant as a proof, I use it as an example of what I prefer to call the poetry of positivism, 'sin e = 1.50 × sin 30', says who? I still remember being called to the front of my fourth-year class in High School to write down one of those proofs that we were encouraged to memorise. Luckily, I had crammed the stuff the previous night and so I got it right down to the Q.E.D. However, I had no clue what it all meant because I was not told that it was poetry. Rather I was taught that it was an invariable law of nature. I now see this as a myth of poetic proportions because as poetry, every equation is open to different interpretations. Our High School mathematics teacher would disagree with us and say that one plus one is always two but the class once conspired to ask him, 'What if it is one apple plus one banana?' 'Two fruits', he answered. 'One human plus one elephant?' 'Two mammals.' 'One human plus one glass of milk?' 'You've got me', he admitted.

Note how the angle 'normal' is placed above and the 'angle of deviation' is coincidentally placed below as if only the subaltern is capable of deviating from the norm. Although this is only an analogy, it is very similar to Talcott Parsons' grand theory of socio-cybernetic functionalism which Pfohl (1994), among others, critiqued as being too mechanistic. According to this model, socialisation is fed to members of a society like goal-directed information that they adopt. Those who conform to the values communicated to them are rewarded and those who resist are persuaded while those who rebel are punished to maintain the balance in the status quo. This is the approach that is common in criminology where the crimes of the powerful are widely neglected while the relatively powerless are over-whelmingly the objects of criminological research. Fortunately for black boys, they are not unconscious glass prisms; masculinity is not a simple matter of mechanically shining a white light, and normality or deviance is not exclusively found along monolithic angles. For that reason this book does not approach the subject of criminological theory through the positivistic philosophy of science that privileges causal path analysis. The study of social relations is not the study of unconscious matter with no self-interests and vested interests in politicised global societies. Bearing this in mind, this book encourages the adoption of a perspective that is sensitive to the fact that even though the attitudes of young black men to masculinity could be measured and analysed, attitudes are ordinal level data and not interval level data. It is a common misapplication of statistical measurement to see attitudes being treated as interval and ratio level data due to the pressure for researchers to quantify their findings (Champion, 2000). If we are looking at race, class and gender constructions of deviance and social control, the statistical precision of Newton's optics becomes increasingly untenable except as poetry.

According to Gleick, one of the advocates of chaos theory, Feigenbaum, was not satisfied with Newton's optics. He discovered in Goethe an extraordinary set of experiments on colours. Goethe also experimented with a prism but instead of casting a beam of white light through the prism, he held it close to his eyes and looked at it. What he saw was a blankness, neither a rainbow nor individual shades of colour. He tried his experiment against a background of a clear blue sky and against a clear white surface and produced the same result. However, when a slight spot interrupted the white surface or a cloud appeared in the blue sky, Goethe saw a burst of colour. He concluded that it is the interchange of light and shadow that causes colour. He confirmed his hypothesis by observing how people perceive shadows cast by different sources of coloured light.

Whereas Newton broke down light to find the smallest unit of colour and expressed this mathematically as a theory for the whole of physics, Goethe studied paintings, walked through colourful gardens and studied how people perceive colour in search of a grand theory of colour. Feigenbaum was convinced that Goethe was on the right track and that his theory was close to the view of psychologists that human perception is not always identical with the hard physical reality that they observe. As Gleick summarised this:

> The colors we perceive vary from time to time and from person to person ... But as Feigenbaum understood them, Goethe's ideas had more true science in them. They were hard and empirical. Over and over again, Goethe emphasized the repeatability of his experiments. It was the perception of color, to Goethe, that was universal and objective. What scientific evidence was there for a definable real-world quality of redness independent of our perception? (Gleick, 1987: 165)

This chaotic theory of colour is relevant, especially when we are talking about the racial classification of human beings based on their skin colour. The people who are commonly called black are in fact brown and the people commonly called white are actually pink. Besides, some people who are called black are almost as white or whiter than some other people called white. This book has not followed Newton down the lane of formulating a mathematical formalism with which to sift through the 'mess' of multiple human perceptions and arrive at universal qualities of blackness or masculinity, for instance. Blackness and masculinity are not specific bandwidths of light, as Newton's optic illusions would have it. On the contrary, masculine blackness, like any racialised-gendered-class-specific category, is a chaotic territory with hybrid boundaries that are impossible to quantify, yet we are certain that we can identify black men regularly and with empirical verifiability, as Goethe would argue. In Australia, South Africa and the United States, we do not need a mathematical formula by which to identify young black men, but we can empirically identify the young men whose racialised identity is black in the three culturally different locations.

Contributing to the development of chaos theory in criminology, or what they call 'constitutive criminology', Henry and Milovanovic (1996: 60) provide a critique of the criminological theories based on the Newtonian philosophy of science. According to them:

In the Newtonian paradigm, the 'point' is privileged. The individual particle, the entity 'person', can be followed through time. Actions, with the correct amount of scientific knowledge, are potentially predictable. For example in positivistic criminology consider how causation is depicted in path analysis diagrams ... In contrast, for quantum mechanics, only probabilities exist. (Henry and Milovanovic, 1996: 60)

They go on to outline the various insights that chaos theory has contributed to a better understanding of society. Chaos theory is explicit or implicit in the work of postmodernist theorists. Such theorists conceptualise social order as the exception in social relations because order has to be imposed against various forms of resistance. This suggests that the social universe is characterised by disorder most of the time, rather than being clean, clear, pure and whole as Newtonian positivism would have us believe. This model of reality appears to be more useful for understanding a phenomenon like black masculinity which is not a single, monolithic whole but is made up of dissipative structures that tend towards order and disorder, with variable fractals that remain unstable and sensitive to their social environment that is full of chance, spontaneity and uncertainty, unlike the rational bureaucracies through which a modicum of order is attempted in the face of chaos.

The approach of chaos theory can be critiqued for privileging chaos in an imperialist, patriarchal, white supremacist world where the people who have been suffering the effects of such chaos yearn for a break into orderly lives (King, 1967). For young minority men, women and the poor who are demonised as bearers of the violent criminal identity (never mind that more people are massacred daily by imperialists than by all the individual murderers in years), it is not very helpful simply to deconstruct the social construction of the hierarchies of criminality when they yearn for an end to racism, sexism and class snobbery. If the world is essentially chaotic, it follows that the organisation of change would also have to be disorganised rather than disciplined. Such an anarchic view of social change could work against the efforts to eliminate oppressive practices which are very much organised, systematic and institution-alised. Henry and Milovanovic try to answer these shortcomings of chaos theory by promising to go beyond deconstruction and begin the task of reconstruction. However, in their postmodernist alternative to modernist criminological theory, they offer an interpretation of the 'Outcome basins of the Mandelbrot set' which remains problematic especially for young black men (Agozino, 1999).[*] According to them the

> area outlined in black represents convergence (those with law-breaking commitment profiles) and the area outside it in white represents divergence (those with law-abiding profiles or other forms of harm). (Henry and Milovanovic, 1996: 166)

To say without any hint of irony that the 'area outlined in black represents convergence (those with law-breaking commitment profiles)' is to offer a lineal and positivistic interpretation that tries to defy the poetic reading which the piece deserves. I use the Set as an example of the poetry of postmodernism in contrast to what I called the poetry of positivism earlier. If you view the Mandelbrot Set from different angles and perspectives, it could look like a sea turtle, love on wings, a bum or a person with an exotic hair style. When I shared the Set with my class, a student came forward with a rap compact disk from the Atlanta, Georgia group, Outkast, who used it on their Stankonia album with a naked black woman whose body was supposedly on fire superimposed on the Set. This was the group that Rosa Parks unsuccessfully sued for using her name in one of their misogynist songs. The interesting coincidence is that I used the same Set to talk about black masculinity and here were two black men using it to represent their masculinity in relation to the sexualised body of a black woman. However, when I searched for the record on-line, the Mandelbrot Set and the naked black woman had been replaced on the cover with the American Flag, either as a ploy to cash into the profitable patriotism that was being marketed after 9/11 or because the suit of Rosa Parks made the group more sensitive about how they represent black women. The point that I am making is that the Mandelbrot Set, as poetry, lacks a monolithic interpretation.

The postmodern interpretation of the Mandelbrot Set sounds too much like the racial profiling that is increasingly being recognised as part of the reason why young black men are over-represented in the justice system. This conclusion departs from such a reading of chaos

---

[*] The Mandelbrot Set can be seen at www.mindspring.com~chroma/mandelbrot.html. Benoît Mandelbrot coined the word 'fractal' to represent the normal curves of infinity that Georg Cantor mistakenly saw as pathological in the Cantor Set (Eglash, 1999).

theory by avoiding the use of representations that could reinforce existing prejudices against young black men. The approach of postmodern chaos criminology is flawed perhaps because it represents an attempt to apply to social relations, the findings of theoretical physicists about unconscious natural phenomena. Hence, although chaos theorists abhor linear Euclidean explanations, their non-linear geometry still approximates a linear explanation or a multi-linear explanation. For example, chaos theorists talk about bifurcations as the things that make up the non-linear geometry of social relations. Elsewhere, I have questioned the privileging of bifurcations in chaos analysis and suggested the conception of social relations as involving, at least, trifurcations if not multifurcations (Agozino, 1997a). One of the leading thinkers of chaos criminology, T.R. Young (1992), outlines the potential contributions of chaos theory to criminology and his outline can be applied to a conclusion of a book like this. As he put it:

A. The geometry of dynamical system varies with scale of observation (this is visible in the Mendelbrot set above but it is also true of black masculinity as a dynamic phenomenon that varies among its fractals).

B. Any given region at any given scale of observation is similar to an adjacent region or the larger region of which it is a part, but it is never identical (this hypothesis can be applied to black masculinities in the US, Australia and South Africa in terms of their similarities even though they are far from being identical).

C. One speaks of degrees of reality rather than Euclidean states of objectivity (are there degrees of the reality of black masculinity or is it a monolithic reality?)

D. Both order and disorder are found together in every region at every scale in fractal structures (we can hypothesise that young black men would be as normal as non-black young men everywhere with some tending towards disorder but most remaining orderly even in the face of racial profiling in the three countries).

E. The amount/ratio of order to disorder depends upon which portions of an outcome basin one samples; precision and replicability are a function of sampling decisions (and so we must endeavour to sample from different socio-economic backgrounds in the different countries before we can begin to understand why

three culturally distinct fractions of black masculinity are similarly
marginalized by the institutions of social control).

The above five points correspond to the five essential components
of fractal geometry that Eglash (1999) found to be more common
in indigenous African design and social thought compared to the
more commonly Cartesian European and Euclidean Native
American designs. The five essential elements are recursion (the
output of black masculinity becomes the input for the reproduction
of African masculinity); scaling (the variations of black masculinity
do not follow smooth straight lines but have jagged edges at the
margins); self-similarity (the patterns of black masculinity do not
have to be identical to qualify as fractals of the same thing); infinity
(although black masculinity can be scaled, it must be noted that its
variations are infinite); and fractional dimensions (the dimensions
of black masculinity are not only whole numbers but fractions of
gender relationships).

The preferred approach in this book has been to follow the theory
of articulation as developed by Stuart Hall (1980, 1996; see also
Agozino, 1997a, 1997b). Although Hall would distance himself from
postmodern thinking, his theory implicitly applies the assumptions
of chaos theory on the analysis of race, class and gender. Like chaos
theory, the theory of articulation assumes that social relations are
not isolated from one another but that they actually intersect or
articulate with one another. For example, it will be impossible to
explain the social relations of young black men simply in terms of
gender or masculinity, exclusively in terms of race or colour, nor
simply in terms of class or socio-economic relations. A poor black
boy in Durban, South Africa, Aboriginal youth in Brisbane, Australia
or African American youth in Pittsburgh, Pennsylvania do not, for
instance, go to one police station to experience their poverty before
going to another police station to experience their masculinity and
to a third police station to experience their blackness. Rather, all
three social relations are articulated, disarticulated and rearticulated
in the significant social relations that impact on the young black
men who are racially profiled as violent criminals by law enforcement
agents and by large sections of the public.

The theory of articulation is also useful because it presupposes that
social change would have to be organised in order to overcome the
disadvantages, direct and indirect, that keep some young black men
trapped in violence within otherwise democratic societies where the

majority of young black men remain overwhelmingly law-abiding. Instead of simply agonising over or celebrating the existence of chaos in the lives of some young black men, the theory of articulation lays emphasis on how to articulate alternative solutions in alliance with interested sections of society through education, social action and differential social organisation.

This perspective is close to the idea of the intersections of race, class and gender domination outlined by Patricia Hill Collins (1990). The major difference is that Collins adopted an individualist conception of agency by emphasising the choices available to her as an individual middle-class black woman whereas the theory of articulation emphasises the building of coalitions and alliances along the race–class–gender axis in the struggle against injustice. What the theories of articulation and intersection share is an understanding that within certain conjunctures, one social relation could relatively disarticulate the others by becoming more prominent or more significant in certain situations or points in time. However, the theory of articulation recognises that disarticulation is always followed by a rearticulation of the disarticulated relations, giving rise to a new view of dominance and resistance. The Cartesian mathematical concept of intersectionality further differs from the fractal linguistic concept of articulation by suggesting that there are areas outside the intersections where pure race, pure gender or pure class relations can be found while articulation assumes the disarticulation and rearticulation of every aspect of the relevant social relations within an articulation of dominance and resistance.

My preference for fractal chaos theory finds support in the work of Ron Eglash (1999) who found that 'while fractal geometry can indeed take us into the far reaches of high-tech science, its patterns are surprisingly common in traditional African designs, and some of its basic concepts are fundamental to African knowledge systems' (Eglash, 1999: 3). I am not surprised at how common fractal designs are in Africa because the very shirt I am wearing as I type these words carries fractal designs from West Africa and, as a young boy, I watched my mother paint fractal motifs on the bodies of mothers who were about to celebrate the first month (28th day) of the newborn.

Eglash went on to do a cross-cultural analysis of the frequency of fractal designs and found that European designs tend to be Cartesian while the designs of Native Americans and South Pacific Islanders tend to be Euclidean. He found that fractal designs appear more common in African cultures. However, he warns against interpreting this empirical evidence in a racist manner to suggest that Africans are closer to nature while Europeans are closer to culture. This warning reminds us of debates between poststructuralists and the advocates of Africentrism. Mudimbe (1988) and Appiah (1992), writing from poststructuralist orientations, warn that Africans differ from place to place and from time to time, just like any other group of people on earth, and so we should not follow colonial and anti-colonial thinking by lumping Africans together for different ideological reasons. On the other hand, writers like Asante and Asante (1985) emphasise the cultural unity of Africa and insist that the differences among people of African descent are insignificant compared to the compelling evidence of similarities. Alternatively, bell hooks (1991) argues for what she calls 'postmodern blackness' by suggesting that postmodernists should conduct their discourse in a language that is not designed to exclude the masses and tackle issues of relevance to the black community.

According to Eglash, paying attention to African fractals would reveal that both sides of the argument have a point. Africa is not the same in every respect and yet there is a family resemblance among Africans just as a family photograph would show likeness among members of the family who are far from being identical. In the project that I am proposing as a way of advancing some of the ideas in this book, there is no assumption that black men are biologically the same everywhere. Rather, the assumption is that despite the differences among black men, their historical experiences in the US, Australia and South Africa are painfully similar. Fractal analysis allows us to theorise the differences in the representation of black masculinity within the three regions of interest while also capturing the similarities. Paul Gilroy (1993) makes use of fractal analysis to explain the dynamism and diversity of African cultures and the cultures of the African Diaspora. The methodological problem that arises here is whether it is valid to compare African American men with South African men and Aboriginal Australian men. Why are these culturally distinct fractions of young black men equally marginalised and oppressed in societies structured in white supremacist patriarchal imperialist dominance? They come from different countries but are all over-represented in the prison industrial complex at proportions that compete to out-scandalise each other. This conclusion is not the place to deal with this question adequately. It is something that I am proposing to take up in a future project. Suffice it to warn that such a project could not be accomplished along the lines of colonialist criminology but along the oppositional perspectives of counter-colonial criminology outlined in this book.

Another social problem that cannot be completely addressed in this book but which should not be completely ignored is the terrorist war against terrorism that is being waged by the new imperialism. Every right-thinking person is against terrorism and so no one should accuse me of not being with 'us' or being against 'us'. The attempts to demonise critics with boasts about European cultural superiority or to use the grief caused by terrorists to justify the terrorising of whole populations with smart and dumb bombs is straight out of the books of colonialist criminology.

Counter-colonial criminology would suggest that the military option is not the only or even the most effective way to prevent security risks to innocent citizens around the world. The colonialist criminological approach simply chooses allies who appear convenient at the moment. They are armed and trained to attack perceived enemies with terroristic tactics. Eventually, the chickens come home to roost in the sense that the same people who are trained and armed to attack the baddies often attack their mentors. What if the huge sums of money being used to seek a military solution to the crime problem were spent on paying reparations to the victims of colonialism and imperialism? Perhaps there would be less need to drop leaflets with bombs and food packages, telling the terrified citizens which packages to open and which explosives of the same colour to avoid opening in a phoney turkey-shoot war.

As usual, criminologists are not intervening in this immense perpetration of human rights crimes. If they respond at all, they will be designing commodified courses on how to win the war against terrorism rather than offering alternative theories of crime in a world where imperialism is globalised. It is left to a courageous politician like Fidel Castro Ruz of Cuba to risk his life by honouring the invitation from the United Nations to speak words of truth about the crimes committed by imperialism against the people of the Third World and against the poor minorities within imperialist countries, against the clearly stated wishes of the forces of imperialism and their lackeys who would rather that Castro did not show up. Come on criminology theorists, one more effort!

While criminologists indulge in their profitable culture of silence on human rights crimes, a Nigerian mathematician who obviously understands fractal thinking, analyses what is going on in his popular weekly column for the *Guardian*, Lagos (Thursday, 18 April 2002).

The writer Dr Edwin Madunagu lost his job as a mathematics professor when the military dictatorship of General Obasanjo sacked him and others for sympathising with students who were murdered by security agents. In the fractally titled article 'The Invisible Encounter', he analysed what happened on 21 March 2002, when Dr Fidel Castro addressed the International Conference on Financing for Development, in Monterrey, Mexico. He quotes Castro as telling the conference that 'The existing world economic order constitutes a system of plundering and exploitation like no other in history.' Castro continued his speech by telling his audience that in the year 2001,

> more than 826 million people were actually starving; there were 854 million illiterate adults; 325 million children do not attend school, 2 billion people have no access to low cost medications and 2.4 billion people lack the basic sanitation conditions. Not less than 11 million children under age 5 perish every year from preventable causes, while half a million go blind for lack of vitamin A; the life span of the population in the developed world is 30 years higher than that of the people living in sub-Saharan Africa.

And criminologists still focus on the POO theory – the punishment of offenders – without raising an eyebrow as to who is responsible for the plundering and exploitation that produces such genocidal results. Such silence is actually underdeveloping criminology by tying it to the apron strings of colonialism and imperialist reason. Madunagu the mathematician was a better criminologist than most criminologists by paying attention to what Castro had to say. He concluded his column by quoting from Castro again:

> In the face of the present deep crisis, a still worse future is offered where the economic, social and ecological tragedy of an increasingly ungovernable world would never be resolved and where the number of the poor and the starving would grow higher, as if a larger part of humanity were doomed. As I have said before, the ever more sophisticated weapons piling up in the arsenals of the wealthiest and the mightiest can kill the illiterate, the poor and the hungry, but they cannot kill ignorance, poverty and hunger. It should definitely be said: farewell to arms. Something must be done to save humanity, a better world is possible.

A better criminology is definitely possible too. Such a criminology would ask why the Third World governments that try genuinely to stop these genocidal crimes are often the targets of imperialist forces. Why would Castro be harassed by his Mexican hosts and forced to leave the international conference before the arrival of the American president, George W. Bush, and why are criminologists not interested in the implications of such undiplomatic conduct for human rights? Some might argue that Third World poverty is the consequence of the ignorance of Third World people and the mismanagement of their resources by their leaders, nothing to do with criminology.

The interconnectedness of the problems of imperialist reason and criminological theory can be made clearer by developing a decolonisation model of deviance and social control. The thesis statement of this model is that crime and punishment are instances of imperialist power relations. Both crime and control seek to exercise colonial power over Others by imperialist force, threat of force or fraud and cunning rather than through the democratic process.

This gives rise to the spiral of imperialism that originates from interpersonal relationships and spreads to inter-group and international relations. All individuals, social classes, gender groups and racial or ethnic categories are capable of colonising the private or collective spaces of Others. Everyone is capable of attempting decolonisation as an understandable response to imperialist power.

Parents and guardians abuse children because of the imperialist power that they wield over them. Juveniles bully others and commit offences because of the will to colonise others and exercise power unjustly. Rapists are the dominant characterisation of imperialists. A man rapes a woman just as Europa rapes Africana. One rapes an individual and the other rapes masses of people. What they have in common is not rape but imperialism. Pickpockets and insider dealers, kidnappers and war criminals, murderers and genocidists, drunk drivers and human rights violators, terrorists and armies of occupation, fraudsters and military coup plotters, environmental polluters and pornographers, drug dealers and hate criminals are all united in the spiral of imperialism.

This is not to suggest that human nature is essentially imperialistic. On the contrary, the vast majority of the masses make society possible by adopting democratic principles in their relationships with others. It is always a minority that wishes to lord it over the majority unjustly who resort to imperialist reason. The masses individually and collectively struggle for decolonisation as part of the struggle to deepen democratic ethos within civil society.

This view can be summarised in a few propositions:

1. The exercise of imperialist power in any relationship is the general form of deviance.
2. The greater the frequency and intensity of imperialist power relations, the more deviant the outcome.
3. The more intense, enduring or persistent the imperialist power relation, the more likely that the victimised will organise decolonisation struggles.
4. The more militaristic the attempt to repress the struggle for decolonisation, the more militant the struggle becomes.
5. The more militaristic the decolonisation struggle, the more likely that the outcome will retain forms of neo-colonial imperialist power relations.
6. The more enduring the militarised power of neo-colonial imperialism, the more likely that the struggle will continue.

Fanon recognised the dangers of militarism as a solution to imperialism and called instead for reparations to be paid for the crimes of imperialism. This is in line with the African fractal belief system in the interconnectedness of humanity in contrast to dehumanising Eurocentric hierarchical reasoning that sustains imperialist hegemony. Similar ideas can be found in the consistent criticism of the abuse of power as the source of crime in the works of Chambliss (1971, 1989, 1995), Pepinsky (1991), Odekunle (1986), Angela Davis (1981), bell hooks (1984), Box (1983) and many others. The solution to the abuse of power is not disempowerment but increased empowerment through intensified democratisation of civil society.

In sum, the book has demonstrated that the silence on the genealogical links of criminology with colonialism has produced two adverse effects: (1) criminological theory has been constrained by the shackles of imperialist reason, and (2) postcolonial countries have generally shunned criminology as an irrelevant colonialist pastime even while continuing to import the nuts and bolts of 'made-for-export' imperialist technology. Both these consequences of the failure of the criminological imagination need to be addressed in order to begin and further the decolonisation of criminology for the good of all.

One immediate consequence of the decolonisation model is that criminologists will no longer focus exclusively on the punishment of individual offenders but will join the millions of people around the world who are demanding reparations for the crimes of the African holocaust (otherwise known as European trans-Atlantic slavery), the genocide against native Americans, Aboriginal Australians and the Maori in New Zealand, the crimes against humanity known as apartheid, the Arab slave trade, the stolen generations of Aboriginal children, the colonial pogroms in Africa, Palestine, Asia and South America and the crimes of the Japanese colonial adventurers in Asia. Such tasks will no longer be abandoned to journalists like Chang (1997), who opened the eyes of the world to the Nanking massacre while criminologists turned a blind eye. As Cohen (1993) and the Schwendingers (1970) have been crying in the wilderness, human rights crimes are also criminological problems which should no longer be excluded from the fat volumes that pretend to be comprehensive handbooks of criminology.

Another consequence would be the establishment of Third World schools of theoretical criminology that could teach the West one or two things about difference, deviance, defiance and social control. It is no longer credible for the imperialist countries that have the greatest crime problems and that perpetrate the greatest crimes to continue to posture as the standard-bearers of criminology from which the Third World should learn. There is an English proverb that you should set a thief to catch a thief, but I have never trusted this proverb since I first read it in primary school. I have always suspected that the imperialist thieves would join forces and conspire to rob you blind. I am sure that western criminologists could learn a thing or two by humbling themselves to listen to Other perspectives. Willem de Haan (1992) stated that there is a need for 'progressive criminology' to be indigenised in the Third World, but he warned that such a project should not proceed along the line of extreme cultural relativism lest it perpetuates stereotypes of the Other. This book suggests that it is not enough to indigenise already existing criminological schools, including progressive criminologies. Instead, western criminologists should remain open to opportunities to learn from the experiences and struggles of others as well through an exchange of knowledge, contrary to the modernist assumption that technology must be transferred from the West to the rest of us.

Finally, let me end with the humorous tale of 'insulting the meat' which Giddens (1994) cited in his essay on what it means to live in a post-traditional society. According to him, the !Khun San Africans who live in the Kalahari desert where game is scarce, developed a technology with which to keep the ego of skilled hunters in check, lest they become proud and begin to will domination over others. According to ethnographic reports, the hunter gets home and sits by the fire silently and humbly. Everyone ignores him at first and then someone casually asks him if he has seen any game today. The hunter is expected to snub himself and say that he is not a skilled hunter, that he did not see anything, perhaps only a very small animal. Then the audience would smile and know that he must have caught a big one, otherwise he would have brought it home by himself. The following day, a party will set out with him to bring home the 'small' catch. On the way back, everyone will be insulting about the meat and chiding the hunter for dragging them all the way from home just to collect a pile of bones. The hunter will keep apologising that he is really no good at hunting and that he is still learning. Westerners are more likely to boast about their big catch.

In line with that African tradition in humility which, like every tradition, was invented at some point, I apologise to my readers for the dry words that I have dragged them out here to read. As you can see, I am no good at writing and I am still learning the craft. Maybe I have learned a little but I hope to keep learning so that some day I will write my big opus. As you must have guessed, this African tradition is now part of the best social science research in the guise of limitations of findings and recommendations for future research. The major limitation of this book is that most of the claims in it have not been empirically tested due to the limitation of funding available at the time of writing. Hopefully, research like this will be more generously funded and more empirically tested in the future, but it would be irresponsible to wait for funding and empiricism before starting the urgent task of rewriting the history of ideas.

Bibliography

Abu-Jamal, M. (1995) *Live From Death Row*, New York, Avon.

Achebe, C. (1975) *Morning Yet on Creation Day*, Edinburgh, Heinemann.

Achebe, C. (1983) *The Trouble with Nigeria*, Edinburgh, Heinemann.

Achebe, C. (1988) *Hopes and Impediments*, Edinburgh, Heinemann.

Achebe, C. (2000) *Home and Exile*, Oxford, Oxford University Press.

Agozino, B. (1991) 'Victimisation as Punishment', *African Concord*, Vol. 6, No. 7, June.

Agozino, B. (1995a) 'Methodological Issues in Feminist Research', *Quantity & Quality: International Journal of Methodology*, Vol. 29, No. 3, 287–98.

Agozino, B. (1995b) 'The Social Construction of Deviance, Psychiatry, Gender and Race in a Feminist Performance', *Journal of Contemporary Health*, No. 3, September, 315–29.

Agozino, B. (1996) 'Football and the Civilizing Process: Penal Discourse and the Ethic of Collective Responsibility in Sports Law', *International Journal of the Sociology of Law*, Vol. 24, No. 2, 163–88.

Agozino, B. (1997a) *Black Women and the Criminal Justice System: Towards the Decolonisation of Victimisation*, Aldershot, Ashgate.

Agozino, B. (1997b) 'Is Chivalry Colour-Blind? Race and Gender Discrimination in the Criminal Justice System', *International Journal of Discrimination and the Law*, Vol. 2, No. 3, 119–216.

Agozino, B. (1997c) 'The Politics of Cultural Identity', W. Ackah and M. Christian, eds, *Black Identity and Organization: Local, National and Global Perspectives*, Liverpool, Charles Wootton Press.

Agozino, B. (1999) 'Social Fiction *Sui Generis*: The Fairy Tale Structure of Criminological Theory', *The Critical Criminologist*, Vol. 9, No. 3, 11–14.

Agozino, B. (2000) 'Beware of Strangers or the Myth that Immigrants are More Likely to be Deviant', in B. Agozino, ed., *Theoretical and Methodological Issues in Migration Research*, Aldershot, Ashgate.

Agozino, B. (2002) 'African Women and the Decolonization of Victimisation: Dazzling Crime Figures', *Critical Sociology*, Vol. 28, Nos 1–2.

Agozino, B. and Idem, U. (2001) *Nigeria: Democratising a Militarised Civil Society*, London, CDD.

Aguda, Justice T.A. (1985) *A New Perspective in Law and Justice in Nigeria*, Kuru, National Institute for Policy and Strategic Studies.

Ahire, P.T. (1991) *Imperial Policing*, Milton Keynes, Open University.

Ake, C. (1979) *Social Science as Imperialism: The Theory of Development*, Ibadan, University of Ibadan Press.

Albanese, J.S. (2000) *Criminal Justice*, Boston, Allyn and Bacon.

Alldridge, P. (1994) 'Forensic Science and Expert Evidence', *Journal of Law and Society*, Vol. 21, No. 1, March.

Allen, H. (1987) *Justice Unbalanced*, Milton Keynes, Open University.

Alschuler, A.W. (1995) 'Plea Bargaining and its History', in R.L. Abel, ed., *The Law & Society Reader*, New York, New York University Press.

Althusser, L. (1971) *Lenin and Philosophy and Other Essays*, B. Brewer trans., New York, Monthly Review Press.

Amadiume, I. (1987) *Male Daughters. Female Husbands: Gender and Sex in an African Society*, London, Zed.

Amin, S. (1977) *Imperialism and Unequal Development*, Hassocks, The Harvester Press.

Amin, S. (1987) 'Democracy and National Strategy in the Periphery', *Third World Quarterly*, Vol. 9, No. 4, 1129–57.

Amnesty International (1992) *Women on the Frontline*, London, A1.

Amnesty International (1997) *Africa: A New Future without the Death Penalty*, London, A1.

Appiah, A. (1992) *In My Father's House*, New York, Oxford.

Archer, P. and Reay, L. (1966) *Freedom at Stake*, London, Bodley Head.

Arrigo, B.A. and Bernard, T.I. (1997) 'Postmodern Criminology in Relation to Radical and Conflict Criminology', *Critical Criminology*, Vol. 8, No. 2.

Asante, M.K. and Asante, K.W. (1985) *African Culture: The Rhythms of Unity*, Westport, CT, Greenwood Press.

Ayu, I.D. (1986) *Essays in Popular Struggles*, Ogata, Zim Pan-African Press.

Back, L. and Solomos, J. (1993) 'Doing Research, Writing Politics: The Dilemmas of Political Intervention in Research on Racism', *Economy and Society*, Vol. 22, No. 2, 178–99.

Badau, H.A. and Radelet, M.L. (1992) *Conviction of the Innocent*, Boston, Northeastern University Press.

Bains, S. (1989) 'Crimes against Women: The Manchester Survey', in C. Dunhill, ed., *The Boys in Blue: Challenges to the Police*, London, Virago.

Baldus, C.D., Woodworth, G.G. and Pulaski, Jr, C.A. (1989) *Equal Justice and the Death Penalty*, Boston, Northeastern University Press.

Baldwin, J. (1961) *Nobody Knows My Name*, Harmondsworth, Penguin.

Bankowski, Z., MacCormick, D.N., Summers, R.S. and Wroblewski, J. (1991) 'On Method and Methodology', in D.N. MacCormick and R.S. Summers, eds, *Interpreting Statutes*, Dartmouth, Aldershot.

Bankowski, Z., Mungham, G. and Young, P. (1977) 'Radical Criminology or Radical Criminologist?' *Contemporary Crisis*, 1, 37–51.

Barak, G. (1991) *Crimes by the Capitalist State*, New York, SUNY.

Barak, G., Flavin, J, and Leighton, P. (2001) *Class, Race, Gender and Crime: Social Realities of Justice in America*, Los Angeles, Roxbury.

Barkan, E. (1992) *The Retreat of Scientific Racism: Changing Concepts of Race in Britain and the United States between the World Wars*, Cambridge, Cambridge University Press.

Barlow, H.D. (2000) *Criminal Justice in America*, Upper Saddle River, Prentice-Hall.

Baudrillard, J. (1995) *The Gulf War Did Not Take Place*, tr. P. Patton, Bloomington, Indiana University Press.

Baudrillard, J. (1996) *Perfect Crime*, London, Verso.

Baudrillard, J. (1990) *Fatal Strategies*, London, Semiotext(e)/Pluto.

Bauman, Z. (1989) *Modernity and the Holocaust*, Cambridge, Polity Press.

Beccaria, C. (1804, 1963) *On Crimes and Punishments*, New York, Macmillan.

Becker, H.S. (1963) *Outsiders: Studies in the Sociology of Deviance*, New York, Macmillan.

Becker, H.S. (1966–67) 'Whose Side Are We On'? *Social Problems*, Vol. 14, 239–47.

Beirne, P. (1993) *Inventing Criminology: Essays on the Sociology of Deviance*, New York, Free Press.

Bell, V. (1993) *Interrogating Incest: Feminism, Foucault and the Law*, London, Routledge.

Ben-Tovim, G., Gabriel, J., Law, I., and Stredder, K. (1986) *The Local Politics of Race*, London, Macmillan.

Bentham, J. (1789, 1948) *An Introduction to the Principles of Morals and Legislation*, New York, Macmillan.

Bhabha, H.K. (1992) 'Postcolonial Authority and Postmodern Guilt', in D. Grossberg, et al., eds, *Cultural Studies*, London, Routledge.

Blaunstein, A. and Zangrando, R. (1971) *Civil Rights and the Black American*, New York, Washington Square Press.

Blumer, H. (1966) *Symbolic Interactionism*, Englewood Cliffs, Prentice-Hall.

Boland, B. (1996) 'What is Community Prosecution?', *National Institute of Justice Journal* Vol. 213, August.

Bolshavkov, V. (1984) *Human Rights American Style*, Moscow, Novosti.

Bottoms, A.E. (1967) 'Delinquency amongst Immigrants', *Race*, Vol. VIII, No. 4, 357–84.

Bottoms, A.E. (1983) 'Neglected Features of Contemporary Penal Systems', in D. Garland and P. Young, eds, *The Power to Punish: Contemporary Penalty and Social Analysis*, London, Heinemann.

Bourdieu, P. (1986) *Distinction: A Social Critique of Judgments of Taste*, London, Routledge & Kegan Paul.

Box, S. (1983) *Power, Crime and Mystification*, London, Tavistock.

Brandt, A. (1978) *Racism, Research and the Tuskegee Syphilis Study*, in Hastings Center Report, 7.

Brown, D. and Hogg, R. (1992) 'Essentialism, Radical Criminology and Left Realism', *Australian & New Zealand Journal of Criminology*, Vol. 25, No. 195–230.

Brownmiller, S. (1975) *Against our Will: Men Women and Rape*, New York, Bantam.

Bryson, N. (1986) 'Two Narratives of Rape in the Visual Arts: Lucretia and the Sabine Women', in S. Tomaselli and R. Porter, eds, *Rape*, Oxford, Blackwell.

Cabral, A. (1972) *A Return to Source*, New York, Monthly Review Press.

Cabral, A. (1979) *Unity and Struggle*, New York, Monthly Review Press.

Cabral, A. (1982) 'Homage to Nkrumah', in A. de Braganca and I. Wallerstein, eds, Vol. 2, *The African Liberation Reader*, London, Zed.

Caesaire, A. (1972) *Discourse on Colonialism*, New York, Monthly Review Press.

Cain, M. (1990) 'Realist Philosophy and Standpoint Epistemologies of Feminist Criminology as a Successor Science' in L. Gelsthorpe and A. Morris, eds, *Feminist Perspectives in Criminology*, Milton Keynes, Open University Press.

Cain, M. (1995) 'Labouring, Loving and Living: On the Policing of Culture in Trinidad and Tobago', in L. Noakes, M. Maguire and M. Levi, eds, *Contemporary Issues in Criminology*, Cardiff, University of Wales.

Campbell, H. (1985) *Rasta and Resistance: From Marcus Garvey to Walter Rodney*, London, Hansib.

Campbell, H. (1986) 'Popular Resistance in Tanzania: Lessons from Sungu Sungu, *Africa Development*, Vol. 14, No. 4, 5–44.

Campbell, H. (1991) 'Africans and the 'New World Order': Democracy or the Globalisation of Apartheid?' An Address to the Holdane Society of Socialist Lawyers Conference, London.

Carlen, P. (1992) 'Women's Criminal Careers', in D. Downes, ed., *Unravelling Criminal Justice*, London, Macmillan.

Carmichael, S. and Hamilton, C.V. (1967) *Black Power: The Politics of Liberation in America*, New York, Penguin.

Caudwell, C. (1975) 'English Poets: (1) The Period of Primitive Accumulation', in D. Craig, ed., *Marxists on Literature*, Harmondsworth, Penguin.

Chagnon, N.A. (1992) *Yanomamo: The Last Days of Eden*, New York, Harvest Books.

Chambliss, W.J. (1971) 'Vice, Corruption, Bureaucracy, and Power', *Wisconsin Law Review*, 1150–73.

Chambliss, W.J. (1989) 'State-Organized Crime', *Criminology*, Vol. 27, 183–208.

Chambliss, W.J. (1995) 'Another Lost War: The Costs and Consequences of Drug Prohibition', *Social Justice*, Vol. 22, No. 2, 101–24.

Champion, D.J. (2000) *Research Methods for Criminal Justice and Criminology*, Upper Saddle River, Prentice-Hall.

Chang, I. (1997) *The Rape of Nanking: The Forgotten Holocaust of World War II*, New York, Penguin.

Chigwada, R. (1991) 'Policing of Black Women', in E. Cashmore and E. McClaughlin, eds, *Out of Order? Policing Black People*, London, Routledge & Kegan Paul.

Chinweizu, (1987) *Decolonising The African Mind*, Lagos, Pero.

Chinweizu (1990) *Anatomy of Female Power: A Masculinist Dissection of Matriarchy*. Excerpts in *African Concord*, Vol. 5, No. 28, 12 November.

Cicourel, A. (1969) *The Social Organization of Juvenile Justice*, New York, Wiley.

Clark, E. (1990) 'Black as Villain in African Literature', Keynote Address to the 4th Annual Conference of the English Department, University of Lagos. Excerpts in *African Concord*, Vol. 5, No. 32, 10 December.

Cleaver, E. (1969) *Soul on Ice: A Collection of Essays on Racial Questions Written from Folsom State Prison*, California and London, Cape.

Clifford, W. (1974) *An Introduction to African Criminology*, Nairobi, Oxford University Press.

Clinard, M.B. and Abbott, D. (1973) *Crime in Developing Countries*, New York, John Wiley and Sons.

Cloward, R.A. and Ohlin, L.E. (1960) *Deliquency and Opportunity*, New York, Free Press.

Clutterbuck, R. (1995) *Drugs, Crime and Corruption: Thinking the Unthinkable*, London, Macmillan.

Cohen, S. (1985) *Visions of Social Control*, Cambridge, Polity Press.

Cohen, S. (1988) *Against Criminology*, New Brunswick, Transaction Books.

Cohen, S. (1993) 'Human Rights and Crimes of the State: The Culture of Denial', *Aust. & NZ Journal of Criminology*, Vol. 26.

Coleman, J.S. et al. (1966) *Equality of Educational Opportunity*, Washington, US Government.

Collard, A. with J. Contrucci (1988) *Rape of the Wild: Men's Violence against Animals and the Earth*, London, The Women's Press.

Collins, P.H. (1986) 'Learning from the Outside Within: The Sociological Significance of Black Feminist Thought', *Social Problems*, Vol. 33.

Collins, P.H. (1990) *Black Feminist Thought: Knowledge, Consciousness and the Politics of Empowerment*, Boston, Unwin Hyman.

Cook, D. and Hudson, B. (1993) *Racism and Criminology*, London, Sage.

Daly, K. (1993) 'Class–Race–Gender: Sloganeering in Search of Meaning', *Social Justice*, Vol. 20, 1–2.

Daly, M. (1978) *Gyn/ecology: The Metaethics of Radical Feminism*, Boston, Beacon Press.

Davis, A. (1981) *Women, Race and Class*, London, The Women's Press.

Davis, A. (1987) 'Rape, Racism and the Capitalist Setting', *Black Scholar*, Vol. 9, No. 7, 24–30.

Derrida, J. (1994) *Specters of Marx*, Peggy Kamuf, trans., London. Routledge.

Deutscher, M. (1983) *Subjecting and Objecting: An Essay in Objectivity*, Oxford, Basil Blackwell.

Dorn, N., South, N. and Murgi, K. (1992) *Traffickers: Drug Markets and Law Enforcement*, London, Routledge.

Downes, D. (1966) *The Delinquent Solution*, London, Routledge & Kegan Paul.

Du Bois, W.E.B. (1992) *Black Reconstruction in America, 1860–1880*, New York, Free Press.

Du Bois, W.E.B. (1994) *The Souls of Black Folk*, New York, Dover.

Durkheim, E. (1965) *The Elementary Forms of the Religious Life*, New York, Free Press.

Durkheim, E. (1973) 'Two Rules of Penal Evolution', in S. Lukes and A. Scull, *Durkheim and the Law*, London, Macmillan.

Durkheim, E. (1982) *The Rules of Sociological Method and Selected Texts on Sociology and its Method*, S. Lukes, ed., W.D. Halls, trans., London, Macmillan.

Eagleton, T. (1976) *Marxism and Literary Criticism*, Berkeley, University of California Press.

Eagleton, T. (1990) *The Ideology of the Aesthetic*, Oxford, Basil Blackwell.

Eaton, M. (1993) *Women after Prison*, Buckingham, Open University.

Edwards, A.R. (1989) 'Sex/Gender, Sexism and Criminal Justice: Some Theoretical Considerations', *IJSL*, 17.

Eglash, R. (1999) *African Fractals: Modern Computing and Indigenous Design*, New Brunswick, Rutgers.

Eide, A. (1984) 'The Right to Oppose Violations of Human Rights: Basis Conditions and Limitations', in *Violations of Human Rights*, New York: UNESCO.

Ekwe-Ekwe, H. (1993) *Africa 2001: The State, Human Rights and the People*, Reading, The International Institute for Black Research.

Ellis, J.M. (1983) *One Fairy Story Too Many*, Chicago, University of Chicago Press.

Emerson, R.M. (1995) 'Holistic Effects in Social Control Decision-Making', in R.L. Abel, ed., *The Law and Society Reader*, New York, New York University.

Engels, F. (1848; 1958) *The Condition of the Working Class in England*, W.O. Henderson and W.H. Chaloner, trans. and eds, Oxford, Blackwell.

Ericson, R.V., Baranek, P.M. and Chan, B.L. (1989), *Negotiating Control*, Milton Keynes, Open University.

Falk, R. (2001) 'The Vietnam Syndrome', *The Nation*, 9 July.

Fanon, F. (1963) *The Wretched of the Earth*, Harmondsworth, Penguin.

Fanon, F. (1965) *A Dying Colonialism* trans. H. Chevalier, New York, Monthly Press.

Fanon, F. (1967) *Black Skin, White Masks*, New York, Monthly Review Press.

Fanon, F. (1970) *Towards the African Revolution*, Harmondsworth, Penguin.

Farrington, D. and Morris, A. (1983) 'Sex, Sentencing and Reconviction', *British Journal of Criminology*, Vol. 23, No. 3.

Fatunde, T. (1986) *Oga Na Tief Man*, Benin City, Adena.

Fatunde, T. (1990) 'Writer as Propagandist', interview with Kunle Ajibade in *African Concord*, Vol. 5, No. 24, 15 October.

Fawehinmi, G. (1993) 'Human Rights are Non-Negotiable', *Nigeria Now*, Vol. 2, No. 6, June.

Finkelstein, N.H. (2001) *Captain of Innocence: France and the Dreyfus Affair*, New York, iUniverse.com

Fitzgerald, M. (1993) *The Royal Commission on Criminal Justice: Ethnic Minorities and the Criminal Justice System*, London, HMSO.

Fitzgerald, P. (1990) 'Democracy and Civil Society in South Africa: A Response to Daryl Glaser', *Review of African Political Economy*, No. 49, Winter.

Fitzpatrick, P. (1980) *Law and State in Papua New Guinea*, London, Academic Press.

Fitzpatrick, P. (1992) *The Mythology of Modern Law*, London, Routledge.

Foucault, M. (1961) *Madness and Civilisation: A History of Insanity in the Age of Reason*, London, Routledge.

Foucault, M. (1977) *Discipline and Punish: The Birth of the Prison*, London, Allen Lane.

Foucault, M. (1980) *Power/Knowledge: Selected Interviews and Other Writings 1972–1977*, C. Gordon, ed., New York, Pantheon Books.

Foucault, M. (1988) *Politics, Philosophy, Culture: Interviews and Other Writings, 1977–1984*, L. Kritzman, ed., New York, Routledge.

Freire, P. (1972) *Pedagogy of the Oppressed*, Harmondsworth, Penguin.

Frugg, M.J. (1992) *Postmodern Legal Feminism*, London, Routledge.

Fyfe, C. (1992) 'Race, Empire and the Historians', *Race & Class*, Vol. 33, No. 4.

Gabbidon, S.L, Green, H.T. and Young, V.D. (2002) *African American Classics in Criminology and Criminal Justice*, London, Sage.

Garfinkel, H. (1974) *Studies in Ethnomethodology*, Upper Saddle River, Prentice-Hall.

Garland, D. (1985) *Punishment and Welfare: A History of Penal Strategies*, Aldershot, Gower.

Garland, D. (1990) *Punishment and Modern Society: A Study in Social Theory*, Oxford, Clarendon.

Garland, D. (2001) *The Culture of Control: Crime and Social Order in Contemporary Society*, Chicago, University of Chicago Press.

Garland, D. and Young, P. (1983) 'Towards a Social Analysis of Penalty', in D. Garland and P. Young, eds, *The Power to Punish: Contemporary Penalty and Social Analysis*, London, Heinemann.

Gelsthorpe, L. (1986) 'Towards a Sceptical Look at Sexism', *International Journal of the Sociology of Law*, Vol. 14.

Gelsthorpe, L. (1992) 'Response to Martyn Hammersley's Chapter On Feminist Methodology', *Sociology*, Vol. 26, No. 2, 213–18.

Giddens, A. (1989) *Sociology*, Cambridge, Polity.

Giddens, A. (1994) 'Living in a Post-Traditional Society', in U. Beck, A. Giddens and S. Lash, *Reflexive Modernization: Politics, Tradition and Aesthetics in the Modern Social Order*, Stanford, Stanford University Press.

Gill, P. (1996) '"Sack the Spooks": Do We Need an Internal Security Apparatus?', *Socialist Register*, 189–211.

Gilroy, P. (1987a) *There Ain't No Black in the Union Jack*, London, Hutchinson.

Gilroy, P. (1987b) 'The Myth of Black Criminality', in P. Scraton, ed., *Law, Order and the Authoritarian State*, Milton Keynes, Open University Press.

Gilroy, P. (1991) 'The Politics of Race and the Criminal Justice System', address to 'Criminology into the 1990s Conference' on *Women and Ethnic Minorities and the Criminal Justice System*, London, 29 May.

Gilroy, P. (1993) *The Black Atlantic*, London, Verso.

Glasser, B.G. and Strauss, A.L. (1967) *The Discovery of Grounded Theory: Strategies for Qualitative Research*, Chicago, Aldine.

Gleick, J. (1987) *Chaos: Making a New Science*, London, Sphere Books.

Goffman, E. (1961) *Asylums: Essays on the Social Situation of Mental Patients and Other Inmates*, Garden City, NY, Anchor.

Gouldner, A. (1961) 'Anti-Minotaur: The Myth of a Value-Free Sociology', *Social Problems*, Vol. 9, 199–213.

Gouldner, A. (1970) 'The Sociologist as Partisan: Sociology and the Welfare State', in J.D. Douglas, ed., *The Relevance of Sociology*, New York, Appleton-Century-Crofts.

Gouldner, A. (1971) *Coming Crisis of Western Sociology*, New York, Avon.

Gramsci, A. (1971), *Selections From the Prison Notebooks*, London, Lawrence and Wishart.

Green, P. (1991) *Drug Couriers*, London, The Howard League for Penal Reform.

Green, P., Mills, C. and Read, T. (1994) 'The Characteristics and Sentencing of Illegal Drug Importers', *British Journal of Criminology*, Vol. 34, No. 4, 479–86.

Greenberg, D.F. (1993) *Crime and Capitalism: Readings in Marxist Criminology*, Philadelphia, Temple University Press.

Gugelberger, G.M. (1985) *Marxism and African Literature*, London, James Curry.

Haan, W.D. (1992) 'Universalism and Relativism in Critical Criminology', *The Critical Criminologist*, Vol. 4, No. 1, Spring.

Habermas, J. (1987) *The Theory of Communicative Action. Volume 2. Lifeworld and System: A Critique of Functionalist Reason*, Cambridge, Polity.

Habermas, J. (1996) *Between Facts and Norms*, Cambridge, Polity.

Hall, S. (1979) *Drifting into a Law and Order Society*, London, Coben Trust.

Hall, S. (1980) 'Race, Articulation and Societies Structured in Dominance', in UNESCO, ed., *Sociological Theories: Race and Colonialism*. Paris, UNESCO.

Hall, S. (1987) 'Urban Unrest in Britain', in J. Benyon and J. Solomos, eds, *The Roots of Urban Unrest*, Oxford, Pergamon.

Hall, S. (1988) *The Hard Road to Renewal*, London, Verso.

Hall, S. (1996) *Critical Dialogues in Cultural Studies*, London, Routledge.

Hall, S. and Scraton, P. (1981) 'Law, Class and Control', M. Fitzgerald, G. McLennan and J. Pawson, eds, *Crime and Society: Readings in History and Theory*, London, Open University/Routledge.

Hall, S., Critcher, C., Jefferson, T., Clarke, J. and Roberts, B. (1978) *Policing The Crisis: Mugging, the State, and Law and Order*, London, Macmillan.

Hammersley, M. (1993) 'Research and "Anti-Racism": The Case of Peter Foster and his Critics', *British Journal of Sociology*, Vol. 44, No. 3, 429–48.

Harding, S. (1986) *The Science Question in Feminism*, Milton Keynes, Open University Press.

Harding, S. (1987) 'Introduction' to S. Harding, ed., *Feminism amd Methodology*. Milton Keynes, Open University Press.

Harding, S. (1991) *Whose Science? Whose Knowledge? Thinking from Women's Lives*, Milton Keynes, Open University Press.

Harding, S. (ed.) (1993) *The 'Racial' Economy of Science: Toward a Democratic Future*, Bloomington, Indiana University Press.

Hargreaves, J. (1988) *Sport, Power and Culture*, Oxford, Polity.

Harlow, B. and Carter, M. (1999) *Imperialism & Orientalism: A Documentary Sourcebook*, London, Blackwell.

Harrison, R. (1986) 'Rape – a Case Study in Political Philosophy', in Sylvana Tomaselli and Roy Porter, eds, *Rape*, Oxford, Blackwell.

Hartsock, N.C.M. (1987) 'The Feminist Standpoint: Developing the Ground For a Specifically Feminist Historical Materialism', in S. Harding, ed. (1993) *The Racial Economy of Science: Toward a Democratic Future*, Bloomington, Indiana University Press.

Headley, B. D. (1983) '"Black on Black" Crime ...' *Crime and Social Justice* No. 20.

Hecter, M. (1975) *Internal Colonialism: The Celtic Fringe in British National Development 1536–1966*, Beverly Hills, University of California Press.

Hecter, M. (1983) 'Internal Colonialism Revisited', in D. Drakakis-Smith and S.W. Williams, eds, *Internal Colonialism: Essays around a Theme*, Edinburgh University, Department of Geography.

Heidensohn, F. (1986) 'Models of Justice: Portia or Persophone?', *International Journal of the Sociology of Law*, Vol. 14.

Henry, S. and Milovanivic, D. (1994) 'The Constitution of Constitutive Criminology: a Postmodern Approach to Criminological Theory', in D. Nelken, ed., *The Futures of Criminology*, London, Routledge.

Henry, S. and Milovanovic, D. (1996) *Constitutive Criminology*, London, Sage.

Herman, D. (1993) 'Beyond the Rights Debate', *Social & Legal Studies*, Vol. 2, 25–43.

Herman, E.S. and Chomsky, N. (1988) *Manufacturing Consent: The Political Economy of the Mass Media*, New York, Pantheon.

Higginbottam, A.L., Jr. (1978) *In the Matter of Color: Race and the American Legal Process*, New York, Oxford University Press.

Hillyard, P. (1993) *Suspect Community: People's Experience of the Prevention of Terrorism Acts in Britain*, London, Pluto.

Hillyard, P. (1994) 'Irish People and the British Criminal Justice System Evidence', in *Journal of Law and Society*, Vol. 21, No. 1, March.

Hirst, P. (1975) 'Radical Deviancy Theory and Marxism: A Reply to Taylor and Walton', in I. Taylor, P. Walton and J. Young, eds, *Critical Criminology*, Boston, Routledge & Kegan Paul.

Ho Chi Minh (1924) 'Lynching', *La Correspondance Internationale*, No. 59.

Hobbes, T. (1650, 1950) *The Leviathan: Matter, Forme and Power of a Commonwealth, Ecclesiastical and Civil*, London, Everyman's Library.

Hochschild, A. (1998) *King Leopold's Ghost: A Story of Greed, Terror, and Heroism in Colonial Africa*, New York, Houghton Miffin Company.

Hood, R. (1992) *Race and Sentencing: A Study in Crown Courts*, Oxford, Clarendon.

hooks, b. (1984) *Feminist Theory: From Margin to Center*, Boston, South End Press.

hooks, b. (1989) *Talking Back: Thinking Feminist. Thinking Black*, London, Sheba Feminist Publishers.

hooks, b. (1993) 'bell hooks Speaking about Paulo Freire – The Man, His Work', in P. McLaren and P. Lepnard, eds, *Paulo Freire: A Critical Encounter*, London, Routledge.

hooks, b. (1994) *Outlaw Culture: Resisting Representations*, London, Routledge.

Hooton, E.A. (1939) *The American Criminal*, Cambridge, MA, Harvard University Press.

Howe, A. (1994) *Punish and Critique: Towards a Feminist Analysis of Penalty*, London, Routledge.

Hudson, B. (1987) *Justice through Punishment*, London, Macmillan.

Hughes, G. (1991) 'The New Left Realist Theory of Crime: A Sociological Revival and Critique'. Paper presented at the British Criminology Conference, York, 19 June.

ICA (1980) 'Peter Tosh – Victim of the Shitstem ... Almost a Year Later the Mystery Unfolds', *Reggae Report*, Vol. 6, Part 6.

Institute of Race Relations (1987) *Policing against Black People*, London, IRR.

Iyayi, F. (1982) *The Contract*, Harlow, Longman.

Iyayi, F. (1991) 'A Stinging Bee', interview with Kunle Ajibade, *African Concord*, Vol. 5, No. 43, 26 February.

Jacobs, S. (1983) 'Women and Land Resettlement in Zimbabwe', *Review of African Political Economy*, Vols 27/28.

Jacobs, S., Jacobson, R. and Marchbank, J. (eds) (2000) *States of Conflict: Gender, Violence and Resistance*, London, Zed.

James, C.L.R. (1980) *The Black Jacobins: Toussaint l'Ouverture and the San Domingo Revolution*, London, Allison and Busby.

James, C.L.R. (1982) *Nkrumah and the Ghana Revolution*, London, Allison and Busby.

Jefferson, T. (1991) 'Discrimination, Disadvantage and Police Work', in E. Cashmore and E. McLaughlin, eds, *Out of Order? Policing Black People*, London, Routledge.

Jefferson, T. (1992) 'The Racism of Criminalisation: Policing and the Reproduction of the Criminal Other', in L. Gelsthorpe, ed., *Cropwood Roundtable on Ethnic Minority Groups and the Criminal Justice System*, Cambridge, Institute of Criminology.

Jenkins, R. (1971) *The Production of Knowledge at the Institute of Race Relations*, London, Independent Labour Party.

Jensen, A. (1967) 'How Much Can We Boost IQ and Scholastic Achievement?', *Harvard Educational Review*, Vol. 29.

Jeyifo, B. (1985) *The Truthful Lie*, London, New Beacon.

Johnson, C. (1982) 'Grass Roots Organizing: Women in Anticolonial Activity in Southwestern Nigeria', *African Studies Review*, Vol. 25, 2–3.

Johnson, E.H. (1983) *International Handbook of Contemporary Developments in Criminology: Europe, Africa, the Middle East and Asia*, Westport, CT, Greenwood Press.

Kalunta-Crumpton, A. (1998) *Race and Drugs Trials: The Social Construction of Guilt and Innocence*, Aldershot, Ashgate.

Kant, I. (1964) *Groundwork of the Metaphysics of Morals*, Cambridge, Cambridge University Press.

Katz, J. (1996) 'Seductions and Repulsions of Crime', in J. Muncie, E. McLaughlin and M. Langen, eds, *Criminological Perspectives: A Reader*, London, Sage.

Keith, M. (1993) *Race, Riots and Policing*, London, UCL.

Kelly, L. and Radford, J. (1987) 'The Problem of Men: Feminist Perspectives on Sexual Violence', in P. Scraton, ed., *Law, Order and the Authoritarian State*, Milton Keynes, Open University.

Kennedy, H. (1992) *Eve Was Framed*, London, Vintage.

Kennedy, M.C. (1976) 'Beyond Incrimination: Some Neglected Facets of the Theory of Punishment', in W.J. Chambliss and M. Mankof, eds, *Whose Law What Order?*, London, John Wiley & Sons.

Kennedy, R. (1997) *Race, Crime and the Law*, New York, Pantheon.

King, Jr, M.L. (1967) *Where Do We Go From Here: Chaos or Community?*, New York, Harper & Row.

Kingdom, E. (1992) *What's Wrong with Rights?: Problems for Feminist Politics of Law*, Edinburgh, Edinburgh University Press.

Kinsey, R., Lea, J., and Young, J. (1989) *Losing the Fight against Crime*. Oxford, Basil Blackwell.

Kitsuse, J. (1975) 'The New Conception of Deviance and its Critics', in W. Grove, ed., *The Labelling of Deviance*, New York, Halstead.

Kuper, L. (1965) *An African Bourgeoisie*. London, Yale University Press.

Lassman, P., Velody, I., and Martins, H. (eds) (1989) *Max Weber's 'Science as a Vocation'*, London, Unwin Hyman.

Lazreg, M. (1994) 'Women's Experience and Feminist Epistemology: A Critical Neo-rationalist Approach', in K. Lennon and M. Whitford, eds, *Knowing the Difference: Feminist Perspectives in Epistemology*, London, Routledge.

Lea, J. and Young, J. (1984) *What is to be Done about Law and Order?* Harmondsworth, Penguin.

Lea, J. and Young, J. (1996) 'Relative Deprivation', in J. Muncie, E. McLaughlin and M. Langen, eds, *Criminological Perspectives: A Reader*, London, Sage.

Lea, J., Kinsey, R. and Young, J. (1986) *Losing the Fight against Crime*, Oxford, Blackwell.

Lemert, E.M. (1951) *Social Pathology: A Systematic Approach to the Theory of Sociopathic Behavior*, New York, McGraw-Hill.

Lenin, V.I. (1996) *Imperialism: The Highest Stage of Capitalism*, London, Pluto.

Lennon, K. and Whitford, M. (1994) 'Introduction' to K. Lennon and M. Whitford, eds, *Knowing the Difference: Feminist Perspectives in Epistemology*, London, Routledge.

Liebman, S.J., Fagan, J. and West, V. (2000) *A Broken System: Error Rates in Capital Cases, 1973–1995*, New York, Columbia University Law School.

Little, K. (1980) *The Sociology of Urban Women's Images in African Literature*, London, Macmillan.

Little, K. (1995) 'Surveilling Cirque Archaos: Transgression and the Spaces of Power in Popular Entertainment', *Journal of Popular Culture*, Vol. 29, No. 1.

Locke, J. (1690, 1988) *Two Treatises of Government*, Cambridge, Cambridge University Press.

Lombroso, C. (1876) *The Criminal Man*, Turin, Fratelli Bocca.

Lombroso, C. (1911) 'Introduction' to Gina Lombroso Ferero, *Criminal Man According to the Classification of Cesare Lombroso*, New York, Putnam, p. xv.

Luhhmann, N. (1995) *Social Systems*, Stanford, Stanford University Press.

Lumumba, P. (1962) *Congo My Country*, tr. G. Heath, London, Pall Mall.

Lyotard, J. (1988) *The Inhuman: Reflections on Time*, Cambridge, Polity.

Lyotard, J. (1990) *Duchamp's TRANS/formations: A Book*, Paris, Lapis.

Mackinnon, C.A. (1987) 'Feminism, Marxism, Method, and the State: Towards Feminist Jurisprudence' in S. Harding, ed., *Feminism and Methodology*, Milton Keynes, Open University Press.

Mackinnon, C.A. (1989) *Towards a Feminist Theory of the State*. London, Harvard University Press.

Mackinnon, C.A. (1993a) *Only Words*, London, HarperCollins.

Mackinnon, C.A. (1993b) 'Crimes of War, Crimes of Peace', in S. Shute and S. Hurley, eds, *On Human Rights: The Oxford Amnesty Lectures*, New York, Basic Books.

Macpherson, Sir W. of Cluny (1999) *The Stephen Lawrence Inquiry: Report of an Inquiry*, London, HMSO.

Madanugu, E. (1982) *Problems of Socialism: The Nigerian Challenge*, London, Zed.

Maden, A., Swinton, M., and Gunn, J. (1992) 'The Ethnic Origin of Women Serving a Prison Sentence', *British Journal of Criminology*, Vol. 32, No. 2, 218–21.

Madhubuti, H.R. (1994) *Claiming Earth: Race, Rage. Rape, Redemption Blacks Seeking A Culture of Enlightened Empowerment*, Chicago, Third World Press.

Mafeje A. (1998) 'Anthropology and Independent Africans: Suicide or End of an Era?', *African Sociological Review*, Vol. 2, No. 1.

Malleson, K. (1994) 'Appeals against Conviction and the Principle of Finality Evidence', *Journal of Law and Society*, Vol. 21, No. 1, March.

Mama, A. (1989) *The Hidden Struggle*, London, London Housing and Race Research Unit.

Mamdani, M. (1983) *Imperialism and Fascism in Uganda*, London, Heinemann.

Mangena, O. (1994) 'Against Fragmentation: The Need for Holism', in K. Lennon and M. Whitford, eds, *Knowing the Difference*, London, Routledge.

Marable, M. (1995) *Beyond Black and White*, London, Verso.

Marx, K. (1904) *Contribution to the Critique of Political Economy*, N.I. Stone, trans, Chicago, Charles H. Kerr.

Marx, K. (1954) *Capital*. Vol. 1, Moscow, Progress.

Marx, K. (1961) *Selected Writings on Sociology and Social Philosophy*, T. Bottomore, and M. Rubel, eds, London, Penguin.

Marx, K. (1980) *The Holy Family or Critique of Critical Criticism*, New York, Firebird Publications.

Marx, K. and Engels, F. (1974) *On Colonialism*, New York, Pathfinder.

Masson, J.M. (1984) *Freud: The Assault on Truth*, London, Faber.

Mathiesen, T. (1983) 'The Future of Control Systems – the Case of Norway', in D. Garland and P. Young, eds, *The Power to Punish*, London, Heinemann.

Matza, D. (1964) *Delinquency and Drift*, New York, John Wiley.

Maxfield, M.G. and Babbie, E. (1998) *Research Methods for Criminal Justice and Criminology*, Boston, Wadsworth.

McCamant, J.F. (1981) 'A Critique of Present Measures of "Human Rights Development" and an Alternative', in V.P. Nanda et al., eds, *Global Human Rights*, Colorado, Westview Press.

Mead, G.H. (1918) 'The Psychology of Justice', *American Journal of Sociology*, Vol. 23, 577–602.

Medford, R. (1992) 'Imprisonment: The Aboriginal Experience in Western Australia' in M. Carlie and K. Minor, eds, *Prisons around the World*, Des Moines, IA, Wm C. Brown.

Meierhoefer, B. (1992) *The General Effect of Mandatory Minimum Prison Terms*, Federal Justice Center, Washington, DC.

Merton, R.K. (1938) 'Social Structure and Anomie', *American Sociological Review*, Vol. 3, pp. 672–82.

Messerschmidt, J.W. (1993) *Masculinities and Crime: Critique and Reconceptualization of Theory*, Lanham, MD, Rowman & Littlefield Publishers.

Mhalanga, B. (1997) *The Colour of English Justice*, Aldershot, Ashgate.

Midford, R. (1992) 'Imprisonment: The Aboriginal Experience in Western Australia', in M. Carlie and K. Minor, eds, *Prisons around the World*, Des Moines, IA, Wm C. Brown.

Miles, R. (1993) *Racism after 'Race Relations'*, London, Routledge.

Miliband, R. (1969) *The State in Capitalist Society*, London, Weidenfeld and Nicolson.

Milne, A.J.M. (1979) 'The Idea of Human Rights: A Critical Inquiry', in F.E. Dowrick, *Human Rights: Problems, Perspectives and Texts*, Aldershot, Saxon House.

Milovanovic, D. (1992) *Postmodern Law and Disorder*, Liverpool, Deborah Charles.

Milovanovic, D. (1997) *Postmodern Criminology*, New York, Garland.

Mirandé, A. (1987) *Gringo Justice*, Notre Dame, University of Notre Dame.

Morrison, T. (1992) *Jazz: A Novel*, London, Chatto & Windus.

Morrison, T., ed. (1992) *Race–ing Justice, En–gendering Power: Essays on Anita Hill, Clarence Thomas and the Construction of Social Reality*, New York, Pantheon Books.

Moyer, I. (2001) *Criminological Theory: Traditional and Nontraditional Voices and Themes*, London, Sage.

Mudimbe, V.Y. (1988) *The Invention of Africa*, Bloomington, Indiana University Press.

Mullard, C. (1985) *Race, Power and Resistance*, London, Routledge.

Murray, C. (1984) *Losing Ground: American Social Policy, 1950–1980*, New York, Basic Books.

Myrdal, G. (1944) *An American Dilemma*, Vol. II, New York, Harper and Row.

Nacro (1989) *Race and Criminal Justice*, London, NACRO.

Naffine, N. (1990) *Law and the Sexes: Explorations in Feminist Jurisprudence*, Sydney, Allen & Unwin.

Nagel, T. (1986) *The View from Nowhere*, Oxford, Oxford University Press.

Nelken, D. (1994) *The Futures of Criminolgy*, London, Sage.

Ngara, E. (1985) *Art and Ideology in the African Novel*, London, Heinemann.

Nietzsche, F. (1969) *On the Genealogy of Morals*, trans. W. Kaufman and R.J. Hollingdale, New York, Vintage.

Nkrumah, K. (1967) *Challenge of the Congo*, New York, International Publishers.

Nkrumah, K. (1968) *Neo-Colonialism: The Last Stage of Imperialism*, London, Heinemann.

Norris, C. (1992) *Uncritical Theory: Postmodernism, Intellectuals and the Gulf War*, London, Lawrence and Wishart.

Norton-Taylor, R. (1999) *The Colour of Justice*, London, Oberon Books, extracted in the *Guardian*, 30 January.

Nwabueze, B.O. (1985) *Nigeria's Presidential Constitution*, London, Longman.

Nzegwu, N. (2000) 'African Women and the Fire Dance' in *West Africa Review*: 2, 1.[iuicode: http://www.icaap.org/iuicode?101.2.1.11

OAU (1981) *African Charter on Human and Peoples Rights*, Nairobi, Organisation of African Unity.

Obasanjo, O. (1998) *Guides to Effective Prayer*, Abeokuta, Olusegun Obasanjo.

Odekunle, F. (1986) 'The Legal Order, Crime and Crime Control in Nigeria: Demystification of False Appearances'. Public Lecture, Centre for Cultural Studies, University of Lagos.

Offiong, D. (1980) *Imperialism and Dependency*, Enugu, Fourth Dimension Publishers.

Omar, D. (1990), 'An Overview of State Lawlessness in South Africa', in D. Hansson, ed., *Towards Justice*, Oxford, Oxford University Press.

Onwudiwe, I. (2000) *The Globalization of Terrorism*, Aldershot, Ashgate.

Opolot, J.S.E. (1982) 'Contributions of the African Novel to the Development of African Criminology', *International Journal of Comparative and Applied Criminal Justice*, Vol. VI, No. 2.

Pashukanis, F.B. (1980) *Selected Writings on Marxism and Law*, London, Academic Press.

Patterson, O. (1998) *Rituals of Blood*, New York, Basic Books.

Pearce, F. (1976) *Crimes of the Powerful*, London, Pluto.

Pepinsky, H.E. (1991) *The Geometry of Violence and Democracy*, Bloomington, University of Indiana Press.

Pepinsky, H. and Quinney, R. (1991) *Criminology as Peacemaking*, Bloomington, Indiana University Press.

Pfohl, S. (1994) *Images of Deviance and Social Control: A Sociological History*, New York, McGraw-Hill.

Pfohl, S. and Gordon, A. (1986) 'Criminological Displacements: A Sociological Deconstruction', *Social Problems*, Vol. 33, No. 6.

Picciotto, S. (1979) 'The Theory of the State, Class Struggle and the Rule of Law', *Capitalism and the Rule of Law*, London, National Deviancy Conference.

Picciotto, S. (1982) 'The Theory of the State, Class Struggle and the Rule of Law', in P. Beirne and R. Quinney, eds, *Marxism and Law*, New York, John Wiley.

Pick, D. (1989) *The Faces of Degeneration: A European Disorder, c.1848–c.1918*, Cambridge, Cambridge University Press.

Pitch, T. (1995) *Limited Responsibilities: Social Movements and Criminal Justice*, J. Lea, trans., London, Routledge.

Pollack, O. (1950) *The Criminality of Women*, Philadelphia, University of Pennsylvania Press.

Porch, D. (1995) *The French Secret Services: From the Dreyfus Affair to the Gulf War*, New York, Farrar, Straus and Giroux.

Porter, R. (1986) 'Rape – Does it have a Historical Meaning?', in S. Tomaselli and R. Porter, eds, *Rape*, Oxford, Blackwell.

Poulantzas, N. (1978) *State, Power, Socialism*, London, New Left Books.

Power, J. (2000) *Amnesty in Africa*, in PROSPECT, November.

Quinney, R. (1974) *Critique of Legal Order*, New York, Little, Brown.

Quinton, A.M. (1969) 'On Punishment', in H.B. Acton, ed., *The Philosophy of Punishment*, London, Macmillan.

Ramazanoglu, C. (1993) *Up against Foucault: Explorations of Some Tensions between Foucault and Feminism*, London, Routledge.

Ratamar, R.F. (1979) 'Against the Black Legend', *Ideologies and Literature*, Vol. II, No. 10.

Rawls, J. (1969) 'Two Concepts of Rules', in H.B. Acton, ed., *The Philosophy of Punishment*, London, Macmillan.

Reich, W. (1970) *The Mass Psychology of Fascism*, Harmondsworth, Penguin.

Reid, S.T. (1976) *Crime and Criminology*, New York, Holt, Rinehart, and Winston.

Reinarman, C. and Levine, H.G., eds (1997) *Crack in America: Demon Drugs and Social Justice*, University of California Press, Berkeley.

Reiner, R. (1992) 'Race, Crime and Justice: Models of Interpretation'. Paper presented at the Cropwood Conference on Minority Ethnic Groups and the Criminal Justice System, Cambridge, 30 March–1 April.

Rescher, N. (1997) *Objectivity: The Obligations of Impersonal Reason*, Notre Dame, University of Notre Dame Press.

Retamar, R.F. (1979) 'Against the Black Legend', *Ideologies and Literature*, Vol. II, No. 10.

Rice, M. (1990) 'Challenging Orthodoxies in Feminist Theory: A Black Feminist Intervention', in L. Gelsthorpe and A. Morris, eds, *Feminist Perspectives in Criminology*. Milton Keynes, Open University.

Rodney, W. (1972) *How Europe Underdeveloped Africa*, London, Bogle-L'Ouverture.

Rodney, W. (1974) 'Towards The Sixth Pan-African Congress: Aspects of the International Class Struggle in Africa, the Caribbean and America', in H. Campbell, ed., *Pan-Africanism: Struggle Against Neo-Colonialism and Imperialism*, Dar-es-Salaam.

Rodney, W. (1975) 'Contemporary Trends in the English-Speaking Caribbean', *Black Scholar*, Vol. 7, No. 1.

Rodney, W. (1981) *A History of the Guyanese Working People, 1881–1905*, Baltimore, Johns Hopkins University Press.

Rodriguez, A.M. (1987) 'Institutional Racism in the Organisational Setting: An Action-Research Approach', in J. Shaw et al., eds, *Strategies for Improving Race Relations*, Manchester, Manchester University Press.

Rousseau, J.-J., (1762, 1968) *The Social Contract*, New York, Penguin.

Roussou, M. (1987) 'War in Cyprus: Patriarchy and the Penelope Myth', in Rosemary Ridd and Helen Callaway, eds, *Women and Political Conflict: Portraits of Struggle in Times of Crisis*, New York, New York University Press.

Rovella, D.E. (1997) 'Danger of Executing the Innocent on the Rise', *The National Law Journal*, Vol. 19, 4 August.

Rubin, A. and Babbie, E. (1989) *Research Methods for Social Work*, Belmont, Wadsworth.

Ruggiero, V. (1992) 'Realist Criminology: a Critique', in J. Young and R. Matthews, eds, *Rethinking Criminolgy: The Realist Debate*, London, Sage.

Ruggiero, V. and South, N. (1995) *Eurodrugs: Drug Use, Markets and Trafficking in Europe*, London, UCL.

Rusche, G. and Kirchheimer, O. (1968, c1939), *Punishment and Social Structure*. New York, Russell & Russell.

Russell, S. (1997) 'The Failure of Postmodern Criminology', *Critical Criminology*, Vol. 5, No. 2.

Said, E. (1978) *Orientalism*, New York, Pantheon.

Said, E. (1993) *Culture and Imperialism*, London, Chatto and Windus.

Schutz, A. (1962) *Collected Papers I: The Problems of Social Reality*, Maurice Natanson, ed., The Hague, Martinus Nijhof.

Schwendinger, H. and J. (1970) 'Defenders of Order or Guardians of Human Rights?', *Issues in Criminology*, Vol. 5.

Schwendinger, H. and J. (1997) 'When the Study of Delinquent Groups Stood Still: In Defence of a classical Tradition', *Critical Criminology*, Vol. 8, No. 2.

Schwendinger, J. and Herman (1983) *Rape and Inequality*, London, Sage.

Scott, R.A. (1969) *The Making of Blind Men*, New York, Russell Sage.

Scraton, P. (1990) 'Scientific Knowledge or Masculine Discourse? Challenging Patriarchy in Criminology', in L. Gelsthorpe and A. Morris, eds, *Feminist Perspectives in Criminology*, Milton Keynes, Open University.

Scraton, P. and Chadwick, K. (1987) 'Speaking Ill of the Dead: Institutionalized Responses to Deaths in Custody', in P. Scraton, ed., *Law, Order and the Authoritarian State*, Milton Keynes, Open University.

Scraton, P. and Chadwick, K. (1996) 'The Theoretical and Political Priorities of Critical Criminology', in J. Muncie, E. McLaughlin and M. Langen, eds, *Criminological Perspectives: A Reader*, London, Sage.

Seller, A. (1994) 'Should the Feminist Philosopher Stay at Home?', in K. Lennon and M. Whitford, eds, *Knowing the Difference: Feminist Perspectives in Epistemology*, London, Routledge.

Sellin, T. (1972) 'Crime as Violation of Conduct Norms', in David Dressler, ed., *Readings in Criminology and Penology*, New York, Columbia University.

Senna, J.J. and Siegel, L.J. (1984) *Introduction to Criminal Justice*, New York, West, 5.

Shaw, G.B. (1938) *Prefaces*, London, Odhams Press.

Shivji, I. (1982) 'Semi-Proletarian Labour and the Use of Penal Sanctions in the Labour Law of Colonial Tanganyika (1920–38), in C. Sumner, ed., *Crime, Justice and Underdevelopment*, London, Heinemann.

Shivji, I. (1995) 'The Rule of Law and Ujamaa in the Ideological Formation in Tanzania', *Social and Legal Studies*, Vol. 4, 147–74.

Sim, J., Scraton, P. and Gordon, P. (1987) 'Introduction: Crime, the State and Critical Analysis', in P. Scraton, ed., *Law, Order and the Authoritarian State*, Milton Keynes, Open University.

Simmons, J.L. (1969) *Deviants*, San Francisco, Boyd & Francis.

Sivanandan, A. (1974) *Race and Resistance: The I.R.R. Story*, London, Race Today.

Sivanandan, A. (1990) *Communities of Resistance: Writings on Black Struggles for Socialism*, London, Verso.

Sivanandan, A. (2000) 'The Lawrence Inquiry: One Year On', IRR, London, 19 February.

Smart, C. (1990) 'Feminist Approaches to Criminology or Postmodern Woman Meets Atavistic Man', in L. Gelsthorpe and A. Morris, eds, *Feminist Perspectives in Criminology*, Milton Keynes, Open University Press.

Smith, D.J. (1994) 'Race, Crime and Criminal Justice', in M. Maguire, R. Morgan and R. Reiner, eds, *The Oxford Handbook of Criminology*, Oxford, Oxford University Press.

Smith, L.T. (1999) *Decolonizing Methodologies: Research and Indigenous Peoples*, London, Zed.

Snell, T.L. (1996) *Capital Punishment 1995*, Washington, DC, US Bureau of Justice Statistics.

Snowden, D. (1988) 'Andrew Tosh Shoulders Reggae Legacy', *Los Angeles Times*, 7 April.

Solomos, J. (1992) 'The Politics of Immigration Since 1945', in P. Braham, A. Rattansi and R. Skellington, eds, *Racism and Antiracism*, London, Sage.

Soyinka, W. (1973) *Season of Anomy*, London, Arena.

Soyinka, W. (1988) *This Past Must Address its Present: The 1986 Nobel Lecture*, Occassional Papers of the Phelps-Stokes Fund, No. 3.

Soyinka, W. (1994) *The Man Died*, London, Vintage.

Soyinka, W. (1996) *The Open Sore of a Continent*, Oxford, Oxford University Press.

Spitzer, S. and Scull, A.T. (1982) 'Social Control in Historical Perspective: From Private to Public Responses to Crime', in P. Beirne and R. Quinney, eds, *Marxism and Law*, New York, Wiley.

Spivak, G.C. (1999) *A Critique of Post-colonial Reason: Towards a History of the Vanishing Present*, Cambridge, Mass, Harvard University Press.

Stanko, E. (1992) 'The Case of Fearful Women: Gender, Personal Safety and Fear of Crime', *Women and Criminal Justice*, Vol. 4, 117–35.

Stanley, L. (1994) 'The Knowing Because Experiencing Subject: Narratives, Lives and Autobiography', in K. Lennon and M. Whitford, eds, *Knowing the Difference: Feminist Perspectives in Epistemology*, London, Routledge.

Stanley, L. and Wise, S. (1983) *Breaking Out*. London, Routledge & Kegan Paul.

Sudnow, D. (1965) 'Normal Crimes', *Social Problems*, Vol. 12, winter, 255–70.

Sumner, C. (1981) 'Race, Crime and Hegemony', *Contemporary Crisis*, Vol. 5, No. 3.

Sumner, C. (1990) 'Reflections on a Sociological Theory of Criminal Justice Systems', in C. Sumner, ed., *Censure, Politics and Criminal Justice*, Philadelphia, Open University.

Sumner, C. (1994) *The Sociology of Deviance: An Obituary*, Buckingham, Open University.

Sumner, W. (1906) *Folkways*, Boston, Ginn.

Sutherland, E.H. (1949) *White Collar Crime*, New Haven, Yale University Press.

Talbot, C.K. (1982) 'The Mirror Image of Crime: A Comparison of Recorded Crime and Crime Recorded in Fiction', *International Journal of Comparative and Applied Criminal Justice*. Vol. 6, No. 2.

Talbot, C.K. (1987) 'The Procedural Perspective on Public and Police Violence', *Crimecare Journal*, Vol. 3, No. 1.

Talbot, C.K. (1988) 'Towards the Criminology of Literature', *Crimecare Journal*, Vol. 4, No. 1.

Tappan, P.W. (1977) 'Who is the Criminal?', in G. Geis and R.F. Meier, eds, *White-Collar Crime*, New York, The Free Press.

Tarzi, A. and Hedges, J. (1990) *A Study of Foreign Prisoners*, London, Inner London Probation Service.

Tatum, B. (1996) 'The Colonial Model as a Theoretical Explanation of Crime and Delinquency', in A.T. Sulton, ed., *African American Perspectives on Crime Causation, Criminal Justice Administration and Crime Prevention*, Boston, Butterworths-Heinemann.

Taylor, I. (1982) 'Against Crime and for Socialism', *Crime and Social Justice*, No. 18, Winter.

Taylor, I. et al. (1973) *The New Criminology*. London, Routledge & Kegan Paul.

Taylor, J. and Chandler, T. (1995) *Lesbians Talk: Violent Relationships*, London, Scarlet Press.

Thompson, E.P. (1975) *Whigs and Hunters*, London, Allen Lane.

Tierney, P. (2000) *Darkness in El Dorado*, New York, W.W. Norton & Co.

Tonry, M. (1994) 'Racial Politics, Racial Disparities, and the War on Crime', *Crime and Delinquency*, Vol. 40, 475–94.

Tosh, P. (1977) 'Can't Blame the Youth/Version', Kingston, JA. Intel Diplo.

Toyo, E. (1984) *The Third Republic and the Working Class*, Calabar, Jusaiah.

Toyo, E. (2001) *The Economic Question in the Third World*, Jos, Academic Staff Union of Universities.

Tucker, N. (1984) 'Freud and the Fairy Stories', *New Society*, 27 September.

Turk, A.T. (1976) 'Law, Conflict and Order: From Theorizing toward Theories', *Canadian Review of Sociology and Anthropology*, Vol. 13, No. 3, August.

Turner, T.E. (1994) 'Rastafari and the New Society: Caribbean and East African Feminist Roots of a Popular Movement to Reclaim the Earthly Commons', in T.E. Turner with B.J. Ferguson, eds, *Arise! Ye Mighty People! Gender, Class & Race in Popular Struggles*, New Jersey, African World Press.

Tyler, F. (1959) *Examples in Physics for First Examinations*, London, Edward Arnold.

Urdang, S. (1983) 'The Last Transition? Women and Development in Mozambique', *Review of African Political Economy*, Vols 27/28.

US Controller-General (1990) *Death Penalty Sentencing: Research Indicates Pattern of Racial Disparity*, Washington, DC, US General Accounting Office.

Usman, Y.B. (1982) *Political Repression in Nigeria*, Zaria, Gaskiya.

Van Onselen, C. (1976) *Chibaro*, London, Allen Lane.

Wa Thiongo, N. (1981) *Detained*, London, Heinemann.

Wa Thiongo, N. (1982) *Devil On The Cross*, London, Heinemann.

Wa Thiongo, N and Mugo, M.G. (1977) *The Trial of Dedan Kimathi*, London, Heinemann.

Walker, A. (1988) *Living by the Word*, New York, Harcourt Brace Jovanovich.

Walker, A. (1992) *Possessing the Secret of Joy*, London, QPD.

Weber, M. (1905, 1958) *The Protestant Ethic and the Spirit of Capitalism*, New York, Scribner.

Weber, M. (1979) *Economy and Society: An Outline of Interpretive Sociology*, Berkeley, University of California Press.

Weber, M. (1989) 'Science as a Vocation', in P. Lassman et al., eds, *Max Weber's 'Science as a Vocation'*, London, Unwin Hyman.

Wells-Barnet, I.B. (1892, 2002) 'Southern Horrors: Lynch Law in All its Phases', in S.L. Gabbidon, H.T. Green and V. Young, eds, *African American Classics in Criminology & Criminal Justice*, New York, Sage.

West, C. (1993) *Race Matters*, Boston, Beacon Press.

White, T. (1987) 'I AM THAT I AM: In the Path of Stepping Razor', *Reggae and African Beat*, Vol. 6, Part 5.

White, T. (1991) *Catch a Fire: The Life of Bob Marley*, London, Omnibus.

Williams, P.J. (1993) *The Alchemy of Race and Rights*, London, Virago.

Wilmot, P. (1986) *The Right to Rebel: The Phenomenology of Student Revolutionary Consciousness*, Oguta, Zim Pan-African Publishers.

Wilson, N.C. (1993) 'Taming Women and Nature: The Criminal Justice System and the Creation of Crime in Salem Village', in R. Muraskin and T. Alleman, eds, *It's a Crime: Women and Justice*, Englewood Cliffs, NJ., Prentice-Hall.

Wilson, J.Q. and Herrnstein, J.H. (1985) *Crime and Human Nature: The Definitive Study of the Causes of Crime*, New York, Touchstone.

Wolpe, H. (1972) 'Capitalism and Cheap Labour in South Africa', *Economy and Society*, Vol. 1, No. 4.

Wright, R. (1972) *Native Son*, Harmondsworth, Penguin.

Young, A. (1990) *Femininity in Dissent*, London, Routledge.

Young, C. and Turner, T. (1985), *The Rise and Decline of the Zairian State*, London, University of Wisconsin.

Young, J. (1986) 'The Failure of Criminology: The Need for a Radical Realism' in R. Matthews and J. Young, eds, *Confronting Crime*, London, Sage.

Young, J., and Matthews, R. (eds) (1992) *Rethinking Criminology: The Realist Debate*, London, Sage.

Young, P. (1987) 'Punishment, Money and Legal Order: An Analysis of the Emergence of Monetary Sanctions with Special Reference to Scotland', PhD thesis, University of Edinburgh.

Young, P. (1992) 'The Importance of Utopias in Criminological Thinking', *British Journal of Criminology*, Vol. 32, No. 4.

Young, T.R. (1992) 'Chaos and Social Control Theory: Mapping Non-Linear Social Dynamics', The Red Feather Institute, http://www.tryoung.com/chaos-crm/004control.html

Index

Jensen, A., 168
Jews, 203
Jeyifo, Biodun, 155
Johnson, E.H., 8
Johnson, Linton Kwesi, 169–70, 224
journalists, 9
judicial process, 13
just desserts, 65
justice, reconceptualised, 120

Kalahari desert, 247
Kant, Immanuel, 16, 21, 93
    race of devils, 103–4
Kaunda, Kenneth, 40
Kelley, Liz, 72, 92
Kennedy, M.C., 125–6
Kennedy, Randall, 175
Kenyan school girls, raped, 85
Kenyatta, Jomo, 40
    Facing Mount Kenya, 62
Kerry, US Senator Bob, 34
Khadi justice, 23
!Khun San, 247
Kimathi, Dedan, 129, 62
King, Martin Luther, Jr, 40, 236
King, Rodney, 206
Kingdom, Elizabeth, 20
Kingston, Jamaica, 219
Kinsey, Richard, 130
Kipling, Rudyard, white man's
    burden, 5
Kitsuse, J., 41
knowledge, dominant forms, 55
knowledge–power axis, 36, 48, 95,
    98
knowledge–power relations, 128
Kuti, Fela Anikolapo, 222

La Guma, Alex, 145
labelling perspective, 40, 41, 45–6,
    49, 50, 56, 63
    situational dynamics, 47
Labour Party, 58, 226
Latino, 186
law and order, 121
Law and Popular Culture, 75
lawlessness, executive, 113
lawlessness, state, 121
Lawrence, Headmaster Stephen, 204

Lawrence, Stephen, 194–213
    racist killing of, 11
Lazreg, M., 161
Lea, John, 130
Lee, Harper, *To Kill a Mocking Bird*,
    79
Lee, Spike, *She's Gotta Have It*, 76
left realism, British, critique of,
    58–60
left realism, questioning, 56
left realists, 63
legal positivism, 118
Lemert, Edwin, 42–3
    idea of societal control culture,
    51
Lenin, V.I., 52–3, 198
Lennon, K., 161
les misérables, 24
lesbian and gay scholars, 52
lesbian metaphor, 74
lesbian rape, 75–91
lesbianism, 65
lesbians, 87–8
Lesbians Talk: Violent Relationships,
    82
lesbofeminists, 78
Leviathan, 51
Liebman, James, 180–2
literary criticism, 7
Little, Kenneth, 149
Live From Death Row, 190
Liverpool City Centre, 115
Living Marxism, 80
Locke, John, 16, 93
Lombrosian School, 92
Lombroso, Cesare, 4, 25–6, 34, 37, 94
    positivism, 65
love, in criminology, 39
Lucretia, 89
Luhmann, Niklas, 105, 107, 198
lumpenproletariat, 51
Lumumba, Patrice, 31–2
    imperialist murder of, 60
Luxemburg, Rosa, 198
lynching, 39
Lyotard, J., 81–2, 198

McCamant, J.F., 135
McCleskey v. *Kemp*, 173–93